A Guide to
The Wars
of the
Roses

A Guide to
The Wars
of the
Roses

Derek Birks

PEN & SWORD
HISTORY
AN IMPRINT OF PEN & SWORD BOOKS LTD.
YORKSHIRE - PHILADELPHIA

First published in Great Britain in 2024 by
PEN AND SWORD HISTORY
An imprint of
Pen & Sword Books Ltd
Yorkshire – Philadelphia

Copyright © Derek Birks, 2024

ISBN 978 1 03612 050 4

The right of Derek Birks to be identified as Author of this work has been asserted by him in accordance with the Copyright, Designs and Patents Act 1988.

A CIP catalogue record for this book is available from the British Library.

All rights reserved. No part of this book may be reproduced, transmitted, downloaded, decompiled or reverse engineered in any form or by any means, electronic or mechanical including photocopying, recording or by any information storage and retrieval system, without permission from the Publisher in writing. No part of this book may be used or reproduced in any manner for the purpose of training artificial intelligence technologies or systems.

Typeset in Times New Roman 10/13 by
SJmagic DESIGN SERVICES, India.
Printed and bound in the UK by CPI Group (UK) Ltd.

The Publisher's authorised representative in the EU for product safety is Authorised Rep Compliance Ltd., Ground Floor, 71 Lower Baggot Street, Dublin D02 P593, Ireland.
www.arccompliance.com

For a complete list of Pen & Sword titles please contact
PEN & SWORD BOOKS LIMITED
George House, Units 12 & 13, Beevor Street, Off Pontefract Road, Barnsley, South Yorkshire, S71 1HN, England
E-mail: enquiries@pen-and-sword.co.uk
Website: www.pen-and-sword.co.uk

or

PEN AND SWORD BOOKS
1950 Lawrence Rd, Havertown, PA 19083, USA
E-mail: uspen-and-sword@casematepublishers.com
Website: www.penandswordbooks.com

Contents

Illustrations vii
Introduction ix

Part One: Origins of the Conflict 1
Chapter 1   The Context of the Wars of the Roses.. 2
Chapter 2   The Minority of Henry VI... 6
Chapter 3   The Personality of King Henry VI.. 9
Chapter 4   Divisions at Court 12
Chapter 5   An Attempted Coup 1452 15
Chapter 6   A Wedding, a Funeral and a Birth... 18
Chapter 7   Fasten Your Seatbelts.. 23
Chapter 8   Bust-up in St Albans, 1455 27
Chapter 9   A Line Drawn in the Sand, 1459... 31
Chapter 10   So, it's War Then, 1459 36

Part Two: The Crisis of 1459–64 41
Chapter 11   Showdown at Ludford Bridge... 42
Chapter 12   A Yorkist Revival? 46
Chapter 13   The End of the 'Old Guard' 50
Chapter 14   Two Battles 54
Chapter 15   The Bloody Meadow.. 57
Chapter 16   Post-Towton Blues 61
Chapter 17   A Lancastrian Revival?.. 65
Chapter 18   Lancaster's Last Chance Saloon 68

Part Three: The Crisis of 1467–71 73
Chapter 19   Wedding Bells 74
Chapter 20   Warwick, the Wedding Planner.. 78

Chapter 21	The Kingmaker Illusion	82
Chapter 22	A Cunning Plan…	86
Chapter 23	The House of Cards, 1470	90
Chapter 24	Return of the King?	94
Chapter 25	The Fog of War	98
Chapter 26	Another Bloody Meadow…	102
Chapter 27	Peace for Our Time…	106

Part Four: The Crisis of 1483–7 ... 111

Chapter 28	Peace, the Final Frontier…	112
Chapter 29	A Surfeit of Brothers…	116
Chapter 30	Trouble with the In-Laws	121
Chapter 31	Richard, Duke of Gloucester	126
Chapter 32	Edward, Prince of Wales	131
Chapter 33	Crisis? What Crisis?	135
Chapter 34	Off with his Head!	140
Chapter 35	When Is a King Not a King?	145
Chapter 36	Richard III… King Slayer?	149
Chapter 37	An Autumn Storm	153
Chapter 38	The Waiting Game	158
Chapter 39	Fake News	164
Chapter 40	A Welshman Comes Calling	168
Chapter 41	Bosworth, Part One	173
Chapter 42	Bosworth, Part Two	179

Part Five: After Bosworth ... 183

Chapter 43	What Next?	184
Chapter 44	Trouble in Ireland	188
Chapter 45	Perkin Warbeck	193
Chapter 46	The Spectre of the White Rose	198

Part Six: Conclusion ... 203

Principal Protagonists of the Wars of the Roses ... 209

Bibliography ... 210
Index ... 211

Illustrations

1. Henry VI of England. (*Poems and Romances* (Shrewsbury book), illuminated by the Master of John Talbot, public domain, via Wikimedia Commons)
2. Edmund Beaufort and envoyés de Rouen. (Philippe de Mazerolles, public domain, via Wikimedia Commons)
3. Richard, Duke of York. (Copyright Derek Birks; the stained glass windows at St Laurence's Church, Ludlow.)
4. Castle Inn, St Albans, marking the death of Edmund Beaufort, Duke of Somerset in 1455. (Spudgun67, CC BY-SA 4.0 <https://creativecommons.org/licenses/by-sa/4.0>, via Wikimedia Commons)
5. Margaret of Anjou. (Talbot Master (fl. in Rouen, c.1430–60), public domain, via Wikimedia Commons)
6. Cecily Neville. (http://www.thebookofdays.com/months/may/31.htm, public domain, via Wikimedia Commons)
7. Edward IV. (Ann Longmore-Etheridge, CC BY-SA 4.0 <https://creativecommons.org/licenses/by-sa/4.0>, via Wikimedia Commons)
8. Elizabeth Woodville. (Unidentified painter, public domain, via Wikimedia Commons)
9. Lady Margaret Beaufort. (Irrilyth, CC BY-SA 4.0 <https://creativecommons.org/licenses/by-sa/4.0>, via Wikimedia Commons)
10. Cock Beck from Old London Road. (Cock Beck c. by Ian S, CC BY-SA 2.0 <https://creativecommons.org/licenses/by-sa/2.0>, via Wikimedia Commons)
11. Cock Beck footbridge. (Footbridge over Cock Beck by Ian S, CC BY-SA 2.0 <https://creativecommons.org/licenses/by-sa/2.0>, via Wikimedia Commons)
12. George, Duke of Clarence. (Unidentified painter, public domain, via Wikimedia Commons)
13. Burying the Earl of Warwick. (M. & N. Hanhart Chromo Lith (floruit 1839–1865)[1], public domain, via Wikimedia Commons)
14. The Siege of London, 1471. (Unknown, possibly Jean Spifame, public domain, via Wikimedia Commons)

15. Rivers and Caxton Presenting a Book to Edward IV. (Lorenzo Lippi, public domain, via Wikimedia Commons)
16. Edward V and Arthur Tudor. (Copyright Derek Birks, taken at the stained glass windows at St Laurence's Church, Ludlow)
17. King Richard III. (Barthel ii, public domain, via Wikimedia Commons)
18. Richard III and Anne Neville. (VeteranMP, CC BY-SA 3.0 <https://creativecommons.org/licenses/by-sa/3.0>, via Wikimedia Commons)
19. Buckingham finds the Severn impassable. (James William Edmund Doyle, public domain, via Wikimedia Commons)
20. Elizabeth of York. (Elizabeth_and_Henry.jpg: Malden, Sarah, Countess of Essex (c.1761–1838) derivative work: Jappalang, public domain, via Wikimedia Commons)
21. Henry VII. (Unbekannter zeitgenössischer Maler/unknown contemporary painter, public domain, via Wikimedia Commons)
22. Perkin Warbeck (Unknown source, public domain, via Wikimedia Commons)

Introduction

IN 2018, I STARTED a series of short podcasts on the Wars of the Roses which in the end amounted to forty-six episodes. The aim at the time was to give readers of my Wars of the Roses fictional series some reliable handholds for negotiating their way through the period. Since then, it has become clear that many thousands of people have used these podcasts as a handy guide to the topic – especially students.

Thus, I've decided to make them available in print for those who don't tend to listen to podcasts. I am aiming to provide a comprehensive, but easy to follow, guide to a subject which has been branded 'confusing' and 'complicated'. I don't see the period that way and I find that if you break it up into manageable episodes it is a lot easier to understand. So the intention here is to help the reader understand what happened and why. Although I have provided a chart of the leading protagonists, it should only be used as a reference point.

Though I've studied this period for about fifty years – both as a student and a teacher – I don't claim to know everything. However, I have read the original sources for the period and, while it is perfectly possible that some will disagree with my conclusions, I stand by them. My understanding of the subject has accumulated over many years from secondary works too numerous to mention – indeed, I have long forgotten many of them. This book has a bibliography to aid further study, though it is by no means exhaustive.

There are several works, however, that I have often relied upon and which I would heartily recommend to readers.

On the whole topic: *The Wars of the Roses* by John Gillingham, 1981 – the best overall account.

On all things Henry VI: *Shadow King* by Lauren Johnson, 2019 – an authoritative and extremely readable account – don't be put off by its size.

On all things Edward IV: *Edward IV* by Charles Ross, 1974 – still, in my view, the best account.

A Guide to the Wars of the Roses

On Richard III: *Richard III and the Princes in the Tower* by A.J. Pollard, 1991, which, in my view, rises above all the 'noise' about Richard.

The Wars of the Roses is one of the greatest stories of English history and I hope that readers will find this book useful and perhaps a spur to further study into this fascinating period of medieval history.

Derek Birks, 2024

Part One
Origins of the Conflict

Chapter 1

The Context of the Wars of the Roses

THE WARS OF the Roses took place in the fifteenth century, so the obvious place to start would seem to be to give you some dates: exactly when did the Wars start and end? But I'm not going to do that because I'll mention plenty of dates as we go along. Instead, I want to explore what happened to England in the fourteenth century, because if you want to understand an event of this scope, it's always as well to look at what came before.

England in the second half of the fourteenth century was a society in flux: a people battered and bruised, a country struggling to come to terms with what had been hurled at it in the middle of the century: the Black Death. The Black Death was the greatest plague Europe had ever seen and it had torn a gaping wound in the body of the English nation. The Black Death struck rich and poor alike, and people died on an unimaginable scale – how could men and women ever make sense of their lives again after that? The disaster asked searching questions, not only about people's faith, but also about their place in the very fabric of society.

After the Black Death there was widespread famine and the economy was sent reeling. The ruling classes panicked and passed strict laws in a futile attempt to bolster the creaking feudal system. As if this wasn't enough, the Hundred Years War against France gradually drained all England's resources. War was expensive, so harsh taxes were levied to pay for it, including a poll tax – a tax on everyone in England. In 1381 the long-suffering peasants rose up in their thousands in an unprecedented revolt against the hated poll tax. This Peasants' Revolt, as it was known, threatened to shake the crown from the head of young Richard II. Though he survived the challenge, by the turn of the century England was in political turmoil. There was faction and rebellion leading to the deposition of the king, Richard II.

But what would happen next? The nation held its breath until, when the dust settled on the bloody battlefield of Shrewsbury in 1403, the House of Lancaster was left in control of England in the person of Henry Bolingbroke, Duke of Lancaster.

At first, it seemed that stability had been restored and, in due course, the new king, Henry IV, passed on the throne more or less peacefully to his son, who would be the young warrior king Henry V, of Agincourt fame. He achieved the seemingly impossible by reviving English fortunes in the war with France, cutting a swathe through French lands and finally imposing a treaty by which he expected, sooner or later, to become king of France. Thus, after decades of uncertainty, English pride had been given a mighty boost.

And at home... on the lower rungs of the social ladder, life was beginning to present a few opportunities that had rarely been possible before the Black Death. Now, a simple labourer might work for wages and, if he earned enough, he might become a tenant farmer and then, who knows, he might sell produce for a small profit. Such an enterprising yeoman might not have any political voice, but he might just be able to improve his lot in life.

On the national stage, however, optimism about political stability was short-lived. When Henry V died young in 1422, he left a male heir barely nine months old. For the next sixty-five years, England was dominated by increasingly powerful nobles and the factions they gathered about them. During that period, the problems of the government mounted. The French war started to go badly, and the rule of law at home gradually broke down so that a fragile king and his disgruntled nobles were obliged to settle their differences on the battlefield.

I remember from my early reading on the subject that the fifteenth-century used to be referred to as 'the decline of the Middle Ages', as if society stood still or stagnated, or as if progress was somehow stalled while the land was ravaged by conflict until the situation was rescued by the arrival of a combination of the Tudors and the Renaissance. This was, of course, a load of tosh.

The fifteenth century was a time of both chaos and opportunity. England was not in decline at all: many towns grew, trade flourished and thus the business of government became more complex – too complex by far for a king to control by the sheer force of his personality – especially if, like Henry VI, he didn't have very much personality to start with.

The name applied to this period, the Wars of the Roses, was coined several centuries after the events and suggests a period of constant war. However, as some historians have been at pains to point out, the fighting was far from continuous. Still, although it was sporadic, it was also pretty explosive and some of the early battles had far-reaching consequences. In the first Battle of St Albans in 1455, for example, the deaths of several key noblemen created personal feuds that would continue for at least another generation as sons vowed to avenge their fathers. Battles sometimes killed off the leaders of one generation of combatants, only to clear the way for their sons to ratchet up the competition a notch or two – what drama!

The battles themselves have also attracted a lot of interest because they were frequently bloody. By the mid-fifteenth century, the way men fought had evolved into a blood and guts contest: two opposing ranks of well-armoured men-at-arms wielding heavy swords, axes and maces on foot. They would hack away at each other until physical – or metal – fatigue decided the outcome. Archers were still a lethal force, and to add an extra bit of spice there was the first use of handguns and cannon. These new weapons could be dangerous to both target and user, but they were there to stay.

It was not simply the means of warfare that led to so many casualties; it was also the mindset of the participants and their battlefield commanders. In an effort to finish the epic struggle, the cry of 'no quarter' was heard on a number of fields, and notably at the bloodiest battle of all, Towton in 1461.

Bringing even more chaos to the battlefield was the glorious English weather, which managed to pull a few startled rabbits out of hats. For example, before the battle of Mortimer's Cross – fought on a cold February morning in 1461 – there was a remarkable rare parhelion: a vision of three suns formed by a combination of the dawn light and ice crystals in the air. The decisive battle of Towton began in a snow blizzard and at Barnet, the opposing forces were fighting in a fog so dense they could not tell friend from foe. Since the latter two battles were pivotal to the outcome of the Wars of the Roses, it is interesting that the weather played a significant role in both engagements.

I think it is probably time to take a brief look at some of the leading players in what became the original 'Game of Thrones'. My first exposure to these personalities was, I suspect like many others, through the history plays of William Shakespeare. But although the plays introduced me to some of what we might call the 'Hollywood stars' of the period, they remained pretty shadowy figures until I began to undertake a bit of research for myself.

What I learned in the course of that research is that studying the politics of fifteenth-century England is not for the faint-hearted. It is a world of riveting personalities, savage battles, sudden switches of allegiance, violent feuds, the murder of innocents – and not so innocents – and Lord knows what other mayhem. You could find yourself up to your elbows in blood and gore…

Strangely, at the centre of this maelstrom of carnage was a vacuum: a weak king.

Henry VI was a man with all the charisma of a sponge and the good sense of a lemming. Around him clustered the main players of the political game, the purveyors of power and intrigue. These were the leading members of the great noble houses of England: York, Lancaster, Beaufort, Neville, Percy and so on. These prominent men and women existed against a colourful tapestry of ambition, betrayal and violence – such twists and turns, you couldn't read about it! Except of course you could, because the dodgy characters and double-crosses are perfect territory for historical novelists like me.

In recent years much more has been written about some of the period's more prominent women – not only in historical fiction, but as the focus of research by historians. We now know a little more about these women and the part they played in the politics of the period, and the more we know, the more we realise how much we don't know.

The Context of the Wars of the Roses

Possibly the most dramatic phase of the Wars kicked off after the untimely death of Edward IV in 1483, leaving two young male heirs. This provoked a power struggle between the dead king's brother, Richard, Duke of Gloucester and the family of the queen, the Woodvilles. In that struggle, Richard has forever been cast as the villain, but for generations the charge has been disputed. Did he kill his nephews? Did he kill his wife? Did he kill his brother, Clarence? Did he kill anyone at all? Is there anyone he didn't kill?

Perhaps he was just an earnest plodder who was a bit unlucky... Either way, it has always seemed to me that, if he was a villain, he wasn't very good at it.

You would think that after over 500 years the world would have had its fill of Richard III, but no: excavate a car park and up he pops. The controversy was refuelled.

People are immediately drawn to the man and public interest in him seems unlikely to wane any time soon. Our fascination with interesting people and what they did in difficult circumstances is timeless.

Indeed, the Wars of the Roses, as a whole, can seem like a great soap opera. At each stage in the drama, just when it appeared that peace had been secured, another crisis came along and all the old rivalries, as well as a few new ones, rose to the surface.

By the time Henry Tudor became king at the end of it all, most of his potential rivals had gone. But he was still not safe because, although all the real male heirs appeared to be dead, a few imposters turned up – but were they really imposters?

Chapter 2

The Minority of Henry VI

I HAVE SET the scene for the period before the Wars of the Roses but, before I start to examine the causes of the wars, there is one more important diversion I need to take. I should explain a little bit about how government worked in the fifteenth century, because a clear grasp of that is essential for understanding both how the Wars of the Roses came about and why they lasted so long.

Let's start by stating the obvious: England, throughout the Middle Ages, was governed by a king. But a monarch was not then, as he might be today, simply a figurehead for government. In the fifteenth century, the king, anointed by God, actually had to rule the country and all the most important decisions rested with him or with those he appointed to advise him.

The role of king was essentially pretty simple: he had to provide the focus of government – to set the agenda, if you like, and formulate policy on matters such as making war and peace, raising taxation, passing laws and so on.

That's all well and good, but to carry out and enforce his decisions, the king of England needed help. He had no standing army and his resources were not much greater than those of his most powerful subjects. So the only way for a king to achieve his objectives was to harness the ambitions of his key noblemen, for they – and only they – had the power, wealth and resources to help him.

Henry V, for example, did exactly that. When he decided to pursue the war with France vigorously, his most powerful subjects – many of whom by the way had lands in France – backed him wholeheartedly.

Though these leading nobles – or magnates – each had enormous power in the far-flung regions of England, they also expected to play an active role in the business of government. These men would be members of the king's council; they would also provide armed retinues of men, if required, for war or to suppress rebellion. They would also manage affairs in parliament, which was an institution very far removed from our parliament today. While the House of Commons appeared to have some powers, in reality, most matters were controlled by the Lords.

However, the nobility did not take part in government out of generosity of spirit: they expected to be rewarded for their time, spending and efforts. Those rewards might take the form of additional grants of land or promotion to higher office. Other privileges, such as the right to collect lucrative customs duties, were also sought after.

Such rewards were known as patronage and lay at the heart of government and society in the fifteenth century. You supported your patron or lord – in this case the king – and he helped you in return. The modern student of history might see this as bare-faced corruption, but as long as it was kept within bounds, it was accepted at the time as the way the world worked.

And in case you're thinking that patronage was only an issue for a handful of noblemen, remember that each one sat at the apex of a social pyramid. When he was rewarded by the king, he passed on patronage to the lesser men who had supported him. It's worth considering then that if a nobleman was out of favour the adverse effects would trickle down to be felt by many others who depended upon him at all levels of society.

So, after this brief lesson on patronage in the fifteenth century, what about the Wars of the Roses? What has patronage got to do with it? Because surely the Wars of the Roses were all about rival claims to the throne, weren't they?

Well...

The Tudor chronicler, Edward Hall, tells us that the origins of this epic struggle began when Richard II was deposed by his cousin, Henry IV of Lancaster, in 1399, thereby passing the throne from one branch of the descendants of Edward III to another. But is Hall's assertion true?

Certainly, Henry IV did depose Richard II and then usurped the throne. True, his actions were resented by several other fellow descendants of Edward III, but then, let's face it, Edward III had a shedload of descendants. So, was there any reaction to this usurpation?

Yes, there was. A major rebellion occurred early in Henry IV's reign and there were several later plots as well, but by 1422, when his son Henry V died, the House of Lancaster was firmly established on the English throne. Having said that, you may recall that I mentioned that the warrior king, Henry V, died young in 1422 and left an heir, Henry VI, who was barely 9 months old on his succession. If ever there was a time when the House of Lancaster was at its weakest, that was it.

This would seem to be the perfect moment for all those rival claims to be put forward. However, they were not. Throughout the long minority of Henry VI, when you would think that the child king was at his most vulnerable, there was no hint of any movement to depose him. He was accepted as the anointed king by just about everyone. So while there were men who might have ambitions to be the heir presumptive – the presumed successor if Henry VI died childless – there was no suggestion that anyone should actually replace Henry.

Nevertheless, logic suggests that this period, when there was no adult king at the helm, and the kingdom was in the hands of the most powerful nobles, must have been the origin of the Wars of the Roses. Given, as I've said, the very personal nature of royal government, clearly a child could not rule. But the nobility could hardly sit around and say: 'Well this chap Henry's too young; there's nothing for it: we'll just have to wait until he grows up.'

Someone had to rule in the young king's stead. One, or perhaps several, of the nobles would have to fill the dangerous power vacuum at the heart of the government. Some of those key nobles, who would normally expect to serve and support the king, now had a different role to play: they were no longer the supporting cast.

For the first fifteen years or so of Henry VI's reign, therefore, power lay in the hands of the king's council. The royal agenda that I referred to earlier was set and carried out by the councillors, not the king.

Taking a controlling influence in government meant raising yourself above your peers, and inevitably some of them were not keen on that. Whichever nobles stepped up, they laid themselves open to charges of treason or corruption simply because they had to wield the power of a king without being the anointed king.

If a king's policies were unpopular, he might be described as 'badly advised', but if a mighty noble ruling on behalf of a king was similarly unpopular, he was at best incompetent and at worst a villain.

However, if you were a nobleman who took a leading role in government during the long minority of Henry VI, it was probably going to cost you a fortune from your own pocket. So, there had to be something in it for you: lands, titles, advantageous marriages and inheritances – the usual patronage. Both the risks and the rewards were great because the power you wielded could make your and your family's fortune for generations, or utterly destroy you.

The period of the king's minority from 1422 to about 1437 was therefore important because it raised some men far above others in influence and power – and these were not men chosen by a king, but men who could command the support of a majority in the council.

So England during the long minority of Henry VI was ruled by the most powerful nobles. Was it therefore a period of political chaos and noble infighting that sent the kingdom spinning inevitably towards the Wars of the Roses?

Well no, it wasn't. In fact, although Henry's minority was longer than any other in English history, for the most part the king's council ruled effectively. Young Henry was fortunate to have two pretty capable uncles – the dukes of Gloucester and Bedford – to run affairs at home and direct the war in France. Though the king's minority was by no means free from political rivalry and disagreement, such divisions and jealousies were perfectly normal. For the most part, there was political balance and consistent government.

As a result, when Henry VI came of age in 1437, England was a relatively peaceful, well-governed country. There were no embryonic squabbles poised to erupt and plunge England into the Wars of the Roses. Sadly, it was only when Henry's long minority ended that the real problems began...

Chapter 3

The Personality of King Henry VI

WE ARE OFTEN presented with the view that the fifteenth century was a century of disorder and lawlessness – it wasn't. Serious outbreaks of violence also occurred in both the previous and the following centuries. Such events were evidence that some elements of society at least were so outraged by the government's policies that they resorted to violence.

Disorder hardly ever meant that there was an intent to overthrow the king. In our investigation into what led to the Wars of the Roses, we must now turn our attention to Henry VI, who from the late 1430s onwards really began to rule in his own right.

Like many figures in history, Henry VI has become something of a caricature, but there are several enduring, if contradictory, impressions of the man. Some will tell you that he was a simpleton, others that he was a saint, and many others assume he was just 'mad' – whatever that actually means.

As I've already indicated, medieval monarchy depended a great deal on the personality and abilities of the king, so for good or ill, the king's personality would have a profound impact on the nation's history.

So, what sort of a man was Henry VI?

He was very clearly not a martial figure like many kings before him. In that respect, he provided a stark and – to the late medieval eye – unfortunate contrast to his father, Henry V, whose military exploits were almost legendary. The son was not warlike, and indeed his unwillingness, or inability, to play the role of war leader confused and disturbed many of his leading subjects.

Those closest to him were churchmen such as his chaplain, John Blackman, who must have known Henry better than anyone. Blackman's description makes him appear most respectful of God in his daily life and in his outlook. So if we are to believe Blackman, then the young king was a very pious, chaste and honest man. Perhaps, as Shakespeare later put it, 'fitter for heaven than earth.' However, Blackman's account of Henry was written many years later to support an application to Rome to make Henry a saint, and thus we might regard it as rather biased.

In sharp contrast, some popular opinions expressed about the king in the 1440s and 1450s suggest that he was regarded as a simpleton. Some of these accusations were taken seriously enough at the time to be contested in the law courts. It was clearly in the interests of Henry's later political opponents to convince people that Henry was so foolish that someone else needed to rule in his stead. If you're trying to unseat a king then you have to make a very strong case for his inability to rule.

Both extremes of opinion – that he was either a saint or an idiot – could therefore be seen as propaganda. Yet if we dismiss both, then what we are actually left with? Well, we are left with what he did. And only by considering his actions can we make any sort of realistic judgement about Henry VI.

Henry was a very pious man who was kind and generous, and he invariably tried to avoid conflict and argument. He had an excellent theoretical grasp of kingship, but he had never witnessed it. He had never seen his father dispense justice, crush a rebellion or lead an army to war. Henry was a very unusual king in that he had no example to follow.

As I have said, the council ruled during his minority and made a reasonable fist of it. But there is no doubt that during the decades that followed – the 1440s and 1450s – England faced some serious difficulties, largely centred around the long and ongoing war with France. Undoubtedly mistakes were made and unsuccessful policies were followed, and the buck now stopped with Henry. Whether or not the mistakes were made by Henry or his advisers, it was the king who was held responsible.

Some have argued that Henry was more concerned with his own spiritual wellbeing than matters of state; such an assertion assumes that the problems built up due to neglect on Henry's part. Years of deferring to his councillors during his long minority had apparently made it hard for him to break free from them.

However, I would argue that it was Henry's direct intervention in policy which proved most costly. Poor decision-making and a lack of willpower to enforce his decisions came to characterise Henry's kingship.

During much of the first decade of Henry's adult rule, the 1440s, his leading councillor was William de la Pole, Duke of Suffolk. Rightly or wrongly, Suffolk and a handful of other councillors were blamed at the time for the failures of Henry's government. Historians have also tended to regard Henry as merely a puppet, who was unable to control these influential advisers. It has become clear, though, that there were times when Henry specifically intervened in policy. An early and telling example of this was his handling of peace negotiations with the French.

In 1445, England still held much of France and thus could negotiate to end the war from a position of strength. It is clear that the king favoured peace, but Suffolk also believed that England's strong position should make an honourable peace possible. Many of Henry's other leading subjects, however, would actually have preferred to press the war effort harder rather than contemplate any sort of peace. Suffolk thus had little room to manoeuvre and it appeared impossible to please both his king and his peers.

Henry, however, by attempting peace at any price, was completely at odds with both Suffolk and the rest of the ruling classes. He wanted peace because he thought that peace was always the best policy. He believed that he and the French king,

The Personality of King Henry VI

Charles VII, both being Christian kings who desired peace, could settle affairs justly between them. Henry was no doubt encouraged – though by no means coerced – by his young French wife, Margaret of Anjou.

Henry decided to extend an olive branch to Charles VII by means of a secret letter. This amounted to the surrender of two of the most important areas held by the English in France: the provinces of Maine and Anjou.

The fact that Henry kept the contents of this letter secret for some time tells us that he was certainly not a fool. He clearly knew that many of his councillors would be very hostile indeed to its contents – and they were. Once the king's true intentions were revealed, English policy in France descended into a chaotic farce, culminating by the early 1450s in abject humiliation. By then France had gained, one way or another, vast swathes of the territory which England had held only a few years before.

While Henry was not solely to blame, his intervention had prompted the collapse of English power in France. As I said earlier, the king needed the support of his most powerful subjects to rule effectively, so you could argue that his policy of peace at any price was doomed because it put him out of step with those influential men.

Nowadays, we might see peace as a laudable aim in itself, but at the time it was at best idealistic and at worst foolish. I suppose it depends where you draw the line between idealism and folly.

So what was the result of the chaos in France? By 1450 England appeared to be losing the war. But why did that matter?

It mattered because the people remembered the conquering years of Henry V and believed that a disaster on this scale must have been the result of corrupt and incompetent government. Since the king could not be deemed incompetent, Suffolk and several of his fellow councillors must be held to account. It did not take long for discontent to turn into revolt.

There were stirrings of unrest directed against the government in Kent which, by February 1450, reached the point where Henry ordered that all his household servants should be equipped with bows. He then declared that no man was to carry arms anywhere in London or the south-east. This of course was nonsense bred out of panic, but it showed the level of alarm that existed at the centre of government.

In July 1450 a rebellion broke out in Kent, led by a man called Jack Cade, and it touched a nerve with folk in other areas of the country, including Sussex, Wiltshire and Essex. If we consider that about 2,000 people were later pardoned for their involvement in the revolt, we can assume that many more must have participated. King Henry fled north to Kenilworth leaving Jack Cade's rebels to force their way into London. Several key members of Henry's government, including the Duke of Suffolk, were brutally killed.

However, Henry VI himself survived, though no doubt somewhat chastened by the experience. He had been given a warning and all of his closest advisers had paid with their lives. The question now was: would this gentle, peace-loving king learn from his mistakes?

Chapter 4

Divisions at Court

AFTER 1450 I think it must have dawned on King Henry VI that ruling England was not going to be easy. In his early years as king he had relied heavily – though, as we have seen, not exclusively – on several of his advisers. The chief among these, William de la Pole, Duke of Suffolk, was killed in the aftermath of Jack Cade's revolt. Would Henry now put his faith in another key individual, or would he decide to rule more broadly using the skills and strengths of a wider range of his councillors?

Let's consider Henry's situation in 1450.

I've already said that the English monarch in medieval times was obliged to rely upon his greatest subjects for support and thus managing them was very important to his own success. But Henry's interest in the management of his leading subjects stemmed only from a sense of duty. He knew he had to do it, but it was not something he enjoyed – nor did he find it easy. The usual rivalries between various magnates had to be nipped in the bud if the king was to maintain control. There were, for example, several damaging feuds brewing up between rival baronial families – notably in the north and the south-west – but Henry lacked the will to settle such disputes. While he did nothing to ease the tensions, such quarrels could only escalate.

Underpinning all his policies was the war with France, but it was going badly and Henry knew that without some notable military successes, he would be hard pressed to negotiate a peace with France which would be acceptable to his own English subjects.

And, in the shadows, lurked another thorny problem. Though Henry was pretty much unchallenged as king, his marriage to young Margaret of Anjou had yet to produce the required male heir. As long as that was the case, there would be uncertainty in the kingdom about the future. After the death of his remaining uncle, Humphrey, Duke of Gloucester, in 1447, Henry had no other close relatives and the royal house of Lancaster had no obvious heir.

One of Henry's most prominent nobles, Richard, Duke of York, had clear royal lineage as a descendant of Edward III. After Humphrey of Gloucester's death, although York did not press any claim to Henry's throne, he wanted to be acknowledged as the heir if Henry died childless – in other words, to be the heir presumptive.

So, what was Henry to do? Well, York was not the only option: there was an alternative.

Henry is called a Lancastrian king because he was descended from John of Gaunt, Duke of Lancaster – one of the numerous sons of Edward III. However, there was another line of descent from John of Gaunt through a later marriage. This was the Beaufort family, who could therefore also claim to be Lancastrian. Though the first Beaufort heir was born out of wedlock, the Beauforts were later legitimised in the eyes of both church and state. However, Henry's grandfather, Henry IV, keen to protect his own bloodline, had stated that the Beauforts could not inherit the throne. Nonetheless, this was not exactly set in stone as there is much doubt about whether his decision had the force of law. At the end of the day, what one king could suggest, another could surely dismiss.

The adult male heir of the Beaufort line, Edmund, Duke of Somerset, was thus, like Henry VI, a direct male descendant of the House of Lancaster – which made him an option for Henry as heir presumptive. The Beauforts had always been steadfastly loyal to their royal cousins, whereas York's forebears had not always been so supportive – indeed Richard of York's own father had been executed for treason by the previous king, Henry V. Perhaps it is understandable then if, from Henry's perspective, Edmund Beaufort appeared to be a better choice than Richard, Duke of York.

As the years passed with no sign of royal offspring, it seemed increasingly likely that either York or Somerset would be king when Henry died. It was also pretty obvious that these two would see each other as rivals for the king's favour, and that dangerous political factions would inevitably form around them.

Understanding how this deep-seated and poisonous rivalry worsened is the key to making sense of the early stages of the Wars of the Roses.

The rivalry between York and the Beauforts had begun long before 1450. In 1440, York was given a five-year appointment as the king's lieutenant in France and Normandy. Given the importance of the war, this was a very prestigious role and exactly the sort of pivotal appointment that York believed was his due.

However, in 1443 Edmund Beaufort's elder brother, John, was given a similar post in Gascony but for seven years. Furthermore, he was provided with a larger army than York and given a great wad of cash – approximately £25,000 – to pay his soldiers. In contrast, during his five-year stint, York would spend almost £40,000 of his own money.

After John Beaufort died in 1444, his younger brother Edmund rose swiftly to prominence at court. He was given the lieutenancy in France, which York regarded as rightfully his, and in 1448 was made Duke of Somerset. York was sent to rule Ireland for ten years, which was a clear attempt to remove him from the royal court. To York this must have seemed like a cruel exile, for he delayed his departure until 1449.

The Crown owed York a fortune but, unfortunately for him, the Crown owed everyone. Only by agreeing to forfeit a large fraction of the total did York get agreement that the Crown would pay its debts to him. Even then he received very little, because whether a creditor was paid or not depended upon whether they had access to the king's inner circle – and York, quite patently, did not.

This brings us neatly back to where we left off in the last chapter: 1450 and the destruction of Henry's closest advisers, notably the Duke of Suffolk. At that critical moment, both of Henry's most prominent nobles, York and Somerset, were abroad – one in France and the other in Ireland.

Henry decided to recall Somerset from France and leave York in Ireland – a decision which was to have considerable repercussions for the kingdom. Somerset's recall presented York with a bitter dilemma: either he could continue to languish in Ireland and watch his rival grow in power at the royal court, or he could return to England. But he was not permitted to return to England without the king's express permission. Doing so would clearly risk Henry's anger – especially if he came in force.

Yet could York afford to leave Somerset unchallenged? And if he came, could he afford to come alone? Without some muscle behind him, he would surely leave himself vulnerable to Somerset.

York did not wait for long and, no doubt spurred on by the July revolt of Jack Cade, he decided that his moment had come and in September 1450 he arrived in England with a growing force of men-at-arms. He believed, like Cade's rebels, that the problems of Henry's government – the failure in war, mounting debts and charges of corruption – were caused by Suffolk and Somerset. To York, Somerset was a traitor and incompetent who belonged in the Tower, but since Somerset had the confidence of both the king, and an increasingly influential Queen Margaret, there was little chance of them agreeing with him.

Though the revolt was suppressed, the winter of 1450–51 brought a tense impasse between York and Somerset and their various groups of supporters. While York had some popular support, notably in the House of Commons, he had surprisingly little support among members of the Royal Council. So while parliament was in session, York could exert some pressure on Henry, as in December 1450 when parliament impeached Somerset and he was sent to the Tower.

Only a few hours later, however, Somerset was released by order of the queen. Once parliament was dissolved – a power completely in the king's hands – York's influence evaporated, which left Somerset with the upper hand. Though York had risked a great deal, he had done nothing to advance his cause and now languished in the political wilderness. With his influence at an all-time low, he must have realised that if he was going to remove Somerset from power, he would have to resort to force. Yet in 1451, with depleted resources and few allies, even that desperate course of action must have seemed a very long way off.

Chapter 5

An Attempted Coup 1452

TO HAVE A civil war – in fact pretty much any war – you need two sides. But in England in 1451 there was really only one side: the good ship Henry VI. His queen, leading councillors and near enough every nobleman – except Richard, Duke of York – supported him. Not only did they support him, but they would also not have seen the events prior to 1451 as any sort of challenge to his right to be king. They certainly didn't entertain even the slightest prospect of Henry VI being overthrown – nor did York himself intend to seize the throne.

But why, you might ask, do I even bother to mention that there was only one side?

The reason is that for centuries the Wars of the Roses have been presented – as they still are by some – as the end product of a series of events which began in 1399, when, you may recall, the Lancastrian Henry IV usurped the throne from the rightful king, Richard II.

In order for this version of history to make any sense at all, there had to be two sides long before 1451: York and Lancaster – two rival houses, as they are often referred to – struggling to win or keep the throne. The old story tells us that these mortal enemies had been chipping away at each other for fifty years or so until it all escalated into the violent warfare of the Wars of the Roses in 1455 at the Battle of St Albans. After that, the two warring houses could not be reconciled until 1485 when Henry Tudor came along.

The trouble with this version of history is that not much of it is actually true. It's the Tudor view of what happened, constructed after the events to explain the Tudor success story.

The reality was rather different, so put out of your mind forever the idea that Richard, Duke of York, was trying to take Henry's throne – because at no point before 1460 did he attempt to do so.

York was certainly acutely aware of his own claim to the throne, but his hope was to succeed Henry, not depose him. And this was not a matter of interest only to York, because as long as Henry was childless, every nobleman in the country wanted to understand who might succeed him. When the monarchy hung by a single thread, it was only common sense to know what would happen if it snapped.

In 1451, Richard Duke of York was festering in the political wilderness with his influence and resources at an all-time low. The story of the politics of the 1450s is the story of York's surprising return to the centre of government and, crucially, the beginnings of some serious noble support to restore him to prominence. This marks the beginning, if you like, of a situation in England where there might actually be two sides rather than one.

So, apart from licking his wounds, what was York up to during the winter of 1451–52?

He was busy making plans to force his way back into the political arena. In York's view his rival, Edmund Beaufort, Duke of Somerset, had to be stopped – both for his own future and that of the kingdom he hoped to inherit. But since he was excluded from political office and power, the only way he could see to achieve his aim was to use the threat of armed force.

York's plan had two elements: firstly, he waged a propaganda campaign across the country to highlight the government's already well-listed failings: uncontrolled corruption, the setbacks in the French War and enormous debts. Thus, to the commoners of England, York presented himself as the saviour of the kingdom: the man who would rid England of the incompetent and self-serving Somerset and give good and honest counsel to his sovereign lord, King Henry VI.

The second part of York's strategy was to raise an army to give some substance and muscle to his cause. He reckoned that if he went to London on a wave of popular support and with an army at his back, then King Henry could not ignore him. Of course, none of this came cheap, but York hoped that when he was back in favour, the Crown would pay back the debts he had been owed since the 1440s. We can be in no doubt about the extent of York's desperation because he was gambling all, as they say, on a single throw of the dice.

During the early 1450s the influence of Queen Margaret over Crown policy grew significantly. Her perspective was clear-cut: she must work to defend her husband's position. He had already shown that he was incapable of managing his most powerful subjects. The queen viewed York as a threat to her husband's authority. Because she had not given up hope of bearing a son, she thought it imperative not to hand the initiative to York. With the support of the Duke of Somerset – who, like York, had a personal interest in the future of the kingdom – she ensured that Henry raised an army to counter any threat from York.

So when finally, in February 1452, York brought his army to south London, the king's army was there too. This means that as early as 1452 the prospect of civil war was real: thousands of armed men were camped outside the capital while the sovereign's most powerful subject challenged his authority.

However, civil war did not break out. Why not?

The simple answer is that York did not intend to fight anyone in 1452 – to do so would alienate any nobles who still had some sympathy for his grievances. Instead, he expected that his show of force would allow him to arrest Somerset and be restored to the king's council. What he got, however, was a stalemate – and in a stalemate, the king held all the advantages.

Not for the first time – and certainly not for the last – the Duke of York had miscalculated badly.

The mass of popular support he envisaged simply did not materialise, and nor, more importantly, did any noble support – and that was vital. While one or two nobles supported York, the rest remained steadfastly loyal to the king. It was not that the nobles were hostile to York, or that they necessarily supported Somerset. They just believed that York was wrong to make a public show of force against the king. With almost all his peers against him, York was forced to accept negotiation, or be destroyed.

Among those on the king's council who tried to hammer out a settlement were the earls of Salisbury and Warwick, father and son, who led the powerful northern Neville family. They were kinsmen of York and certainly not his enemies. York's principal demand was the arrest of Somerset and this was agreed.

On the strength of this promise, York disbanded his army. However, it was not Somerset, but York, who was promptly arrested and imprisoned. Though his imprisonment lasted only ten days or so, York was forced to take a public oath of loyalty at St Paul's. Arguably he got off lightly. He had taken up arms against his king and had thus committed high treason; noblemen had been executed for far less in the past.

Nevertheless, York felt humiliated. Furthermore, the Duke of Somerset and Queen Margaret remained in the ascendant at court. Edmund Beaufort, thinking his position was now impregnable, proceeded to rub York's nose in it, by prosecuting some of his retainers at the very heart of York's power base in Ludlow. York, his political career in tatters, withdrew once more and cursed his ill fortune.

As the months passed, he could only look on when, in October 1452, England's fortunes in the French war improved as the hero John Talbot, Earl of Shrewsbury, began to roll back French control of Bordeaux. Despite York's absence at the helm, it seemed that the war was actually going better for the English.

Then in the late spring of 1453 came the stunning news that Queen Margaret was pregnant at last. At that moment in time Richard, Duke of York, seemed finished and what we know as the Wars of the Roses could therefore never have happened.

But fate was not finished with York. In the summer of 1453, the entire political climate of England would change and he would have his chance once again.

Chapter 6

A Wedding, a Funeral and a Birth

IN THE WINTER of 1452 Richard, Duke of York, appeared to have neither the resources nor the support to return to the centre of power. However, a series of events in the summer of 1453 produced a seismic shift in the English political landscape. Few could have seen it coming, though a pessimist might have thought that sooner or later Henry VI's incapacity would overwhelm him. What took place in 1453 though, as so often during his reign, was not really Henry's fault.

Like seismic activity, trouble was already brewing beneath the surface well before the ground began to shake. In order to grasp the significance of what took place in 1453, we have to turn first to the north of England, where a long-running feud, entirely unconnected to the rivalry between York and Somerset, was about to escalate into open warfare.

As long as anyone in the north could remember, two of the leading noble families, the Percys and the Nevilles, had been at each other's throats. The Percy family had long been the dominant power in the north as the hereditary Earls of Northumberland, while the Nevilles had only really begun to challenge them towards the end of the fourteenth century.

Though they were by no means the only powerful families in the region, they could both draw on enormous resources. Their lands were scattered across the north from east to west and thus there were many areas where their estates sat side by side. They were always on the lookout for an opportunity to increase their holdings – preferably at the expense of their chief rivals. If you were a Percy tenant, then you were a Percy and you would have no doubt where your loyalties lay.

Something which makes little sense to the modern mind, but was fundamental to life in the fifteenth century, is that tenants would have put their loyalty to their noble lord far above any loyalty to the king. This was partly due to the simple fact that their lord held power of life and death over them, while the king was far away in London.

Why, you might wonder, did any king allow a handful of noblemen to wield such power and engender such loyalty from his own subjects?

The answer is twofold, but simple. In the first place, a king in London, who had few men-at-arms of his own, was in no position to challenge these mighty nobles. And, as long as they recognised his authority, he had no need to do so. Nor did he want to, because the security of his kingdom depended completely upon the power and resources of such families. The Percys and the Nevilles, along with lesser northern lords, formed a powerful and essential bulwark against a Scottish invasion – which was always a very real possibility.

The land south of the Scottish border – known as the northern marches – was divided into two: east and west. For the most part, the Percy and Neville families shared the responsibility of defending the kingdom. For example, in 1453 Richard Neville, Earl of Salisbury, was Warden of the West March, and Henry Percy, eldest son of the Earl of Northumberland, was Warden of the East March.

These posts were not sinecures because the holders of these prestigious titles were expected to defend the border rigorously. Since the wardens even had the authority to raise men at the Crown's expense, there was never a time when either family was short of armed men. Bearing in mind the fierce rivalry between the two factions, the scope for an argument to turn into a skirmish was always there.

During the first fifty years of Lancastrian rule, the fortunes of the Percys and the Nevilles had – as one might expect – fluctuated. At first, the Percys, who were instrumental in putting the Lancastrian Henry IV on Richard II's throne, were in the ascendant., But their ill-fated rebellion against Henry later on led to disastrous royal confiscations of their land. Thus the Percys were weakened, while the Neville family was on the up. Two of the most advantageous marriages of the period increased the lands of Richard Neville, Earl of Salisbury and his son – also confusingly called Richard Neville – the Earl of Warwick. The latter is known to history as the 'Kingmaker' – with remarkably little justification in my view – but much more about that later on.

The two Richard Nevilles, father and son, were amassing enormous amounts of land and wealth at a time when the Percys were still attempting to repair the damage caused by the previous generation's rebellion. But although the Percys were not such dominant players on the national stage at that point, in the north they were still very much a force to be reckoned with.

Interesting though this is, you may well ask: what has it got to do with the Wars of the Roses?

As I mentioned above, Henry VI was not great at managing his nobles at the best of times, and we have already seen how close to open conflict York and Somerset had come in London. But what about the north? Well, for Henry, the north was a closed book and so the Percy–Neville rivalry was allowed to fester unchecked. Though one side or the other might petition the Crown to redress a grievance, they soon came to realise that under Henry VI they would have to settle their squabbles themselves.

In August 1453, an opportunity presented itself for the Percys to knock the Nevilles off their lofty perch – an event which might well have been the inspiration for the so-called 'Red Wedding' in George Martin's *A Game of Thrones*. But don't get too excited about the comparison, because you'll only be disappointed.

There certainly was a wedding – of one of the Earl of Salisbury's sons, Thomas Neville – which took place in the middle of August 1453 at Tattershall Castle in Lincolnshire. The wedding itself went ahead without a hitch – as it were – but the journey of the Nevilles back to their stronghold of Sheriff Hutton Castle in Yorkshire was rather more eventful.

What objection did the Percys have to this particular wedding?

The bride, Maud Stanhope, was the heiress to several pieces of land which had once belonged to the Percys before being confiscated by Henry IV after the aforementioned Percy rebellion against him. The Percys, who wanted all their lost lands back, most certainly did not want any of them to end up in Neville hands – and Maud's marriage to Thomas Neville would mean exactly that.

But what were they prepared to do about it?

The second son of Henry Percy, Earl of Northumberland, was Thomas, Lord Egremont, who was not a young man inclined to shirk conflict. Indeed, one could argue that he went looking for it. He planned to ambush the Nevilles as they returned to Yorkshire after the wedding. This could hardly have been a spur of the moment incident, since Percy retinues were summoned from as far away as Cumberland. Nor was it a minor affair: the Percys brought at least 700 and possibly as many as a thousand of their tenants.

Though the Nevilles would also have had a considerable retinue, it seems very likely that they would have been seriously outnumbered when the attack began at Heworth Moor – then just outside York. The Nevilles managed to escape to reach Sheriff Hutton without injury to any of the family members, but a number of their retainers were killed or wounded. So while not exactly a red wedding, it was certainly tinged with scarlet.

To Richard Neville, Earl of Salisbury, this was a declaration of war, because the Percys had clearly attempted to eliminate their rivals. More importantly, it was clear to the earl that the Nevilles could expect no support from the king's government. This division in the north struck a devastating blow at the unity of the nobility under Henry VI's kingship. The potential for chaos was plain for all to see, but the king was unable to deal with it.

Why then did Edmund Beaufort, Duke of Somerset, the king's leading councillor, not urge Henry VI to act in support of the Nevilles? Well, as with most relationships between nobles in the Middle Ages, the key lies in land ownership. Only a month or so earlier, Somerset had had a major falling out with Richard Neville junior, the Earl of Warwick, about land in south Wales.

Let's briefly consider this from Edmund Beaufort's point of view. The Beaufort family, despite their close proximity to the Crown, had very limited land holdings and Somerset was therefore always keen to extend them – and thus his income – whenever he could. Unfortunately, on this occasion he acquired some lands in Glamorgan which had previously belonged to the Earl of Warwick. Where matters of land ownership were concerned, few noblemen were of a forgiving nature and

Warwick was less forgiving than most. By falling out with the richest earl in the kingdom, Somerset was making a powerful enemy. It does help to explain, though, why he was unwilling to help the Nevilles in their dispute with the Percys. Indeed, he may have decided that any enemy of Richard Neville was likely to be a potential friend for him.

None of these feuds between nobles actually *caused* the Wars of the Roses, but they had several significant effects: one of which was to promote division rather than harmony among the ruling classes. It's important to grasp that this was not an argument between a few individuals; this was discord between rival households which comprised a host of knights, tenants and many other beneficiaries of the patronage of these great men. Such fractured relationships therefore stretched from the top of society to the very bottom.

The most specific and damaging effect was that the Nevilles, having found no support from the Crown or Somerset, decided that they would have to look elsewhere for help.

Ordinarily, a king would have recognised the seriousness of the situation and intervened. Perhaps it would have been possible to re-establish the previous – albeit precarious – balance in the north between Percys and Nevilles. But sadly 1453 was no ordinary year.

While mayhem was escalating in the north, a thunderbolt of misery struck the good ship Henry in late July, with the news of a calamitous defeat in France. The hero John Talbot, Earl of Shrewsbury, starved of resources and reinforcements, was defeated and killed at the Battle of Castillon. At a moment when England faced complete annihilation in France, the squabbles in the north seemed pretty unimportant.

Then in August 1453 King Henry himself had some sort of mental breakdown, which left him incapable of speech or movement. He was unable to communicate his thoughts – if he had any – nor could anyone communicate with him. It was as if the king was absent, and it was catastrophic for his kingdom. Whatever faults Henry possessed as king, he did act from time to time and he was also there to preside over government. Remember what I said at the start about the English king being at the centre of government – it follows that without a king no government had any authority to rule.

While Queen Margaret and the Duke of Somerset continued to act as the key drivers of royal policy, they could not do so for long without a king. The government was paralysed, with the king's councillors waiting into October for the king's condition to improve. During that time, on 13 October, the queen gave birth to the long-awaited Lancastrian son and heir. Now that Henry had a direct male heir, all claims about who the presumed heir might be were suddenly irrelevant.

All the same, in the autumn of 1453 the king's council had to make a decision about what was to be done if the king could no longer rule. If he could not, then they must choose one of their number to act as protector of the realm at this moment of crisis. It would need to be a senior nobleman, a man of title and wealth who could command the respect of his peers and who could direct the government until either Henry recovered, or his son came of age – which would be another fifteen years!

Amid this burgeoning crisis in London, events in the north escalated further. By 20 October the Percys and the Nevilles had gathered all their supporters and were camped only a few miles apart in north Yorkshire. This time there was no bloodletting, but it was surely only a matter of time before the conflict escalated. The Nevilles decided they must find a powerful ally if they were to defeat the Percys.

At this point, the faction leaders rode south to London to join the Great Council summoned to decide who should be protector of the realm. Who would the council choose? Would it be the obvious candidate, Edmund, Duke of Somerset? Or perhaps the queen herself could act as regent? But even Henry Holland, Duke of Exeter, who was a Lancastrian descendant through a female line, might be considered.

The upshot of the meeting was that council decided that, to help them make such an important decision, they should seek the advice of the senior peer of the realm. Step forward Richard, Duke of York, whom Somerset had not invited to the Great Council – though, as a leading peer, he was perfectly entitled to attend.

Richard, Duke of York, was back.

Chapter 7

Fasten Your Seatbelts...

HENRY VI'S INCAPACITY in the autumn of 1453 meant that the king's council had a decision to make – and not one they relished. His councillors were well aware that whatever they decided might well have significant political fallout for many years to come, so when we consider their task, it is easy to understand their reluctance to act.

The council had to choose a regent, or protector of the realm, to rule in the king's stead for as long as Henry VI remained ill, or until his newly-born son, Prince Edward, came of age – possibly as long as fourteen or fifteen years. Such a man would need to be in it, therefore, for the long haul; he would need to have a proven commitment to good government. What's more, whoever was chosen was unlikely to be universally popular. As protector, he would be using the power of a king, yet he would not *be* an anointed king.

So who were the potential candidates for this tempting, but ultimately poisoned chalice?

One obvious candidate was Edmund Beaufort, Duke of Somerset, since he was already acting as the leading minister of the Crown. But there were some reservations within the council about Somerset's ability to rule wisely and, since the flare up between the Nevilles and the Percys, some – notably the powerful Neville earls of Warwick and Salisbury – would not countenance Somerset in the role of protector.

Another possibility was Queen Margaret, who had gradually become more directly involved in politics since 1450. She certainly saw herself as an ideal candidate since, in her homeland of Anjou, it was not so strange for a woman to take such a role for an absent husband, or a young son. However, many lords were unconvinced, because her hostility to the Duke of York and her close ties to Somerset suggested that her rule would be partisan. There was also some distaste for her forthright personality, which some noblemen found difficult to accept in a world normally dominated by men.

An outside contender was Henry Holland, Duke of Exeter. Like Somerset, Holland was a relative of the king – descended through a female line from John of Gaunt's first wife, Blanche. Though Exeter may have harboured the somewhat optimistic notion that he might be declared protector, he was a far less suitable candidate than either York or Somerset – as his later antics would show.

So the council had three possible candidates, and there was also York himself. Embittered and chastened by his experiences in the past three years, York must have thought his chances of power were gone. But the Nevilles' need for action to be taken against their northern rivals, the Percys, played a key part in York's return to favour. Already linked by family ties – York's wife, Cecily, was sister to Richard, Earl of Salisbury – they decided to make a political alliance. The Nevilles would help York to be appointed protector and in return he would deliver strong action against the Percys.

Though the support of the Neville lords was vital, they were by no means the only members of the council who thought York was the right man for the task. We should not underestimate York's qualifications for the post because, despite his recent setbacks, he was still England's leading peer and he was accustomed to leadership, military command and administration. After his lavish propaganda campaign in the early 1450s calling for 'good government', he would be expected to deliver what he had demanded from the king.

York was not being made king, and he never would be, assuming Prince Edward survived to manhood. As protector, he would simply be acknowledged as 'first among equals' – a safe pair of hands in desperate times.

Yet a vote for York was inevitably a vote against Somerset and the queen. Again, it's easy to see why the council dragged its feet. As 1453 drew to a close, preparations were made for parliament to meet in February 1454, where York, usually considered popular with the Commons, would expect to have the upper hand. If anyone was uncertain about what his ascendancy would mean, all doubt was removed before Christmas when York revived his charges against Somerset for incompetence and failure in the French war. As a consequence, Somerset was sent to the Tower – though in truth he was probably safer there than anywhere else.

If you think back to our earlier digression on the importance of patronage, you can see that if York was appointed protector then his supporters stood to gain a great deal. York would be able to act with the power of the king, whereas in comparison, those who backed King Henry's noble favourite, the Duke of Somerset, stood to lose out heavily.

With Somerset imprisoned, the queen assumed control of what historians sometimes refer to – for convenience rather than accuracy – as the 'court party'. (Political parties did not exist at that time at all.) To the queen, York still presented a threat to her extremely young son. She might have a male heir, but, as she saw it, he was extremely vulnerable.

As parliament gathered in London in late February and early March 1454, the atmosphere was pretty poisonous, with supporters of both factions flooding into the city. Many others – including many lords – stayed away, reckoning it was wise to wait and watch what happened from a safe distance. The large number of absentees can be judged by the fact that York fined peers for not attending – the only time that has ever happened.

Though York had been granted the authority to open parliament, he was not yet protector. In the early days of the parliamentary sessions, both sides had their small political victories and there was an uneasy lull – a stalemate of sorts. The council was as reluctant to appoint a protector in March 1454 as it had been in October 1453, and members still hoped and prayed for the king's recovery.

However, matters were given new impetus by the death of the Chancellor, Cardinal Kemp. Though the council had muddled through until then, appointing one of the key officers of state was quite simply beyond their powers. Thus, on 25 March a dozen lords were sent to make one last desperate attempt to communicate with the king. Although they tried everything and spent hours with him, they could get no sign or reaction of any sort from the poor man. At this pivotal moment in the politics of the period, the council was truly on its own. The king's silence left the councillors no choice and, whatever the consequences, they would have to act.

York was duly appointed protector with a responsibility – clearly stated – for dealing with the king's enemies both at home and abroad. It did not take too much imagination to work out who the king's enemies at home might turn out to be.

Only days after his elevation to the protectorate, York appointed his brother-in-law and chief ally, Richard Neville, Earl of Salisbury, to the vacant key post of Chancellor. Nor was it long before the Duke of York made good his promise to the Nevilles and took action against the Percys. He was, in any case, keen to demonstrate how strong central government could ensure that law and order prevailed – by sharp contrast with what he regarded as Somerset's misrule in previous years.

The head of the Percy family, Henry, Earl of Northumberland, had remained aloof from the affairs of government for many years, preferring instead to consolidate his northern influence. However, his second son, the antagonistic Lord Egremont, showed no such reluctance to exert the family's dominance. Quite early in 1454 Egremont had made an alliance with Henry Holland, Duke of Exeter. Holland, as already mentioned, was a relative of the king, but his ambitions were sadly not matched by either his abilities or his resources.

Holland and Egremont were determined to make mischief in the north and for a few days in May 1454, they took control of the great city of York. Perhaps a little too eagerly, Richard, Duke of York rushed north, but found that Holland and Egremont had escaped. He then found himself trapped inside the city while the troublesome pair created havoc in the area around it. Eventually, the protector brought up sufficient men and the ne'er-do-wells fled. So incensed was York that when Holland took sanctuary in Westminster Abbey, he had him dragged out and imprisoned – which was setting rather an interesting precedent...

Meanwhile, despite York's intervention, Egremont remained at large in the north and so, late in the autumn of 1454, the Nevilles took matters into their own hands. At a skirmish near Stamford Bridge, Egremont was captured and later fined so heavily he ended up in Newgate gaol for debt.

So by the end of 1454, we no longer have a nobility united behind the king with the exception of Richard, Duke of York. What we have – for the first time in our story – is two rival groups among the nobility. Several of the key players on one side – Somerset, Holland and Egremont – might be locked up, but they are still hanging in there. There is currently peace between the factions, but very much on York's terms.

What is the difference, you might ask, between the situation at the end of 1454 and that of 1452? Surely the only difference was that in 1454 York, rather than Somerset, was on top? No, there was a much more important difference. In 1452, York had few allies and none with any genuine clout, but by 1454 he had some very powerful allies who now had a vested interest in his continued ascendancy. You might wonder what would happen if that support was suddenly taken away.

Well, wonder no longer. In December 1454, Henry VI's unerring sense of tragic timing meant that his sudden recovery enabled him to snatch chaos from the jaws of stability. While on a human level this was good news for Henry himself, it was surely a Christmas present the nation could have done without...

Chapter 8

Bust-up in St Albans, 1455

DURING 1454, Richard, Duke of York had acquired some very influential allies: most notably the Neville family. For the Nevilles, it was undoubtedly a gamble; but one they believed they had been forced to take. What it meant was that their prosperity – perhaps even their very survival – now depended upon York's continued dominance in the government.

But when, in December 1454, to the surprise of everyone, the mind and body of King Henry VI were restored, York was no longer needed as protector. The king's recovery was received with great rejoicing – and why not? The king's illness had been a personal tragedy and now he could meet his young son, Edward, who would grow up having some sort of relationship with his father. What could be better?

In normal circumstances, the recovery to good health of a king would have been celebrated on a political level too, as it should have brought certainty and leadership – but of course in Henry VI's case, the opposite happened. Where there had been stability under York's steady, though partisan, control, there was now discord among the leading nobles, overseen by a monarch whose failure to manage his greatest subjects was already manifest.

The removal of York from power was followed in early February 1455 by the release of Edmund Beaufort, Duke of Somerset, from the Tower. Soon after, Richard Neville, Earl of Salisbury, surrendered the pivotal office of Chancellor in a council now once more dominated by Somerset and his own northern allies: Henry Percy, Earl of Northumberland, and Lord Thomas Clifford.

What were York and his allies, the Nevilles, to do in the face of this catastrophe? Since they expected the queen and Somerset to move swiftly against them, the first thing they did was to leave London in haste. But what then for these disaffected, but enormously powerful, noblemen? They had tasted great power and the question was: were they prepared to relinquish it? Even hundreds of years later, we can see that this was a no-brainer, as it must have seemed to them. Several times York had tried to remove his enemy, Somerset, by political means, and each time the king had restored his favourite to power. If persuasion had had repeatedly failed, perhaps it was time for coercion.

Somerset, however, with the king once again in his pocket, was equally determined to destroy his enemies. The Percys too, eager to seize the chance to annihilate Neville power in the north, were willing allies. Thus in April 1455, York, Salisbury and his son Warwick, were summoned to a great council to be held on 21 May.

This was not to be a proper parliament where the Commons might favour York; instead, the only commoners present would be court nominees. Nor was it to be held in London where York was popular, but in Leicester, far enough away from the centre of government. The declared purpose of the council was to 'provide for the king's safety'. York and his allies assumed – rightly – that, in the eyes of the 'court party', it was they who represented the threat to his safety.

For York and the Nevilles to attend the council would have been political, and perhaps actual, suicide. But equally, the duke could not just ignore it, for it was likely that a refusal to attend would simply lead to condemnation in their absence.

Perhaps York had already decided – after Somerset's return to favour – that he must resort to force; or perhaps it was the summons that made him do so. Either way, he and his allies began to raise an army in the north. By May they had put together an armed force which they hoped would demonstrate their power and enable them to overthrow Somerset's government.

Somerset still appeared to believe that he could remove York and his allies by political means, because he seemed singularly unprepared for this resort to force. He only started to raise a royal army when York was already on his way south. Evidence of his growing concern, however, is shown on 21 May, when he decided to take King Henry and the leading councillors out of London and head for St Albans. Though Northumberland, Clifford and Somerset's other close allies were prominent, those who accompanied the king were by no means all supporters of Somerset. Some were still well-disposed towards York and the Nevilles, notably the Earl of Devon and Salisbury's own brother, William Neville. There were also some heavyweight 'neutrals' like the Duke of Buckingham, who was loyal to the king but would not gladly take up arms to support Somerset.

So, what was the situation on 21 May? The York–Neville army was heading south at pace, while the court was making a slow progress towards St Albans, where it would await the arrival of the elements of a royal army hastily summoned to meet York's challenge.

It is important to emphasise at this point that there was absolutely no intention to depose Henry VI – it was Somerset and Northumberland who were the principal targets. York's chief aim was to remove Somerset permanently and the Nevilles too had their own specific targets.

The really odd thing about the sequence of events that followed is that all the urgency and sense of crisis seemed to come from York's side. On several occasions he sent letters to the king – even in the middle of the night of 21/22 May at Watford – protesting his loyalty and asking for a council including those of whom his faction approved. But his letters bore no fruit, because Somerset and the queen had already convinced the king that York intended to seize his throne. To be fair, York's behaviour in 1452 certainly gave credence to their fears.

York and his allies followed so close behind his messengers that when the king approached St Albans on the morning of 22 May he found York already there. York's forces outnumbered the king's significantly and there was confusion among the councillors attending Henry as to exactly what he should do.

The moderate Duke of Buckingham advised the king that York was only trying to exert pressure – as he had done in 1452 – and would not press matters to a fight. Somerset, perhaps understanding his old opponent rather better, insisted that York would use force if the king did not accept his terms. Buckingham suggested that they should proceed into the town of St Albans rather than preparing for a pitched battle. There they could continue to negotiate with York to reach a settlement.

Buckingham's advice was utterly reasonable but completely wrong. What he failed to consider was that although York had conceded without resorting to battle in 1452, the result had been an ignominious political defeat for York. The proud duke was not prepared to risk a repeat of that humiliation. This time – one way or another – Somerset would have to go.

While Henry moved his men into the town, heralds passed between the two sides – as was customary – in the hope of avoiding any actual fighting. York's message was both consistent and imperative: hand over Somerset or else. Since the king was not willing to meet this demand, the failure of the negotiations was inevitable, and, belatedly, the royal army prepared to defend the town.

Though the exchange of heralds continued, it must have been obvious to York that the defences were being strengthened. Any further delay would mean that assaulting the town would be more difficult and more costly in lives. So, at ten o'clock in the morning, York ordered the advance.

St Albans, ringed by houses and with its entry roads now barricaded, proved very difficult for York's soldiers to breach. The royal commanders were confident that they could repel all attacks and many did not even bother putting on their armour. They appeared to believe that York, once his military assault was blunted, would return to negotiation.

However, they reckoned without the ruthless determination of the younger Richard Neville, Earl of Warwick. Thwarted at the barricades, Warwick sent his men through the back gardens of several houses with orders to break through and thereby create a breach into the centre of St Albans. As might be expected, the sudden arrival of Warwick's men inside the town caused havoc and men scattered before them.

During the ensuing skirmish, both King Henry and the Duke of Buckingham received wounds before scurrying to hide wherever they could. The victory was swift and overall, the casualties were few, perhaps under a hundred – but three deaths had more significance than all the others. Somerset, Northumberland and Clifford all perished – Somerset in a desperate last stand at the Castle Inn.

While the York–Neville army plundered the town, York went to meet the king. King Henry, with York kneeling before him, had little choice but to pardon him and all those who had fought against him. Thus the following day the king was escorted back to London by the victors, whose entry into the city had much in common with a Roman triumph.

The skirmish which has become known as the first battle of St Albans may have been relatively small, but its impact was enormous. The key enemies of York and the Nevilles had been killed – they would not come back this time. Within days, York and his supporters were in total control of the government and the chief offices of state. St Albans may have been a minor battle, but it was a major coup d'état.

York had risked everything on the streets of St Albans and, on the face of it, his victory was absolute. The king was forced to accept him as his leading councillor and it seemed that York was in an unassailable position. In one short, but brutal exchange, it seemed that a full-scale civil war had been averted because one faction had been shorn of its leadership.

York's success appeared to be set in stone, but fifteenth-century England was a funny old place…

Chapter 9

A Line Drawn in the Sand, 1459

AS WE HAVE seen, after the Battle of St Albans in May 1455, York's position appeared impregnable. One morning's savage blood-letting had left the York–Neville faction unchallenged and it seemed that at least the dire prospect of all-out civil war had been averted.

Sadly, this was only a cruel illusion, because the battle of St Albans settled nothing. Although York had cleared out some of his enemies, there was nothing to stop King Henry VI appointing anyone else he liked to his government. So unless York was prepared to limit or – whisper it softly – remove the king, then sooner or later he was likely to face a similar problem.

Not only that, but the brief battle also had some rather darker consequences. Clearly, it irreparably damaged the relationship between King Henry and York. After all, if you were Henry, would you put any trust at all in York – a man who had twice taken up arms against his anointed king and most recently caused him to be wounded and in fear of his life? Henry was not a fool and he rightly feared York's power – especially since his own son was not yet three.

Consequently, he did not require too much persuasion to counter York's influence from the queen, Margaret of Anjou, who now felt vindicated as her warnings about York seemed to have been proven right. Although her 'court party' had been shorn of its leadership, the queen remained and she was even more hostile to York than before.

In her quest to find some allies to counterbalance the power of York and the Nevilles, Margaret did not have to look too far. Somerset, Northumberland and Clifford might be dead, but their sons were very much alive and thirsting for revenge – another dark consequence of St Albans. As far as those bereaved sons were concerned, there was much unfinished business.

Another leading nobleman was also forced to rethink his attitude towards the Duke of York. The Duke of Buckingham – like York and Warwick – was one of the wealthiest and most powerful men in the kingdom, but for him St Albans had been a disaster. Not only had he taken several wounds during the fighting and been forced to seek sanctuary, but also, belatedly, he realised that his counsel to the king that he should trust York had backfired badly. When, a little later, he was forced to choose sides again, Buckingham was not prepared to trust York a second time.

So, after May 1455, rather than a settled court, we have a hotbed of intrigue and plotting. But St Albans was not just some back-alley scuffle; it was a full-on skirmish fought with serious intent. Important men had been killed and someone had to take the blame. Since York had won, it certainly wasn't going to be him. Instead, he ensured that it was recorded in parliament that the Duke of Somerset was to blame. York's forces were exonerated for any actions they took at St Albans – such as, I suppose, fighting against and wounding their king...

Against this grim background, York attempted to consolidate his position. At the centre of power the important offices were given to York's allies, the usual suspects: Salisbury, Warwick and a few other loyal supporters. Warwick became Captain of Calais, which was the main prize because it was a post which offered much independence.

It is difficult from our vantage point in the early twenty-first century to grasp the significance of Calais in the fifteenth century. It was not the fag end of the English empire in France, no longer relevant to England after defeat in the Hundred Years' War. No, Calais was crucial: it was the only part of England that had a standing army, possibly as many as 1,000 men strong. It had resources for war and shipping – both of which were necessary for its defence – and it was a major centre of trade. However, despite its importance, there were serious financial problems with Calais, for – as with many areas of Henry's government – it had often been starved of the money it required to function. Someone needed to take it in hand, but because of the uncertainties at court, Warwick delayed his departure.

York knew that no matter how many pardons were awarded or offices gained, he was not secure. As a result, in November 1455 he decided to get himself appointed protector again. Since parliament was in session, this was proposed by one of York's own clients in the House of Commons, the excuse being King Henry's poor health and the outbreak of a feud in the south-west between two rival baronial families in Devon, the Courtenays and the Bonvilles. Though this feud was not quite on the epic scale of Neville versus Percy, it would certainly need a firm hand to control the two families. No one believed that Henry could bring the unruly barons to heel.

The council, despite its misgivings, acquiesced – as did Henry. But the second protectorate only lasted three months and after that York had to try to work with the rest of the council and hope to counteract the queen's hostility. Overall, despite Queen Margaret's attempts to re-establish a 'court party', the period 1456–7 saw a good degree of compromise and good sense in the measures the council was undertaking on the king's behalf. As a result, in the summer of 1456 Warwick felt able to take up his new post in Calais and by 1457 he had been given authority for protecting the sea routes around Calais. As usual he was given authority, but precious little cash to achieve the task.

During the periods when the Duke of York ruled there can be little doubt that he was a good deal more effective than his rivals, yet the nobility as a whole never really warmed to him. He was a difficult man to like. He had integrity and gravitas, but he possessed very little charm or charisma. Though his fellow councillors might respect his status and abilities, they did not seem to like him very much.

Those nobles who really did not trust him, rather like the queen, found it difficult to believe that York did not want more than just the position of chief councillor.

At the same time as Warwick was taking up his position in Calais, Queen Margaret was working to create a new power base and, in the process, strengthen the position of her young son, Edward of Westminster. London had never offered her much support in the past, so she took Prince Edward out of the capital and toured the north and west of England so that the new prince could be seen by some of his subjects.

Margaret set up her headquarters at Kenilworth and, from there, she cemented her ties with key loyalists such as Jasper Tudor, Earl of Pembroke. Jasper was King Henry's half-brother – they had the same mother, Catherine of Valois – and he became the linchpin of royal power in much of Wales and the west. Other nobles in the region, such as the disgruntled Buckingham and the Earl of Shrewsbury, were also wooed into the royal fold.

Critically, by August 1456 Margaret had contrived to move King Henry himself to Kenilworth and this enabled her to influence royal appointments once again. Though a new chancellor, William Waynflete, Bishop of Winchester, was appointed, he should be seen as a neutral appointment, acceptable to both sides. However, the appointment of the Earl of Shrewsbury to the other key post of Lord Treasurer might be seen as a win for the queen.

Her previous allies, the Percys, began to re-establish their influence: young Henry Percy, the new Earl of Northumberland, came to court while his younger brother, the troublesome Lord Egremont, escaped from gaol. Their ally Henry Holland, Duke of Exeter, was then released from prison. Meanwhile, behind the scenes, Henry Beaufort, the heir of Somerset, and John Clifford, whose father was also killed at St Albans, were encouraged in their hostility to York. The queen's direct involvement in factional politics was calculated to destroy York, but all was not yet lost. There were still lords who were attempting to preserve unity between the rapidly diverging factions. Even the Duke of Buckingham, despite his closer connection to the queen's supporters, was still a force for moderation.

In 1457 it would have been obvious to all at court that the York–Neville axis was in decline; but was that decline permanent, or simply a bump in the road? The exact situation would not have been clear because, although York had been outmanoeuvred by the queen, he still had much to offer the kingdom, as was demonstrated in August that year when a French raid on the south-east coast required action to defend the realm. The ineffective Duke of Exeter was hastily replaced as admiral by Warwick, who confidently assumed control and dealt with the French incursion. So, despite what happened next, we cannot say that the demise of York was inevitable.

In March 1458 came one of the most bizarre events of the whole Wars of the Roses period. Henry VI, who cherished peace above most things, summoned a Great Council of the nobles in an attempt to reconcile the two sides, but the leading men did not dare to come alone. While some were merely suspicious, others were bitter and vengeful. Either way, the leading players brought hundreds of retainers with them. In order to keep the peace, the city authorities housed York's retainers inside the city and the Lancastrian ones outside. It didn't stop the more determined hotheads, but it helped.

The grudges the two factions held against each other were made all the more tangible by some huge outstanding fines imposed in earlier years by York and the Nevilles on their vanquished enemies. However, after much discussion, a form of words was produced which said that many of the fines would be reduced or removed altogether.

To celebrate these pretty empty words, a ceremony called Loveday was held on 24 March 1458. It is pure Henry VI: a fantasy of peaceful intent engineered by a king in a weak position, who could only ask for promises and hope for the best. The two sides processed to St Paul's in an outward show of unity: the queen alongside York, Warwick with Northumberland, and young Henry Beaufort, Duke of Somerset, with Salisbury. But it was all a tragic sham. None of them had any intention of keeping their promises.

Loveday, Henry's vain attempt to paper over the cracks with gossamer, fooled no one and changed nothing. It only served to demonstrate the deep chasm of division between the two rival factions because, beyond the outward show, thousands of retainers on both sides were spoiling for a fight.

In such a situation, anything – even something quite trivial – could have fired the powder barrel. In the event it was the queen's hostility towards Warwick which did the trick. Warwick had become her prime target. Not only did she blame him for the deaths of her noble favourites at St Albans, but she also saw him as the most potent threat to her success because he held the pivotal base at Calais.

In July 1458 he was summoned back from Calais to London and the situation quickly got out of hand. Fighting broke out between supporters of Warwick and the queen. Warwick returned once more to Calais but the queen ensured that the funds he needed to pay the garrison there were never sent to him. The Earl of Warwick's response was typically direct: he embarked on a piracy spree to raise his own cash – and it turned out he was very good at it.

When Warwick was recalled to London again in the autumn – because of his piracy – there was more trouble between retainers. Once again, he escaped to Calais, but the first blows had been struck in the civil war. By May 1459, it was clear that the queen's party was actively preparing for open war and in June she went for the jugular at a Great Council summoned to meet at Coventry. Though

York, the Nevilles and their allies were invited, they did not attend because the whole set-up must have seemed all too familiar. If they had attended, they would have been arrested; as it was, the council indicted them in their absence.

The king and queen had now drawn a line in the sand and the likes of Buckingham now had to choose a side. Buckingham chose the king and his support gave the court party added momentum, which probably convinced a few waverers.

From this point on, war could only have been avoided by the utter capitulation of one side or the other. The king and queen were sure of their ground and, after what had happened in the previous decade, we can see that Richard Duke of York could not afford to concede defeat. The rivalry which had played out so often in the council chamber was now going to be decided on the field of battle.

York arranged to meet his allies at Ludlow, which was close to his power base in the Welsh Marches. Warwick sailed with an armed force from Calais and his father, the aged Earl of Salisbury, set out with an army from his northern stronghold of Middleham Castle. The Wars of the Roses were about to begin in earnest.

Chapter 10

So, it's War Then, 1459

SO, AFTER NINE chapters, we appear to have reached the start of the Wars of the Roses. That seems to me like a good point at which to step back a little and ask ourselves what those who were about to fight each other were actually fighting for.

I read so frequently that the Wars of the Roses were a struggle for the throne between the houses of York and Lancaster, yet surely nothing I have said so far bears that out. So, let's consider the motives of the main combatants.

King Henry VI was a peace-loving king, so why was he going to war?

Firstly, Henry felt much aggrieved that, despite what he saw as his best efforts, Richard Duke of York still refused to accept his decisions. Twice at least York had taken up arms against his sovereign lord – perhaps not to unseat the king, but certainly to compel him to submit to York's point of view. Whatever York's reasons, this was manifestly treason and a stronger, more vindictive king would have dismembered York for that long before 1459. But by then even Henry's patience was exhausted. His over-ambitious subject needed to be taken down.

In the back of Henry's mind was the fear, or at the very least the suspicion, that York coveted the throne. While Henry was childless, this was understandable, since York saw himself – as many others did – as the heir presumptive. However, the birth of Prince Edward changed all that. Henry had a male heir and he also had every right to assume that his leading subjects would accept and support him. The overwhelming majority did – as is shown by the strong noble turnout for the king in 1459: almost every one of them backed him. If some had a little sympathy for York and quite possibly some doubts about the wisdom of the queen's policies, they still backed their anointed king.

What about Queen Margaret, who played an increasingly important role in events during the 1450s? What was she fighting for?

Much vitriol has been directed at Queen Margaret and Shakespeare is often blamed for that, but it seems to me that only lazy historians use a character in a play as their starting point.

From her perspective, she was fighting for her husband's crown and her son's legacy; it's arguable that, without her tenacity and strength of purpose, Henry might have become a 'puppet king', acting at the whim of the Duke of

York. Margaret was concerned that, if York ruled for her husband, then her son's succession would not be secure. Finally getting rid of York would leave the path of succession clear.

The queen had also – like almost everyone else – been shocked by the events of St Albans in 1455; in particular the death of Edmund Beaufort, Duke of Somerset, and the wound sustained by her husband. Yorkist propaganda would have us believe that she and the Duke of Somerset were lovers. This seems most unlikely to me, but even so his death would have been both a personal and political blow.

As I see it, the queen felt that, before 1455, her warnings about York had fallen pretty much on deaf ears, but after St Albans, the king himself and many among the nobility might well be have been thinking that she was right all along about York. So while St Albans weakened the 'court party', it also vindicated Margaret's concerns.

So when in 1459 the 'force was with her', so to speak, it was not that surprising that she wanted to destroy York once and for all. The Neville leaders too would have to go: partly to keep the support of her Percy and Clifford allies, but also because they had sufficient power to disrupt the kingdom even without York as their figurehead.

Now let's examine the enigma that was Richard, Duke of York. If only we could look inside his mind and see what he was thinking in 1459. Ah, the unsolved mysteries of history – but that's why we like it so much!

For me, York's views evolved during the 1450s. At first he simply wanted to take his place at the top table – to be able to exert a level of influence in the council that he believed was his due as the kingdom's leading nobleman.

His difficulties in achieving that arose from his increasingly bitter and savage dispute with Edmund Beaufort, Duke of Somerset. Ask yourself the question: are we to believe that York's hostility towards Somerset was entirely to do with corrupt and incompetent government? Are we to accept that York's motives were only for the common good? Well, I don't think we can. We can't simply dismiss the fact that Somerset was the Beaufort heir to the throne – whether such an inheritance was legal or illegal was as irrelevant then as it is now. Laws can always be changed. The bold truth was that Somerset was a rival to York for the role of heir presumptive – in other words, possibly the next king. Everyone at court knew that; it was hardly a secret. Thus, every time the pair clashed it was seen as a trial of strength for a time to come.

When Prince Edward arrived in 1453, the goalposts shifted; but the intense rivalry between the two men remained because, given the king's failing health – especially his mental state – they were now rivals for a possible regency.

As we have seen, the quarrel escalated, with each man trying to crush his opponent until St Albans when York decided that there was only one course of action left: Somerset had to be taken out. But after Somerset was killed, what next?

York found that his actions in 1455 destroyed forever any lingering trust the king might have placed in him. Thus, the king would never entrust his son to York's keeping – and nor would the queen. There was even less enthusiasm for York's second protectorate than the first. Apart from the Nevilles, York lacked support even from those who might otherwise have supported him. In 1459, the queen cleverly backed him into a corner so that he must capitulate or fight.

Even if he won the fight, he would have to secure his future by placing strict controls on the king, the queen and the prince. Otherwise, history would simply repeat itself: the king would reject him and the queen would try to destroy him.

But how could York control the anointed king? He must surely have considered the options at that point, if not before. What would he need to do, if he won? Whether he took the throne or not, he would surely need to act with the power of a king.

What then of York's vital allies, the two Neville earls: Salisbury and Warwick? Without their support, Richard, Duke of York would probably only merit a footnote in history. One could go as far, I think, as to suggest that without the actions of the Nevilles there would have been no Wars of the Roses at all – or at least not in the form they took.

The father, Richard Neville, Earl of Salisbury, had his eyes firmly on the north for that was where – despite his confusing title – much of his power lay. His war was with the Percys and the Cliffords for northern dominance. His political alliance with his brother-in-law, York, had delivered that prize to him because Henry Percy, Earl of Northumberland, was slain at St Albans along with Lord Thomas Clifford. But although the two northern families were weakened, as events in 1457 to 1459 showed, Northumberland's heir, Henry Percy, and Clifford's son, John, were not prepared to surrender their influence so easily.

Salisbury realised that in 1459 his situation was actually worse than in the middle of the decade. In 1453 the Crown might have been unwilling to act against the Percys, but now the Crown positively supported them. Given the long, and sometimes violent, feud between their families, it is not that surprising that both Salisbury and his counterpart, Henry Percy, thought that only war could solve their problems.

If we turn to Salisbury's son, the younger Richard Neville, Earl of Warwick, his motives were a little different. Warwick – thanks to the most lucrative marriage of the century – had immense landholdings and income from many areas of England, eclipsing those of his father and rivalling those of York himself. The north was of concern to him, but he was Captain of Calais so he saw himself as a player on the national stage – a man who might influence kings.

Warwick was not averse to the use of force – as his leading part in the Battle of St Albans showed – but I suspect that he and York were not quite on the same page in 1459. If York was contemplating removing the king, Warwick certainly had no intention of doing so at that point. Warwick did not carry the same baggage as York since he had no claim to the throne. Thus, for such a man as Warwick – only recently appointed as Captain of Calais – the move to war, however inevitable it might seem, would also be most regrettable if it ended his own political ambitions.

So, as York and the Nevilles headed for Ludlow where they were to assemble their forces, they were probably a little muddled as to what they hoped to achieve there beyond personal survival.

Nevertheless, the fate of the kingdom hung by a thread: as uncertain as it had been at any time since the deposition of Richard II in 1399 almost sixty years before.

But 1459 was not in any sense a continuation or a revisiting of 1399. Don't let anyone tell you that, because to those about to fight each other in 1459, the events of 1399 were ancient history. They were focussed on where they were going, not where others had gone. And, trust me, where they were going was quite bad enough.

Part Two
The Crisis of 1459-64

Chapter 11

Showdown at Ludford Bridge

IN THE AUTUMN of 1459, the talking stopped and the fighting began. Well, it's rarely ever as simple as that, is it – especially where people are concerned? But certainly, that was the point after which battles seemed to come along fairly regularly. My purpose here is not to describe battle after battle in all its gory detail. I am much more concerned with *why* the battles were fought and, in particular, what political impact they had. All I can hope to do is to provide a coherent overview that encourages the pursuit of further details elsewhere.

As I have said before, the Wars of the Roses were most definitely not a single, continuous event. Rather they can be broken down into three separate, though related, political crises. You might see it as a series of historical novels in which some cast members are retained from one book to the next, but the stories are complete in themselves.

We have now arrived at the first of these three crises, which lasted from 1459 to 1464.

As you will recall, this crisis had been brewing for several years following the Battle of St Albans. As far as Queen Margaret, Henry Beaufort, Duke of Somerset and the Percys were concerned, it was payback time. York and his allies were on the defensive and hastily trying to gather enough military might to balance that of the king.

One of the features of the Wars of the Roses that fascinates the student of history is the way in which the fortunes of the two sides rose and fell. It's almost as if some wicked puppet master was controlling events so that one moment York was triumphant and the next he was utterly lost. Thus it was during the 1450s when so many times the Duke of York thought he had achieved a position of dominance only to find that he really hadn't.

The prime reason for the ups and downs of the 1450s was unquestionably the limited managerial skills of King Henry VI himself. Nevertheless, once war broke out at the end of the decade, one can hardly blame the king for the continuing fluctuation in fortunes. At the time, of course, such things were often put down to the surprisingly capricious will of God; but I prefer to see it as the random consequences of several quite different factors: the unpredictability of battle, bad luck, even bad weather – but mostly, the fickle loyalties of powerful and ambitious men.

In the late summer and autumn of 1459 no one was sure exactly what was happening. Most people were probably not expecting that there would be more than the odd skirmish – an upgraded version of St Albans perhaps. Certainly very few would have wanted an all-out war against the king because – and this is vital for us to grasp – hardly anyone at all actually wanted to fight against Henry VI.

But men also owed loyalty to lords who could determine their fortunes rather more directly than the king. Bear in mind that if, say, you were a knight who owed allegiance to the Earl of Salisbury, and you were summoned with thousands of others to his stronghold of Middleham Castle in Yorkshire, you did not know at that point that you would have to fight against the king himself – to whom you also owed allegiance. It was one thing to take up arms to support your lord against another lord's men, but it was something else entirely to fight against an army flying the royal standard and led by your king in person. It required a fundamental change of mindset – and it also required some hefty justification. The importance of this conflict of loyalties was amply demonstrated when the York's forces met in 1459 at Ludlow.

York's allies had followed different paths to reach Ludlow. The Earl of Salisbury had to dodge past Queen Margaret's army and fight off another royal army at Blore Heath in Staffordshire – indeed he was lucky to get through at all.

Here we have an early example of how fluid alliances were during this period. Lord Thomas Stanley – a name to remember – was a growing power in Cheshire and the north-west of England, but from the start he gained a reputation for sitting on the fence. With his brother, William Stanley, he often had the power to intervene on one side or the other, but only rarely did he ever commit himself.

What happened in September 1459 in the West Midlands is the first example of his duplicity. On the one hand he was sending assurances to Queen Margaret that he was on his way to help prevent the Earl of Salisbury from reaching the other Yorkists in Ludlow, while in fact his brother actually joined forces with Salisbury on the way. Much more will be said about the Stanley brothers later on, but this episode set the pattern for their actions throughout the period.

Salisbury eventually reached Ludlow but lost some of his men at the Battle of Blore Heath – about which we know very little except that the royal commander, Lord Audley, was killed and, at some point in the aftermath, two of Salisbury's sons, among others, were captured.

The Earl of Warwick arrived from Calais in rather better shape, with half the garrison led by one of the most capable and respected soldiers of the day, Andrew Trollope – now, there was a man to have with you in a tight corner!

So early in October 1459, Richard, Duke of York, was camped at Ludlow with his two teenage sons Edward and Edmund, and his allies, the two Neville earls. He drew up his combined force south of the town – just beyond Ludford Bridge with the River Teme at his back. His defences, including his cannon, faced his opponents to the south: a full-scale royal army boasting a very generous sprinkling of peers and with the king and queen at its head.

It is difficult to believe that York really thought this would be St Albans round two. He had tried a show of force several times to get his way with the king – and each time his success had been short-lived. This time, as so often before, York wrote to the king to explain his warlike actions – he was loyal, he claimed, but had been provoked by his enemies; he only wanted good government, removal of corrupt advisers, and so on...

Surely Henry must have wearied of receiving such letters but, being a most forgiving man, he offered a pardon to all those willing to lay down their arms, except those responsible for the death of Lord Audley – one imagines that this single condition might have been intended as something of a catch-all for the ringleaders, because I can't imagine that Henry's leading advisers intended York and his cronies to escape with their lives.

York knew that many of his soldiers would be reluctant to fight their king directly so rumours were spread among his army that Henry VI was dead and – in a nice touch – masses were even sung for his soul. One of the aspects of the wars which I find especially impressive is the depth of loyalty to Henry VI. Few of his subjects saw him as an effective leader, yet they were prepared to fight, and die, for him anyway.

The proof of this is in what happened next: Andrew Trollope – soldier extraordinaire – took his Calais garrison, the steel backbone of York's army, and defected overnight to the king. Without them, York knew that he could not win a military engagement and the following night, anticipating further desertions, he and the other leaders fled, abandoning their cannon and leaving their confused men to make their own peace with the king. The duke also left behind his duchess, Cecily, and his two youngest sons: George and Richard.

The immediate result was that the unfortunate town of Ludlow was ransacked by the jubilant Lancastrian soldiers who had won a victory with virtually no fighting at all. They pretty much drank the town dry and pillaged it so mercilessly that it took years for Ludlow to recover from the beating it took in 1459.

York and his son, Edmund, fled to Ireland while his eldest son, Edward, Earl of March, hurried away with Warwick and Salisbury to Calais. All the leaders escaped with their lives but precious little else – they had abandoned everyone and everything, including their honour.

On 20 November, parliament met at Coventry: notice that London is once again avoided as being too partisan towards York and Warwick. This was the first parliament since York's second and short-lived protectorate in 1456 and there appear to have been some anomalies in the elections, but it hardly mattered because the parliament was only really called for one reason, which may be pretty clear from the name it was later given from the Yorkist perspective: the 'Parliament of Devils'.

This parliament passed an Act of Attainder condemning York and his leading supporters. For those who aren't sure about an attainder, it was a process whereby parliament passed an Act which basically said that someone was a traitor, condemned them – without trial or much in the way of evidence – and ordered the confiscation of their lands. It was therefore a very blunt political weapon of the government, but because it was agreed by parliament, it carried the force of law. It could of course – like any Act of parliament – be reversed by a subsequent parliament.

In any case, by the end of 1459, York and his few allies were abroad and attainted. A casual observer of the period might assume that, since the queen now controlled the government, the matter was settled, but of course, if you've been paying attention, you will know that as long as York was alive, there could be no peace…

Chapter 12

A Yorkist Revival?

THE FIRST CRISIS of the Wars of the Roses was far from over – in fact, it had scarcely begun. The fleeing Duke of York found a welcome in Ireland and his cousin, the Earl of Warwick, still held the vital base of Calais.

York's success in Ireland has always puzzled me a little. Here was a man who appeared to lack charisma, and found it very difficult to win support among his own English peers, yet he was apparently popular with the commons and with the Irish lords. My gut feeling is that the English commons loved the 'idea' of York – a man who would promote the holy grail of 'good government' – or who at least said he would. Most of them would never have seen him – let alone conversed with him. So, for the commons, he was a sort of figurehead in whose name a variety of grievances might be raised. We saw this right back in 1450 when York's name was used by some of the rebels during Jack Cade's rebellion.

For the Irish, I think it was similar: if they backed York, they were supporting a sort of 'alternative' English government, from which concessions might later be gained. However, it seems to me that as a general rule, the more people got to know the Duke of York, the less they warmed to him.

Meanwhile his ally, Warwick, with his back to the wall in Calais, was in his element. Henry Beaufort, Duke of Somerset, was, in theory, appointed by the king to replace Warwick as the new Captain of Calais and was tasked with capturing it. And – bless him – he tried very hard, but his attempts were hamstrung by the usual combination of inadequate resources, poor co-ordination and military incompetence. Calais was a hard nut to crack in any case: no surprise really, since it was designed to be exactly that. Even when Andrew Trollope and some former members of the Calais garrison were employed, there was no success and the royal losses were heavy.

As long as Warwick could pay his garrison, he was secure – but how did he do that? Well, the same way as he had before: by piracy and pillaging, mainly against the French. Such activities not only gave him resources that Somerset could only dream of, but also made him very popular in southern English coastal counties such as Kent, which had suffered from French raids in the past. Indeed, so highly esteemed was Warwick in those parts that he was kept fully informed of every step the Lancastrian government planned to take against him. The result of this was that in January 1460, when a significant expedition was assembled at Sandwich to be launched against Calais, Warwick sent a force of his own there and – aided by a few locals –captured the ships and took them away for his own use. I'm tempted to say that ships didn't grow on trees, but I suppose they did...

Anyway, Warwick's actions brought the government – poorly organised, poorly resourced and poorly informed as usual – to the verge of panic. In March 1460, Warwick felt secure enough to leave Calais for two months to confer with York in Ireland. But what, one wonders, were they planning? Naturally they intended to restore themselves to the government, but beyond that, how far did their ambitions stretch? We've already seen that despite York's success at St Albans in 1455, his situation quickly became untenable. Surely a repeat of that scenario would cost a fortune and gain York and his allies nothing.

Late in May 1460, Warwick returned to Calais, no doubt with Yorkist plans firmly in place, but there was an interesting encounter on his way back. Henry Holland, Duke of Exeter, who had been replaced by Warwick as Admiral in 1457, was presented with an opportunity to prove his worth against his rival. Exeter, whom you may recall had a trickle of royal blood running through his veins, was given command of a sizeable fleet, specifically assembled to catch Warwick in the English Channel. But Exeter was a rather weak reed, as was demonstrated by what happened next. Though faced with a superior fleet, Warwick nevertheless decided to attack and, when he did, Exeter fled. I mention this only because it is one of many such episodes, which taken together helped to create the living legend that was Warwick: a man of decisive and effective action, who cut through all the clutter to 'get the job done.'

When Warwick returned to Calais, Somerset was still waiting for new resources to try again to dislodge him. One almost has to feel sorry for Somerset, because his reinforcements were at Sandwich poised to sail across to join him, when – have a guess – yes, Warwick sent another force there to scatter them. But this was not just a raid, as had occurred in January; this was stage one of an invasion. Sandwich was taken by Warwick's uncle, William Neville, Lord Fauconberg – yes, another Neville. By the end of June, the earls of Warwick and Salisbury, together with York's son, Edward Earl of March, were all in Kent with an army of close to 2,000 men.

Within hours they were at Canterbury and their numbers swelled to tens of thousands as they marched on to London. But why was there so much support for them so quickly? Well, the Yorkist earls relied on their tried and trusted weapon of propaganda – spread throughout the south-east before they even landed. To us, the tired old promises of reforming a corrupt government might be wearing a bit thin, but at the time examples of government corruption and incompetence were probably obvious enough to all.

The City of London authorities tried to remain independent by striking an initial pose of resistance, only to submit to the inevitable on 2 July 1460 and allow

Warwick across London Bridge into the capital. The Lancastrian garrison under Thomas, Lord Scales, withdrew into the Tower and waited for King Henry to come to their aid. Good luck with that.

Once the Yorkists were in London, the city had little option but to support them with money and men. Thus, London was being inexorably drawn into the Yorkist camp. Though Warwick spoke a lot about reconciliation and peace, he was gathering his resources for war. And he was not a man to hang about, so within days of his arrival – on 5 July – his army headed out of London again leaving his father, the Earl of Salisbury, to hold the City.

What was the king doing all this time? Well, contrary to popular rumour spread at the time, he was not fleeing. Instead, leaving the queen and his son at Coventry, King Henry was heading south to London until he halted his advance at Northampton, probably hoping to gather more men from his northern supporters.

As so often before, Henry's councillors were divided about what he should do next. Now if you are beginning to think that the nobles of this whole period were a rather spineless shower, I think that would be a bit harsh. The council wanted to avoid wholesale slaughter and some thought that hearing what the rebels had to say was still worthwhile. Others, such Humphrey Stafford, Duke of Buckingham – who, as you will recall, had got it badly wrong at St Albans – were not prepared to be duped again.

By 10 July, the earls of Warwick and March had reached Northampton, where the Lancastrian defences were very strong and ringed with trenches and cannon. In the morning, a final attempt at peace was made to no avail and so, in the afternoon, the Yorkists attacked.

Let's pause for a moment to consider what the Yorkists were trying to achieve by fighting the king himself at Northampton. Since they gave specific orders to spare the king, they certainly weren't trying to kill him. But if they did not, then how would anything be different, even if they won? The rest of the order gives us a hefty clue because, although the soldiers were also told to spare common men, they were ordered to kill the lords and knights. The aim was clearly a major regime change – the pro-Lancastrian upper echelons were to be destroyed.

All of that, of course, assumed that the Yorkists would win, but the odds were heavily stacked against them because Northampton seemed too strong. But as I've mentioned before, there were many factors which contributed to triumph or disaster, and a common one was the weather.

For several days and nights there had been heavy rain at Northampton, to such an extent that the roads were very difficult to use. More importantly, the king's artillery, with its powder damp, was rendered useless.

Despite this setback, the king might well still have won at Northampton but for the actions of one of his trusted lords: Lord Edmund Grey of Ruthin – not to be confused with a dozen others by the name of Grey. Lord Grey made a secret deal with Warwick to defect with his men at the moment of the Yorkist attack. Since his men were in the Lancastrian vanguard defending a steep and entrenched position, it seems reasonable to assume that, without their treachery, the king might have had a better than decent chance of defending the town successfully. As it was, the Lancastrian army was taken utterly by surprise and swiftly routed – probably in less than an hour. Several earls fought to defend the king and died for their loyalty, including Buckingham, Shrewsbury and Lord Egremont, brother of Henry Percy, Earl of Northumberland, and always hostile to York and the Nevilles.

Warwick now had possession of the king – a vitally important piece in the game, because he could now claim to be acting with royal sanction. Arriving back in London with Henry VI in tow on 16 July 1460, Warwick continued to profess his loyalty. Nevertheless, in practice he quickly took over the government and appointed Yorkist men to key positions of influence. A parliament was called, mainly because there were some attainders to reverse. But after that, what next?

Richard Duke of York was not yet in England, but presumably Warwick was following an agreed plan – or was he? We'll probably never know what York had originally intended, but he wasn't there and Warwick was. Warwick must have felt that his success had been achieved not simply by military muscle, but also by careful diplomacy and skilful propaganda. He had gathered more supporters at the heart of government – more nobles and bishops – who believed his claims about loyalty and good government. The clever Warwick was probably loathe to destroy that embryonic coalition by any talk of replacing the king or disinheriting Prince Edward. Also, Warwick was anxious to return to Calais to ensure that Somerset did not capitalise on his absence. In the event, Somerset made a deal with Warwick and escaped to France; after that, the Lancastrians holding the Tower under Lord Scales soon gave up too.

So, even before York himself returned, the Yorkists were in the ascendant once more and all was well. Er, well, not exactly…

Chapter 13

The End of the 'Old Guard'

SO, WE'VE REACHED the height of summer in 1460 and several battles have been fought. Yet the Duke of York and the queen seem no closer to any sort of resolution of their differences. The Yorkists are in the driving seat, but apparently without a road map to follow. Isn't it therefore just 1455 all over again?

No, it's not.

The state of affairs in summer 1460 was a world away from that of May 1455. True, both years saw pitched battles between the court and Yorkist factions, but the situation was very different, not least because neither faction could claim control over all of England. While Warwick held most of the south-east and had strengthened his grip on Calais, the queen's forces, though somewhat disorganised, were strong in much of the north where the Percys and the Cliffords held sway, and also in the south-west.

Though Warwick held Henry VI and thus could act with legal authority on his side, his control was limited. Queen Margaret had been forced to flee into Wales, but she still had her son, Edward, Prince of Wales, with her if anything should happen to King Henry.

So the situation was far more equally balanced than it appeared at first sight, and of course, there was the 'elephant in the room' – or rather out of the room – because Richard, Duke of York, in whose name all of this chaos had been undertaken, was still in Ireland. The sixty-million-dollar question was, therefore: what was York going to do?

Early in September 1460, York made his dramatic entrance when he landed at Chester. What became clear almost at once is that York was entering the ring as world champion, not a contender. To those who joined him as he made his way through the Marches and across the Midlands, he made it clear that he was coming as king, not subject. Such ideas were conveyed in those days by meaningful signs, and I don't mean placards reading 'York for King', because most folk couldn't read anyway. But they certainly would have recognised the royal coat of arms displayed by York and the fact that his sword was carried upright before him as he processed towards London. The latter was a clear indication of kingship and everyone would have taken note.

The End of the 'Old Guard'

In October York, accompanied by hundreds of supporters, finally reached Westminster, which was then outside the walls of the city of London. The next scene is very well known: York went into the parliament chamber and approached the royal throne, resting his hand upon the seat and apparently expecting that those present would at once acclaim him as the rightful king. They didn't. Instead, the Archbishop of Canterbury broke the awkward silence to enquire whether York had come to see King Henry…

Not for the first time, Richard Duke of York had made a bad political misjudgement, for among the lords there was no enthusiasm at all to force out King Henry VI. But clearly York had decided that the only way he could stay in power was to press his claim to the throne. We can certainly understand that, because several times before he had made agreements with the king only to see them overturned in favour of his enemies. Thus he had come to believe that no lasting settlement could be reached as long as Henry remained king.

In this York may well have been right, but unfortunately for him, hardly anyone agreed and, most notably, one of those who disagreed was the Earl of Warwick. Whatever the leaders had agreed in Ireland, Warwick was pursuing a far more conciliatory policy than York appeared to expect.

As long as York's claim remained theoretical, it could be ignored; it could be stuffed into a dusty drawer somewhere and filed under 'A for Awkward'. But once that claim was formally lodged, the highest law court in the land – the Lords in parliament – was obliged to make a decision about it one way or the other.

Put yourself in their shoes: they had sworn oaths of allegiance to King Henry and the throne had been in Lancastrian hands for three generations. Henry VI also had a legitimate male heir so the future of his dynasty was assured.

However, despite the fact that few folk in 1460 knew anything about the events of 1399 when the first Lancastrian king took the throne from Richard II, York claimed that the throne was his by right. As he argued: 'Though right for a time… be put to silence, yet it rotteth not, nor shall not perish.'

Fine words, but was York right?

Well no, not really. York's actions, as ever, were underpinned by his basic belief that he ought to be king. Since he was of royal blood, it was unfair that he had to put up with all this political manoeuvring just to have some say in the affairs of the kingdom.

However, while he had wealth, power and a genuinely important role in the government, York accepted that Henry VI was his anointed king. But during the 1450s, years of struggle and rejection by the crown had eroded his sense of loyalty. The trouble was that no one else saw it that way and they viewed with distaste his willingness to overthrow the king. This was a king, let's remember, who was not going to be awarded any 'best king ever' medals. Yet still the lords supported him.

Thus there was a new impasse: York was not prepared to submit to Henry, and the lords were not willing to depose Henry. What was needed therefore was a compromise – some sort of flexible filler to cover the cracks for a while. That compromise was the optimistically named Act of Accord, passed by Parliament on 24 October 1460. It decreed that Henry would retain the throne during his lifetime but that after his death, York and his heirs would succeed him.

Sounds good? No, not really. The act ought to have been called the Act of Discord, because it divided political opinion very sharply. It required men of all ranks to decide whether it was fairer that Edward, Prince of Wales, should be disinherited rather than Richard, Duke of York. So although it certainly was a compromise, it was one that provided the queen with a purpose and a rallying cry. Somehow, despite having possession of London, the king and all the machinery of government, the Act of Accord seemed to turn opinion against York.

Margaret, as ever, tried to seize the initiative. While King Henry's half-brother, Jasper Tudor, gathered support in Wales, she took ship to Scotland, where she bought some support by the fairly extreme measure of surrendering the border town of Berwick-upon-Tweed to the Scots. Meanwhile Henry, Duke of Somerset, returned from France, landed in Dorset and, with the support of the Earl of Devon, raised the south-west for King Henry.

By November, Somerset and Devon were marching north to join with other Lancastrian forces under Henry Percy, Earl of Northumberland, at York. The Yorkist-controlled government in London was powerless to stop them and soon realised that, if it did not take action, it would be swept aside by the incoming Lancastrian tide.

Suddenly it was all happening. Richard, Duke of York, with his closest ally, Richard Neville, Earl of Salisbury, decided to head north since that was where the main threat seemed to lie. With them went York's second son, Edmund, Earl of Rutland, and Salisbury's son, Thomas Neville.

York's eldest son, Edward, Earl of March, still only eighteen years of age, was dispatched to Wales to counter the forces of Jasper Tudor, while Warwick remained to keep control in London with King Henry.

Winter – as has been said quite a lot in recent years – was coming; and December was not the ideal time to begin a military campaign, especially in the north. York's army of several thousand was harried on its journey northwards and, though one suspects the losses were not great, they were still not good for morale. Nevertheless, York reached Sandal Castle near Wakefield by 21 December, with his forces more or less intact. The problem was that with the main Lancastrian force so close by at Pontefract, York was surrounded by hostile forces and short of supplies – after all, he had an army to feed. Christmas 1460 must have been very uncomfortable for York and his men. They were frequently obliged to forage away from the castle in the most dangerous of circumstances.

What happened next is now unlikely ever to be explained fully – like much that happened in the fifteenth century. Half a dozen reasons have been suggested as to why the Duke of York left the relative security of Sandal Castle to meet the

Lancastrians in battle. Take your pick: he was rash, he was betrayed, he was badly informed, he was provoked by insults, or he went to rescue some foraging troops. The primary sources we have are – as ever – fragments which offer no conclusive explanation.

Much has been made of all this but for me, whatever the reason for his final act, it does not change my assessment of the man as a whole. Many seek to defend York and I do have some sympathy for his unique and awkward position. But York was a proud man whose pride sometimes got in the way of his success. He was a far from charismatic leader and his frequent misjudgements about how other men would act often led him into trouble.

On 30 December, York led his army out to battle and he, along with possibly several thousand of his men, was killed. His son Edmund was also killed in the rout, as was Salisbury's son, Thomas. Salisbury himself was later captured and put to death.

This was a cataclysmic blow to the Yorkist cause. York and Salisbury, the twin pillars of the Yorkist edifice, had been brought crashing down. Surely this must mark the end of the Yorkist opposition to the court of Henry VI and Queen Margaret.

But let's not forget that the powerful Richard Neville, Earl of Warwick, still held London as well as the king himself. And the Duke of York's eldest son, Edward Earl of March, was in Ludlow, gathering men to him.

Though both Warwick and March had both just lost a father and a brother, they had by no means given up the struggle. The crisis was not yet over…

Chapter 14

Two Battles

BY THE START of 1461, Richard, Duke of York, and his chief ally, Richard Neville, Earl of Salisbury, were dead and the forces of York, though not broken, were certainly scattered. The Earl of Warwick still held London and critically, the king himself. But outside London, only Edward, Earl of March – York's eldest son – had any sort of an army and he was far to the west at the great Yorkist stronghold of Wigmore Castle near Ludlow.

Realising that she was on the cusp of victory, Queen Margaret did not hesitate. Though it was deep in winter, she amassed a vast northern army, bolstered by Scots, and in February began the long march south to retake London and free her husband. At the same time, she ordered Jasper Tudor, Earl of Pembroke, to stop Edward, Earl of March, from moving east to support Warwick.

As neither Warwick nor March was able to support the other, they were on their own.

At Ludlow, young Edward was gathering his Marcher allies to Wigmore, knowing that Jasper Tudor was approaching through Wales. He dared not set out for London until he had dealt with the advancing Lancastrian army.

At dawn on a crisp morning on mostly likely the 2nd, but possibly the 3 February, St Blaise's Day, Edward drew up his men in their battle array. As they stood there, a remarkable – and to the medieval eye – terrible sight greeted them. Ice crystals in the air formed what we would call today a parhelion: three suns low in the freezing sky. At the time, many must have thought that the strange sight was an ill omen, but Edward, showing his characteristic coolness under the most severe pressure, turned the awkward moment to his advantage. It was, he claimed boldly, a manifestation of the Holy Trinity in the sky and was thus a sign of God's support for their cause. In an age when God's favour was much in demand, it was a powerful symbol.

Did that episode make much difference to the outcome of the impending battle? I doubt it, but Edward himself always made a difference in any battle. No man could mistake him on the field, for he was an exceptionally tall, well-built warrior, encased in the finest armour and wielding weapons of devastating power.

The Lancastrian army that faced him that day, where two roads met at Mortimer's Cross in Herefordshire, was rather disorderly. There were Welshmen under Jasper Tudor and his father, Owen, but the weakest link was on the left flank where James Butler, Earl of Wiltshire, led a ragtag assortment of foreign mercenaries and Irishmen. Little detail is known of this battle. The Irish appear to have fought savagely and noisily but wore little body armour and used darts and spears rather than the heavy bludgeoning weapons employed by the English. Though brave, they were slaughtered by Edward's infantry and, while the Welsh fought well, they too were eventually overwhelmed and destroyed, with many being hounded into the nearby River Lugg where they either drowned or froze to death.

The Earl of Wiltshire escaped – indeed, he gained something of a reputation as a 'runner'. Jasper Tudor also managed to get away, but his father was not so fortunate. Edward, no doubt still seething about the death of his father and younger brother, Edmund, to whom he was especially close, executed Owen Tudor and the other captured leaders at Hereford.

But because Jasper Tudor and Wiltshire had escaped, Edward could not assume that the way was clear for him to advance towards London. Also, the battle had been hard fought and he needed time to replenish and strengthen his army. As a result, he waited in the west during most of February for news of how Warwick was faring against the queen's army.

Queen Margaret's army thundered south, like some great juggernaut, carving such a path of destruction that many fled before it, arriving as refugees with lurid tales which grew ever more terrible with the telling. Panic gripped those in its path, although the evidence we have suggests that it behaved very much like other large armies on the move. It needed to be fed, watered and amused... It suited the Yorkist propagandists, however, to present the queen's army as a murdering horde of northerners.

The Lancastrian army boasted not only the queen, the Prince of Wales and the northern lords, Northumberland and Clifford, but also the dukes of Exeter and Somerset, and the earls of Devon and Shrewsbury, all of whom, remember, had already marched their men north to support Queen Margaret in the first place.

Meanwhile, Richard Neville, Earl of Warwick, had assembled a strong army of his own, with the support of the Duke of Norfolk, the earls of Suffolk and Arundel and his own brother, John Neville, Lord Montagu.

Warwick set out on the road north from London to meet the Lancastrians head on. With him went the king, in whose name – in theory – he was still acting. The two armies met on 17 February 1461 at St. Albans, where you will recall Warwick was victorious in 1455.

This time, Warwick was significantly less successful. It was a brutal and confusing affair – like every other battle! But I shall say little about it here because, as ever, the evidence for what actually happened is both patchy and conflicting. Suffice to say that Warwick lost the battle – probably without most of his army engaging with the enemy at all.

The brunt of the Lancastrian assault was borne by his vanguard under the command of John Neville. Against such a large force, the vanguard was obliterated and the rest of the army disintegrated in panic. Warwick also contrived to lose possession of Henry VI, which meant that the Yorkists could no longer claim to be anything other than traitors. The second battle of St Albans was most definitely not Warwick's finest hour, and his defeat left the way open for the queen – reunited with King Henry – to march on London.

When, on 19 February, news of the disaster reached Edward, Earl of March, he set off eastwards at once with every man he could gather and a few days later he met up in the Cotswolds with – one hopes – a rather chastened Earl of Warwick.

With the Lancastrian army at the gates of London, Edward had a defining decision to make. The Act of Accord, agreed by the lords the previous year, had made his father Richard, Duke of York, the heir apparent. Edward inherited that right to the throne, but it was clear that the moment the queen arrived in London, the Act of Accord would be torn into tiny little pieces and cast into the wind.

If Edward and Warwick continued to fight against the queen now, they would be forced to depose Henry VI and put Edward in his place. The alternative was to flee the country forever. Edward's decision would bring either peace at last, or plunge the country into another bout of warfare. I'm afraid there's no prize for guessing what he chose to do…

Chapter 15

The Bloody Meadow

WHERE WOULD WE be in our study of history without an appreciation of irony?

Just as Edward, now assuming the title of Duke of York, must have feared that Queen Margaret's army would take London and thereby seize control of all the resources and engines of government to add to her possession of the king himself, he received a surprising present. Scarcely had he learned of Warwick's defeat at St Albans, when the astonishing news reached him that Queen Margaret, with the city of London at her mercy, had decided to withdraw her army to Dunstable. Now, whatever the attractions of Dunstable, it wasn't London. So why did she withdraw?

Well, the City of London authorities – like many of their counterparts across the land – were anxious not to annoy either faction in this dangerous struggle for power. So they sent representatives, led by a couple of heavyweight widowed duchesses – those of Bedford and Buckingham – to inform the queen that she could have entrance to the city provided that there was no pillaging.

Margaret, so often portrayed as the queen from hell, agreed to this, but, like everyone else, she knew that simply telling her soldiers to behave would be completely ineffective, so she withdrew the army to Dunstable to reassure the city authorities and the good folk of London. This was a considered and honourable decision, but she reckoned without the speed of Edward of York's reaction to the changing events.

Hindsight is a wonderful thing of course. Yes, it turned out to be an error on her part – and quite a big one too – but I've no doubt that if her army had entered London, there would have been trouble. Why? Because Edward's father had always been popular in the capital, and what happened next showed that the good folk of London were, at heart, still supportive of York.

When the city leaders issued a proclamation appealing for calm to allow the royal army into the city, all hell seems to have broken loose. Though there was certainly a strong whiff of Yorkist propaganda in the air, there is no denying that there was genuine support among Londoners for Edward of York. Many men took up arms and by that point, even if the mayor and aldermen had wanted to open the gates to Queen Margaret, it wasn't going to happen.

Meanwhile, Edward, buoyed by his victory at Mortimer's Cross, was marching fast to London with an army at his back. When I read about this critical moment in English history, I find it a constant source of annoyance that Warwick is often credited with the elevation of Edward to the throne and given the flattering nickname of 'Kingmaker'. Are we really to believe that Warwick said to Edward: 'Here's an idea: why don't you become king?'

If the events of 1461 tell us anything about the relationship between the two men, it is that all the energy comes from Edward. Yes, Warwick was a key adviser; yes, Warwick possessed enormous resources; but Warwick had also just lost a major battle – and control of the king. His reputation was a little dented, while the military power of Edward had been greatly enhanced. Edward may have been barely nineteen, but he did not need Warwick to tell him that the throne could be his. By late February 1461, Edward was entering London unopposed and in the first few days of March he was acclaimed as king. In the coming months and years, Warwick would be a brave ally, but Edward was always his own man.

Of course, saying he was king was not quite the same as being king, and the odds of success were still heavily stacked against him. Queen Margaret still had a large army in the field, though she had withdrawn it to the Midlands. Margaret also had the king with her, so she could act with confidence and authority. Most of the nobility still sided with Henry VI, despite his obvious failings and their lingering mistrust of the queen. So often when people talk about this period they emphasise how frequently nobles changed sides, but if you want a powerful demonstration of loyalty and commitment then you have it in this deep-seated allegiance to the anointed king, however flawed he was.

Yet, for all the Lancastrian advantages, they lacked a personality and a cause to die for. In Edward, the Yorkists had the ideal candidate as king: physically tall, well-built and handsome, but with a lively, engaging manner which attracted both men and women. He was also a very able soldier and a sensible tactician. Small wonder that he inspired both confidence and loyalty.

In March 1461 the mood in London was upbeat despite the powerful forces Edward faced. But he had to seize the moment and had to move fast if he was to maintain the momentum he had initiated at Mortimer's Cross. The longer a stalemate continued, the weaker Edward's position would become as his supporters realised that he could not deliver the 'new dawn' that he had promised. All Queen Margaret had to do was wait, but Edward had to act.

So what did he do? Firstly, Edward needed cash so he squeezed a few thousand pounds more out of the city of London. He also needed to raise more men, because the Marcher army which had won at Mortimer's Cross was nowhere near large enough to take on the royal host. His allies – Warwick, Norfolk, Fauconberg and others – were swiftly despatched to raise men. He offered a pardon to any Lancastrian supporters below a certain income level if they submitted within ten days. Why? Because Edward knew that, though he was unlikely now to persuade any of the most powerful nobles to join him, he could appeal to the gentry and other commoners. He was right because such men were the backbone of any army. Indeed, the sustained and widespread support of the gentry for Edward was notable in 1461 and throughout his reign. Edward also put a bounty on the heads of a select few Lancastrians, such as their leading military strategist, the veteran Sir Andrew Trollope.

On 13 March, Edward led his army northwards out of London, but not too quickly as he wanted to give every opportunity for new supporters to join him. Thus he did not arrive at Pontefract in the north until perhaps 27 March.

What happened next is, as ever, shrouded in a lot of uncertainty. One thing everyone can agree on, however, is that it was very cold and therefore not great weather for fighting battles, fording rivers, and foraging for food, animal fodder and other necessities. As to the military action which took place, culminating in the battle of Towton, I tend to share the long-held view that it was a two-day affair – though I know that a recent scholar has suggested otherwise.

On 28 March, the Yorkists crossed the River Aire at Ferrybridge. It was not easy and it cost many lives – Warwick himself received a leg wound in the action and, on the Lancastrian side, it appears that Lord John Clifford, who had been a fierce opponent of the Yorkists since St Albans in 1455 where his father perished, was trapped and killed.

Having crossed the river, Edward was able to move his army closer to the Lancastrians, who were camped across the road north from Ferrybridge to Tadcaster and ultimately York itself. Low on supplies, Edward could not afford to delay, but the Lancastrians must also have been in similar difficulties since they had occupied the area for much longer. Thus both sides were desperate to resolve matters swiftly, which is presumably why both sides were apparently content to begin their battle early on the morning of 29 March, Palm Sunday, in a snow blizzard.

I've noted before that the weather sometimes played a significant role in decisive battles and, in this case, though the conditions may not have decided the outcome, they certainly determined the course of the early stages of the fighting.

Of the battle itself we know next to nothing and there are no eye-witness accounts. Any description of the battle is therefore an attempt to patch together a few fragments with the inevitable risk that one might emphasise one particular aspect and play down others of which we know little or nothing. But hey-ho, we have to say something.

How many men fought that day? Well, pick a number. Both armies were large by late medieval standards but, as always, contemporary estimates by people who were not even present have to be regarded as very suspect. Certainly, it was the largest battle of the Wars of the Roses period and, since many of the most powerful men took part, one can suppose that the retinues they commanded were considerable. Many thousands took part on both sides and, if I had to guess, I would say about 25,000 on each side. It could have been more, but even that is an awful lot of soldiers.

The battlefield was between the Yorkshire villages of Saxton and Towton. The Yorkists seem to have held the higher ground and it appears that the battle began – as was customary – with an exchange of arrows. Here a strong wind seemed to play its part, as the Lancastrian arrows fell consistently short, while those of the Yorkists did not. The apparent consequence was that the Lancastrians were taking heavy fire and casualties while the Yorkists received almost none. It seems that this prompted the Lancastrians to launch an attack. They seemed to have initial success, pushing back the Yorkist battle line, especially on one flank, but then the battle dissolved into the usual bloody press of men-at-arms bashing lumps out of each other with poll-axe, mace and sword.

We are told this carnage went on for hours – perhaps all day – but if so, they would have needed a tea break now and then. The two lines must have fought to a standstill for much of the time, but it seems to me that Edward's role in the heart of the battle would have been crucial, as at Mortimer's Cross. Even more important though was the arrival – late in the day – of fresh Yorkist troops led by the Duke of Norfolk. Those reinforcements gave renewed impetus to the Yorkists and they drove their enemies back. The rout that followed was both savage and deadly. If men were not cut down, they were drowned in nearby rivers, such as Cock Beck, as they tried to flee. The death toll among the vanquished was very great indeed, and not without reason was the area called the 'Bloody Meadow' for a long time afterwards. Though we may argue about the numbers, there can surely be no doubt that thousands were killed, making Towton one of the bloodiest battles ever fought on English soil.

But it was the permanent removal of some of Edward's greatest enemies which made the battle so decisive: Lord Clifford had been killed earlier; Sir Andrew Trollope – wounded at St Albans – did not survive Towton; the Earl of Northumberland was killed in the field and the Earl of Devon was executed afterwards. Queen Margaret and her husband escaped to Scotland, as did the dukes of Somerset and Exeter, but the Lancastrian cause was fatally wounded.

Edward was now *de facto* king and had defeated his enemies, but he was still far from secure. The crisis was not quite over, because Queen Margaret was not the sort of person to give up even after such a colossal disaster.

Chapter 16

Post-Towton Blues

WE'VE SEEN HOW Edward, Earl of March, bounced back from the despair of his father's defeat and death in the winter of 1460. Through his sheer force of personality and his military prowess he had dragged the Yorkist cause back to its feet and managed, very much against the odds, to defeat the majority of the English nobility at the bloody battle of Towton. Edward had already been acclaimed as King Edward IV in London and had effectively sealed his crown with the victory at Towton, but that did not mean that he was universally accepted as king.

There were essentially two reasons why. Firstly, King Henry, Queen Margaret and Edward, Prince of Wales, were all still very much alive, so the Lancastrian cause still possessed a royal figurehead, a passionate champion and a male heir.

Secondly, the dispute had gone on for so long that some men might now be described as 'diehard' Lancastrians. They were utterly committed to King Henry's cause and only his death, or theirs, could put a stop to their intransigent opposition.

So although Edward had defeated his enemies and nominally controlled the kingdom, he still had some work to do before he could rest a little easier on his new throne.

Edward remained in the north for long enough to establish his control and, incidentally, to execute that serial escapist, the Earl of Wiltshire, whose luck finally ran out. Then King Edward headed back to London – after all, he had a coronation to arrange. He also needed to enshrine the Lancastrian defeat in parliamentary law by passing attainders against the leading rebels. Some men would have to be punished, but in general, a consistent feature of Edward's kingship was to build bridges with former Lancastrians. He recognised that the weakness of his father's position in the 1450s was its narrow base of support and thus Edward made overtures to several influential enemies in the early years of his reign.

Of course, some enemies would never be reconciled and though on the one hand Edward wore a rather fetching kid glove, on the other he used a much uglier mailed fist. The most difficult areas of the kingdom to control would always be the far-flung parts: the north, Wales and the south-west. Of these, the north was the most dangerous, because, as we have seen, it was far enough away from London that local lords like the Cliffords, the Nevilles and the Percys could basically do what they liked. After Towton, the heartland of Lancastrian opposition lay in the Percy lands. Who better then to employ the new king's mailed fist, than their perennial rivals, the Nevilles? Rooting out lingering Percy opposition was a task tailor-made for the Neville brothers, Richard, Earl of Warwick, and John, Lord Montagu.

If there were problems in the north, it was inevitable that the Scots would also be involved. Not only had cross-border raiding been a way of life for the folk on both sides for hundreds of years, but King Henry had also taken refuge in Scotland after Towton. Whether the Scots offered Henry support or not would clearly have some impact on how much resistance he could muster against Edward.

At this point, it may be helpful if we take a brief look at what was going on in Scotland. The king of Scotland during the 1450s was James II, who was no stranger to royal family power struggles. By the mid-1450s he felt secure enough to embark on raids into England, hoping to take advantage of English divisions. After the Battle of Northampton in 1460, when the Lancastrian cause seemed to be on the point of collapse, he decided to strike hard at one of the few remaining English-held strongholds in Scotland, Roxburgh Castle.

James besieged Roxburgh with a strong army, bristling with the new military technology of the age: cannon. But it was this weapon, however, which brought about his downfall. Unfortunately, he was standing close to one when it exploded while being fired to celebrate the arrival of his queen, Mary of Guelders. A chunk of cannon cut deep into his thigh and he died shortly afterwards. It did not help Roxburgh Castle, however, as Queen Mary later had it pounded to bits. James II was succeeded by his eight-year-old son, who became James III.

The point of this little diversion into Scottish history is to observe that, at the very moment when King Henry was looking for help, the Scots had a royal minority government. As is often the case, such interim governments are made up of folk who disagree about policy and so it was in 1461 when Henry VI came calling. The Scots were divided about what to do and the result was that, in order to get any help at all from the Scots, Queen Margaret had to make them an offer that was too good to pass up. So in April 1461, the desperate queen gave them the towns of Berwick and Carlisle, which were the key fortresses at the east and west ends of the border. Though Berwick was handed over, Carlisle put up a fight and was never taken by the Scots.

All the same, Edward could hardly ignore the danger signs and so he decided to bring forward his coronation to allow him to deal with the problem. The fact that he did not rush north probably has everything to do with the effectiveness of the Nevilles in strengthening the border and suppressing pockets of Lancastrian resistance.

Edward also had other problems to contend with because an ally of Queen Margaret in Normandy, Pierre de Brézé, decided to attack the Channel Islands. Now you might wonder why that was important, but remember that Lancastrian support in the south-west had been strong and, from Jersey, Brézé would have been well placed to support a Lancastrian rising in Cornwall or Devon. However, here again Edward had a bit of good fortune, because in July 1461 the French king, Charles VII, died and his son, Louis XI, was more well disposed towards the new Yorkist king. De Brézé was therefore recalled, though the threat of a French invasion would re-emerge several times later because Louis XI's neutrality did not last long.

In England itself, Edward was slow to establish his authority and, if you think about it, this was not that surprising, because for thirty-five years or more, Henry VI had been the anointed and undisputed king. For most people, Edward was a completely unknown quantity. Who was this young nineteen-year-old whippersnapper who said he was now the king? Aside from any difficulty the bulk of the population had in realigning their allegiance, there were plenty of individuals who were more than happy to take advantage of any chaos – administrative or legal – to promote their own interests.

So Edward had to do what kings had done for centuries; he had to go on the road. He had to show himself to as many of his subjects as possible: we're not talking here about your average ploughmen, but influential local knights, gentlemen, merchants and such like. He had to dispense law and make decisions in local areas to demonstrate that he was in control.

In August 1461, Edward IV set off from London, accompanied by, among others, his best friend and ally, the newly-promoted Lord William Hastings. He progressed through several of the counties of southern England from east to west as far as Bristol and then north into the familiar territory of the Welsh Marches and back to London via the Midlands. In the meantime, he launched a campaign to destroy Lancastrian power in Wales, where the loyalist, Jasper Tudor, Earl of Pembroke, and Henry Holland, Duke of Exeter – among others – held several key strongholds including Harlech Castle.

As I said before, Henry Holland was, like Jasper Tudor, related to Henry VI but by a different Lancastrian branch. He was, however, a great deal less effective than Jasper and you may recall that he was the one who scuttled away from Warwick in the Channel.

A successful Welsh campaign was led by two up-and-coming Yorkists, Lord William Herbert and Lord Walter Ferrers. They defeated Jasper Tudor and the Duke of Exeter so that, by 1462, only the castle of Harlech was left in Lancastrian hands and, on its own, that was little more than an irritation.

But what about the north? There, matters had not yet been truly resolved. Warwick had been given virtually a free hand in the region by being appointed Warden of both the East and West Marches. In September, all seemed to be going well when the main Percy stronghold of Alnwick Castle surrendered and then Sir Ralph Percy handed over the great fortress at Dunstanburgh. However, to the surprise of the Nevilles, Edward decided, as part of his policy of reconciliation, to hand Dunstanburgh back to Ralph. One can imagine that Warwick was far from pleased, but it was an early – and noteworthy – sign that Edward would not be ruled by Warwick.

The rather fluid situation was likely to remain so as long as there was any Scottish support for the House of Lancaster. Edward placed much faith in diplomacy, so he schemed with Scottish rebels and negotiated with the French king Louis XI and with Duke Philip of Burgundy in the hope of putting more pressure on the widowed Scottish queen, Mary of Guelders. Mary paid for Margaret to go to France to see Louis XI, but was that to help her or to get rid of her? Rumour had it that Margaret's general at Towton and fellow exile, Henry Beaufort, Duke of Somerset, had seduced the Scottish queen, but then such stories seemed to follow him about…

One imagines that Margaret's presence anywhere tended to ramp up the pressure and certainly, while Margaret was absent during the summer of 1462, seeking support in France, the Yorkists gained more success in Northumberland. But upon Margaret's return in October, Lancastrian fortunes improved again, bolstered by a little – but only a little – French support in the form of several hundred men led by De Brézé. Pausing in Scotland to pick up Henry VI, the Lancastrians landed at Bamburgh Castle, which surrendered at once. Ralph Percy, restored by Edward to Dunstanburgh, returned to the Lancastrian fold and Alnwick was besieged and swiftly capitulated.

In a few short days, Margaret had regained the three great Percy strongholds and raised the royal standard in the north. So it seemed that the Lancastrian cause was not so dead after all.

Chapter 17

A Lancastrian Revival?

ONE OF THE things which drew me to the Wars of the Roses in the first place was the fact that there are so many twists and turns over such a short space of time. We've already witnessed plenty of those, but the years 1462–64 present an excellent example of how these events occurred. This period also demonstrates the gulf in the depth and quality of leadership between York and Lancaster.

In October 1462, when the indefatigable Queen Margaret and her husband Henry VI landed at Bamburgh on the north-east coast of England, one wonders quite what Henry made of it all. Given his mental frailty in the 1450s, one would have thought that a combination of the loss of the bloody battle of Towton and his throne, along with the sudden flight into exile, might have tipped him over the edge. Was he a quivering, confused wreck of a man, or was he clearly aware of events, retaining both his dignity and the belief that he would eventually regain his crown? I rather fear the former, but I would like to believe the latter. Certainly, Henry's impact on what happened – as before – was minimal, which is why the leadership skills of those around him mattered even more.

By the end of October 1462 Henry was back in England raising his standard and in possession of three formidable fortresses. The trouble was he had little else: a few ships, not many men-at-arms and not much interest being shown by the battle-weary Northumberland gentry.

To make matters worse, Warwick, in his usual energetic manner, was heading north within days of the Lancastrian landing. The royal ordnance – that's cannon to the uninitiated – were despatched by ship to Newcastle and, by early November, Edward IV himself was on his way north calling upon his nobles for support. The Yorkist war machine was getting into gear – and it needed to, for November was hardly an ideal time to wage a military campaign in the north.

At this point, with only a tenuous hold on the north-east coast, Queen Margaret decided to leave and sail to Scotland, leaving Henry Beaufort, Duke of Somerset, in charge. Since Margaret was by no means a fool, I can only assume that she felt that, without more help, they would fail. So, being Margaret, she sailed off with Henry to get it. However, I don't think her departure could have helped the morale of the Bamburgh garrison, which was then commanded by the Duke of Somerset and Jasper Tudor, Earl of Pembroke. One of the reasons why Margaret's energy shines through was that she was the only one among Henry's supporters who could make a decision. She wasn't always right, but at least she did something.

With the sort of luck which seemed to dog Henry VI wherever he went, I suppose it was inevitable that his ships were hit by a storm and scattered. Four ships sank, including Henry's, and the royal couple, accompanied by their French ally, De Brézé, finally arrived in Berwick in a small boat. Most of their men were washed up on the coast near Holy Isle and one supposes they were not feeling particularly chipper about that.

Meanwhile, Edward IV caught measles – yes, really – and was laid low in Durham. Now here's the key point about leadership: in theory, the Yorkists were leaderless but in practice they had a whole bunch of capable leaders. Warwick assumed command, but to support him he had his experienced uncle, Lord Fauconberg, his brother John, Lord Montagu, John Tiptoft, Earl of Worcester, and the formidable knight – until only recently a Lancastrian – Anthony Woodville, Lord Scales.

The Lancastrians just did not have such heavyweight leaders to match their opponents. Even so, Warwick could not attack all three Lancastrian strongholds; it would simply be too costly in both men and supplies. All he could do was attempt to starve them out, so as long as he could keep his own armies supplied and fed, he could just wait.

What, you might ask, was the point of sending the royal ordnance all the way north and then not using it to batter down the walls of Alnwick? The answer is simple: Edward did not want to capture three heaps of rubble; he wanted the castles as intact as possible. The threat of the large cannon was there and, if push came to shove, he would use them; but he would rather not.

There was also another dimension to this siege – remember the Scots? They were supposed to be helping Henry VI, weren't they? Well, late in November, they promised – after a few inducements – to send an army to relieve Alnwick. The men did set out before Christmas 1462. Unfortunately, the Lancastrian defenders, not knowing that help was on its way and with their food exhausted, decided to surrender.

By 27 December, Edward held Dunstanburgh and Bamburgh again. In return, he agreed to pardon the Duke of Somerset and allow the restoration of his lands and titles. Sir Ralph Percy too was pardoned and though Jasper Tudor, Earl of Pembroke, was not prepared to accept a pardon, he was given safe conduct to Scotland.

Why was Edward so generous to his enemies? Could he really trust these men? There are a couple of reasons – one pretty sensible, the other a bit dodgier. To persuade the defenders to give in, Edward had to offer terms which would be accepted quickly before the Scottish relief army could arrive, and the offer of a pardon seemed to do the trick. As we have seen before, Edward's natural inclination was to recruit his enemies rather than execute them – a policy which has a lot to be said for it – but whether it was wise to return Dunstanburgh and Bamburgh to Sir Ralph Percy was questionable and was certainly a considerable risk.

However, this did mean though that the Yorkist forces, now including, remarkably, the pardoned Duke of Somerset, could concentrate on capturing Alnwick. But just when they thought they had the advantage, the Scottish relief army finally arrived. This was a pivotal moment: would the Scots force Warwick to fight outside Alnwick or not? And would Warwick, in any case, risk everything in a pitched battle in which he might be outnumbered by his enemy?

Warwick decided to pull back from Alnwick and wait, which was not exactly typical of him. Perhaps he felt that his soldiers, after a couple of months' siege in the cold and damp, might not be up for a bloody hand-to-hand struggle with an army of eager Scots. On this occasion, waiting proved to be a masterstroke. While he waited, most of the Alnwick garrison marched out to join the Scots, who then promptly returned to Scotland without taking on Warwick's army.

This was very much a 'nearly moment' because most of the Yorkist military might was gathered in Northumberland, while Lancaster had an army of Scots; yet there was no great battle. Warwick's uncharacteristic caution allowed him to walk into Alnwick virtually unopposed.

But why did the Scots, having raised such a large force, not press home the attack? The answer, I suspect, is that, having fulfilled their promise by going to relieve the Alnwick garrison, they saw little to be gained and much to be lost in a pitched battle. It would have been a tough fight, not just some border raid for plunder. For those on both sides who watched from a safe distance, it was probably a disappointment, but perhaps common sense had prevailed. Make a note of that, because it's pretty rare in this period.

Only the Welsh castle of Harlech now held out against the Yorkist king and Edward could afford to return to London, where he was joined a little later by the Earl of Warwick.

But of course, that was not the end of it, because these are, after all, the Wars of the Roses. In March 1463, Sir Ralph Percy, generously permitted by Edward to retain his castles of Dunstanburgh and Bamburgh, decided to give them back to Lancaster. Alnwick followed his example and so, despite a long winter campaign to regain the castles, by May 1463 all three were once again garrisoned for Lancaster.

Chapter 18

Lancaster's Last Chance Saloon

BY MAY 1463, Edward IV still did not have full control of his kingdom and the past year or two had established a pattern of apparent Yorkist success followed by a rather unlikely Lancastrian revival. Clearly, Edward could not allow this dangerous cycle to continue. Aside from the expense and effort it required, such a situation only prolonged uncertainty in the north and caused alarm everywhere else.

In theory, Warwick was responsible for the security of the north but, like his king, he preferred to live in the south. Someone, however, who seemed quite happy in the north was Warwick's brother, John Neville, Lord Montagu. His apparent hostility towards anything associated with the name Percy was ample motivation for him to act firmly against them. So Edward decided to appoint him Warden of the East March, which was where the trouble mostly lingered.

Although the Lancastrians still held the three coastal castles, they would need to capture other important centres if they were to extend their control in Northumberland. Chief among these was the key port of Newcastle. But although a Lancastrian attack on the city was attempted, the local folk were having none of it and repulsed it.

Meanwhile, in early June, Warwick set off north – again – and when he arrived in Northumberland, he must have been horrified to see that the situation was worse than he expected. Early in July, it got worse still when the Scottish king, James III – still a boy – led an army into England. With him came the whole pack of cards: Henry VI, Queen Margaret, and the boy king's mother, the widowed Scottish queen, Mary of Guelders. Their aim was to besiege the English border castle of Norham with a large army supported by cannon.

On the face of it, this seemed a genuine threat and, when the Neville brothers, Warwick and Montagu, set out to relieve the siege, they expected to be harried all the way there by men from the Lancastrian-held castles on the coast. In fact, they reached Norham unopposed and the Scottish army – taken by surprise – simply disintegrated and fled. The Nevilles then pursued the Scots across the border, laying waste to a swathe of territory. For Scotland, it was an unmitigated disaster and it spelt the end of any more Scottish support for Henry VI.

Although the three northern castles were still in Lancastrian hands, Henry's cause was at its lowest point, with few resources and no Scottish support. Queen

Margaret departed by sea with her son and De Brézé, to seek help elsewhere while Henry remained in Scotland. As it turned out, Margaret was destined never to see her husband again.

In August 1463, Edward IV sought grants of cash from parliament to seize the initiative against the Scots and launch a new attack. But although he moved men and artillery north and spent months there himself, no attack was ever made and, in January 1464, Edward returned to London. This caused some annoyance because the king, having been given funds to finance his campaign, had in fact done nothing. Edward, however, rather cleverly, used the money in other ways, for example by paying the wages of the vitally important Calais garrison.

Why did Edward change his mind? Well, he didn't really. The threat of military action was there but he decided that negotiation was a better policy than war. In this he was helped by a serious change of mind on the part of another monarch, Louis XI. The latter was a tricky customer at the best of times and it would have been unwise to trust him much, but on this occasion, Louis's interests aligned with Edward's. Without going into the fine detail of French policy, the upshot was that Louis wanted good relations with both England and neighbouring Burgundy, whose duke was already well-disposed towards Edward. So Louis rejected the entreaties of Queen Margaret – as did the Duke of Burgundy – and instead the three countries held peace talks, which by October 1463 had led to an agreement not to support each other's enemies. This partly explains why Edward did not attack Scotland, since it had close ties to France. On the contrary, in this new spirit of congeniality, Edward negotiated a truce with the Scots as well in December 1463. By the terms of that truce, the Scots agreed not to help Henry VI and to send him out of Scotland to Bamburgh, where, of course, he was much more vulnerable. It was also agreed that further negotiations for a more permanent peace would be held in March 1464.

Thus it looked as if the crisis was over, and it was only a matter of time before the three castles capitulated. Er, no. Because just when complete victory was within the Yorkist king's grasp, one of his earlier decisions blew up in his face.

Henry Beaufort, Duke of Somerset, after a year or more in close companionship with his new king, did a runner. Remembering how vitriolic the relationship had been between their fathers, it seems incredible that Edward had even attempted a rapprochement with Somerset. He made every possible effort to keep Somerset on side, putting much personal trust in him. But there was, perhaps inevitably, continued hostility towards the duke from other less forgiving Yorkists. In the end, Edward had a hard job keeping Somerset alive. To protect the duke, he had sent him to north Wales, but around Christmas 1463 Somerset escaped and headed north. Apparently he intended to turn the Newcastle garrison, capture the town, and declare for Henry VI.

I doubt we can ever be sure why Somerset decided to betray Edward and return to the Lancastrian fold. Perhaps he just regretted his decision to surrender in the first place, though he could have chosen a better time to turn up and help. It has been suggested that the timing owed much to riots and unrest against the new king's taxes, yet many of these took place after Somerset had actually escaped. Indeed, his escape might have stirred up the unrest further.

At first, Edward left his able lieutenants to deal with the troubles, but at the end of March 1464, he decided to go north once more to crush any risings orchestrated by Somerset, who had somehow evaded capture and arrived at Bamburgh. Let's not forget that the three major coastal castles were still in Lancastrian hands, and another rather disturbing development had also occurred. The Cliffords – remember them? – had retaken their old castle at Skipton in Yorkshire, and although this was an isolated event, it seemed indicative of a shift in momentum in the north. More worrying was that Somerset and Ralph Percy moved out of their strongholds to attack and capture a number of places inland including Norham, Hexham and Bywell – the next stop would be Newcastle.

Another result of these Lancastrian successes was to threaten the outcome of the Scottish peace talks which were to take place in Newcastle. With the talks already delayed from March to April, Edward was desperate to make sure they took place. Moving the venue to York, he sent Lord Montagu to escort the Scottish envoys from the northern border. Montagu only narrowly made it as far as Newcastle, where he gained reinforcements and pushed on north beyond Alnwick into the area where the Lancastrians had more control.

On 25 April, Lord Montagu found himself under attack from a large Lancastrian force under the Duke of Somerset, Ralph Percy and several other recalcitrant Lancastrian lords. We know almost nothing about this battle except that it was fought at Hedgeley Moor, west of Alnwick, and the Lancastrians lost. How or why is a matter for conjecture, based on very limited scraps of evidence.

One suggestion is that several of the lords did not share the enthusiasm of Somerset and Percy for the fight. During the battle, Ralph Percy was killed along with most of his retinue, apparently in a bold but futile charge. I doubt that John Neville was overly keen to spare any Percy supporters.

With King Edward gradually amassing a large royal army at Leicester and the Scottish envoys safely conveyed to York, Somerset and the remaining Lancastrians were in the 'last chance saloon.' But, to be honest, they had been ensconced in that saloon for quite some time.

Having swiftly re-formed his army, Somerset gambled all on a quick, sharp strike. Moving south to Hexham, he hoped to surprise Lord Montagu. By moving Henry VI from Bamburgh closer to Bywell he perhaps hoped that the king's presence alone would rally more to his banner. If he did he was delusional, and Montagu was too intelligent a commander to be taken unawares by Somerset's ramshackle army.

On 15 May it was Lord Montagu who sprang the surprise and annihilated the Lancastrians near Hexham, after which he zealously tracked down the fleeing lords. The Duke of Somerset and his allies, lords Hungerford and Roos, were taken and summarily executed. Another thirty or so rebel leaders were similarly treated. John Neville did not mess about – he did not issue pardons. His men, stumbling upon a Lancastrian carrying Henry's war chest, of which a staggering £2,000 remained, divided it up between them. Quite a windfall! For the next year or so, Henry VI himself managed to escape capture by hiding in private houses.

In June 1464, the three fortresses in Northumberland, where we began this part of the story, were faced by the Earl of Warwick with a large army and three enormous cannon. Dunstanburgh and Alnwick surrendered pretty much at once, but another diehard, Sir Ralph Grey, held out at Bamburgh knowing there would be no pardon for him. For the first time the royal ordnance was used and Bamburgh was severely damaged. In the end, with Grey wounded, his comrades sued for peace and Bamburgh was taken. Grey was condemned by the king in person and executed at Doncaster.

The final fall of Bamburgh marks the end of the crisis in the north and the point at which Edward might have regarded himself as true master of his kingdom. In addition, a fifteen-year peace was agreed with the Scots. Lord Montagu was rewarded for his efforts with the great prize of the earldom of Northumberland, traditionally held by his arch-enemies the Percys – how sweet that must have been for him.

Everyone else went home and that's something which is often ignored. The soldiers, raised mostly from south and middle England, had traipsed north to meet the last Lancastrian threat. Having taken part in virtually no fighting, they then trudged back south again. I'm sure there's at least one novel about what those thousands of men got up to on their journeys home.

Queen Margaret, who had been seeking help elsewhere, took her young son, Edward, to her father's house in Anjou while, in July 1465, her husband Henry was eventually captured and taken to the Tower of London. A few years later, even the Welsh fortress of Harlech was taken.

So King Edward had finally won the war. Now all he had to do was, as they say, win the peace.

Part Three
The Crisis of 1467–71

Chapter 19

Wedding Bells

FROM THE FIELD of Mortimer's Cross, it had been a long and bitter struggle for Edward, Earl of March, to win the throne of England for the House of York, but he managed it. After the failures of his father, Richard, Duke of York, there were times when the Yorkist cause must have seemed utterly hopeless. Yet by the mid-1460s Edward IV ruled the kingdom pretty much unchallenged. The previous king, Henry VI, was still alive, but he was safely housed in the Tower of London. Henry's heir, Edward of Westminster, was lodged in France with his mother, the embittered former queen, Margaret of Anjou – and in 1464 he was only eleven years old.

Edward's willingness to build bridges with his former opponents, while it had caused him some problems – notably in the case of Henry Beaufort, Duke of Somerset – also enabled him to gain the support of many ordinary knights and gentry who had once fought for Henry VI. Although there were a few exceptions, such as Jasper Tudor, Earl of Pembroke, Edward IV had gained the support of most of the political classes, at least for the time being. If he was successful, he was likely to retain their support, but what would peacetime success look like?

First and foremost, Edward had to act like a king – an area where his predecessor had been seriously deficient. Edward had the advantage of charm and good looks, plus his abilities as a warrior and general. He looked like a king ought to look, which was, in itself, reassuring for his subjects. But for all that, he was still an unknown quantity. Could he rule more effectively than Henry VI, or was he just good at winning battles?

Top of the list of royal priorities was to restore the rule of law after a long period of disorder. Moreover, Edward had to be seen making judgements and putting an end to some of the baronial feuds which had fuelled much of that lawlessness in the 1450s. The prosperity of the kingdom – and the king himself – would depend on trade and commerce, which could only flourish in a peaceful environment. Having said that, we should not imagine that the Wars of the Roses caused the sort of major disruption to trade that some would have us believe. England was not exactly devastated by the Wars of the Roses. Throughout the crisis of 1459–64, for many folk in England life went on as usual. In the areas where much of the fighting and movement of armies occurred that was clearly not the case, but elsewhere England was not a burning land, laid waste by war. One or two places were very badly affected – such as Ludlow – and it would be many years before the town recovered from its sacking by Lancastrian soldiers in 1459. But generally, life went on. Let's put it in perspective: an exceptionally harsh winter or relentless summer rains would have had far more impact on most local communities than the Wars of the Roses.

There was, of course, some rebuilding to do, but in many respects people just wanted to be left alone to get on with their lives. One thing they did not want was more taxes: that had been a constant source of complaint during Henry's reign, especially when the king's government seemed to be wasting its resources. Edward, however, had spent a great deal in the early years of his reign as he endeavoured to stamp out the last embers of Lancastrian resistance. Thus, he asked parliament for taxes to pay for his campaigns. A pragmatist like Edward was inclined to divert any surplus cash to pay for other pressing needs, but such behaviour did not endear him to many taxpayers.

Aside from restoring what folk tended to call 'good government', Edward needed to cement Yorkist control of the throne for the future. What does that mean? Well, he was unmarried and he needed sons – quickly - because the House of Lancaster already had an eleven-year-old male heir waiting in France.

If a sudden accident or illness should strike Edward down, the country would be plunged into chaos once more. The Yorkist heir presumptive was Edward's younger brother George, Duke of Clarence, but he was only 15. So Edward needed a quick marriage and then a period of stability so that he could establish himself. Spoiler alert: he didn't get it…

What happened in the second half of the 1460s demonstrates how fragile the new Yorkist regime actually was – and how much it depended on several key powerful individuals. This dependence on such men was a situation Edward was stuck with for the time being. Though his success had been achieved very much by his own efforts, he had relied heavily upon the energy and resources of a few close supporters. Foremost among this happy band was Richard Neville, Earl of Warwick, who had been directly involved in the ongoing political and military struggle since the early 1450s.

History has awarded Warwick the wholly undeserved nickname of 'Kingmaker' and he is still frequently referred to by that name – but more of that later. There were other men upon whom Edward relied, including several of Warwick's relatives: his brother John Neville, Lord Montagu, and his uncle, William Neville, Lord Fauconberg. Others included John Howard, a growing presence in East Anglia who played a critical role at Towton, and Lord William Hastings, Edward's closest friend and ally. Vital to Edward's success as king would be to retain the continued support of all these men until he could establish a much wider base of support.

The king's marriage was vital and everyone urged him to marry as soon as possible – but then courtiers always do that, because they are on top of the pile and they'd quite like to stay there. Edward gave them a marriage in 1464, but it was rather a case of be careful what you wish for. As Star Trek's Spock might have said: 'it's a royal marriage, Jim, but not as we know it.'

So, what was the problem with Edward's marriage? Well, where do I start?

Traditionally, at all levels of society, the marriage convention was that you married for your family's advancement, whether by means of a likely inheritance, or increased political influence or wealth. Warwick himself had pulled off the most spectacular marriage of the century, which gave him the landed wealth and power that I have talked about so often. So if anyone knew the importance of a great marriage, it was Warwick. For kings, marriages were usually to foreign princesses who might bring with them an alliance and a handsome dowry. Marrying a foreigner also prevented the king from raising one of the English noble families to royal status.

In summary, Edward married the wrong girl – and he knew it – which was why he married her in secret.

Both before and after his marriage, Edward was not exactly the most chaste individual on the planet. He had several mistresses and more than likely quite a few 'one-night stands'. Not only was he serially attracted to women, but it appears that they were equally attracted to him – long before he wielded the power of a king.

There are two ways of looking at this: on the one hand he might be seen as a dissolute stalker of women, careless of whether or not they were married, and some historians, especially during the Victorian period, have taken that view to a lesser or greater extent. His kingship was lumped together with his licentious morality and he was thus branded a failure.

I don't take that view, because there is no evidence at all that he ever forced a woman to his bed and, judged by the morality of his time – which, in my view, is the only yardstick against which he can be judged – he was hardly the only powerful man to have mistresses.

When Edward announced his marriage to the world at Reading in September 1464, it caused ripples of shock across the court, the country and even as far as the Continent. So who was she, and what was wrong with her?

Elizabeth Grey, née Woodville, was probably about twenty-six years old when she married Edward, while he was only twenty-two. She was a widow whose Lancastrian husband, Sir John Grey, had been killed at the second battle of St Albans in 1461. She was not truly of noble, let alone royal, birth because although her mother Jacquetta of Luxembourg was of good lineage, her father Richard Woodville was a mere gentleman. From the perspective of men like the Earl of Warwick, the king's marriage to Elizabeth Woodville was incomprehensible because she brought nothing to the marriage but problems.

So why did Edward marry her? We are told that it was the oldest story in the book: he was in love. We are told that he was so smitten by her beauty that he had to have her – and since, it is alleged, he was not going to get her unless he married her, he took the plunge, albeit in a secret ceremony attended by her mother, a priest and precious few others.

The fact that the king married in secret tells us that he knew the marriage would not go down well at court. Did he think that he might be able to wriggle out of this clandestine liaison later once he had had his wicked way with Elizabeth? We don't know – and in fact, there's a lot we don't know about the marriage, including the date. Tradition has it that he married on 1 May, though it could easily have been months later. If, for example, it was in August, then keeping it a secret for a few weeks does not seem quite so sinister as four or five months. The useful details are, however, obscured by the same great black hole in historical evidence that afflicts numerous other interesting events in the fifteenth century.

One effect of the marriage was to raise to prominence the entire Woodville family. Elizabeth came with two sons from her first marriage, a great many brothers and sisters, and two rather pushy parents. So Edward was not marrying just one leading lady, he was taking on a whole cast. There were suddenly a number of important courtiers to promote and find wives for – and there were numerous sisters to arrange suitable marriages for. A sister-in-law of the king couldn't marry just anyone – though of course Edward himself had done just that.

Marriages, as I've said, were very important to the nobility, especially to Warwick who had no sons but two daughters. As the co-heiresses to his vast fortune, they had to be found suitable husbands. Though the arrival of the Woodvilles saturated the marriage market, the king had two brothers of his own: George, Duke of Clarence, and Richard, Duke of Gloucester – surely the marriage of at least one of those dukes to a daughter of Warwick would do very nicely? Warwick thought so, but Edward flatly refused to allow such a match, much to Warwick's fury.

The marriage of Warwick's daughters was not his only concern, as, despite his meteoric success, the earl was not a happy man. His position under Edward IV was not as influential as he would have wished, and his dissatisfaction – as well as an over-inflated opinion of his own worth – was soon to bring an end to Edward's all too short period of stability. This being the Wars of the Roses, one thing led to another and pretty soon the Yorkist house of cards was in trouble.

Chapter 20

Warwick, the Wedding Planner...

MUCH HAS BEEN made by historians of the Earl of Warwick's growing irritation during the 1460s, especially over the king's secret marriage to Elizabeth Woodville in 1464. We are also told that Warwick was 'disappointed' that Edward did not give him the influence over policy that he believed he deserved. But yes, you're right: Warwick had an ego to die for – and sooner or later he would…

In his 'disappointment' Warwick began to consider a possible alternative to Edward. After all, if one powerful duke could seize the throne, why not another? His attentions were therefore focused on the heir presumptive, Edward's younger brother George, Duke of Clarence. He seemed an obvious choice because his claim to the throne was just as good as Edward's – especially if Edward was without Warwick's support. An obvious choice then, except that what was equally obvious was that George was not the man Edward was. Only a desperate man would seek to supplant the king with his younger brother.

Unfortunately for England, Warwick was beginning to feel desperate by about 1468. Why? It had a lot to do with sons and daughters – Warwick had no sons and two daughters.

As I've said before, a favourable marriage was a major tool in noble advancement as Warwick found with his own marriage, which had added enormously to his power and wealth. Thus, at least one of his daughters would have to secure a great marriage and the best – perhaps the only – option amongst the higher nobility would have been Henry Stafford, Duke of Buckingham, since he had royal lineage as a descendant of Edward III. Yes, I know… almost everyone seemed to be one of that king's descendants; but Buckingham also had enormous landholdings, which, if combined with the Warwick inheritance, would create a very effective power base for a new Neville/Buckingham family.

However, one tiny detail derailed this grand design: in 1465 Buckingham, aged eleven, had been swiftly married off to one of the new queen's Woodville sisters, Katherine, aged six – they married early in those days. So Buckingham was unavailable, and if the noble line of Richard Neville, Earl of Warwick, was not to be subsumed into a lesser noble house, his daughters must marry up – i.e. into royalty. Enter George, Duke of Clarence: available, eligible and royal. This would be the perfect match to secure the future power and prosperity of the Neville family.

King Edward, however, dismissed out of hand the idea of a Neville marriage to either of his brothers. Perhaps Warwick did have genuine cause for complaint since, in his eyes, the king had denied him Buckingham and was now ruling out the two royal dukes as well. But from Edward's point of view he, like Warwick, had two daughters and no sons. How dangerous would it be if the heir presumptive, his brother George, married into the most powerful noble family in England, while Edward still had no male heir of his own? A further hurdle was that a papal dispensation would be required, since George and Warwick's daughters were cousins. The church did not normally allow marriages between first cousins but, if kings asked nicely, exceptions could be made and a dispensation given.

In spite of the king's opposition, Warwick persisted with the project through 1467 and at some point began secret negotiations with the Pope for the necessary dispensation. The summer of 1467 marks the first really low point in the relationship between the king and Warwick.

By the end of the summer, Warwick's favoured foreign policy of an alliance with France was demolished when Edward opted instead for an alliance with the enemy of France: Burgundy.

Here is not the place to discuss the relative merits of the two foreign policies, but suffice to say that the Burgundian alliance was not exactly a terrible idea. However, for Warwick, who saw himself as a great diplomat astride the continent of Europe, this was a great humiliation. At least, that was how he saw it, and this set the earl on a collision course with the king.

Though Warwick went home to his estates to lick his wounds, that does not mean that he had already decided upon rebellion; all it means is that he was considering his options. Warwick had other gripes because apart from the French fiasco, he was also resentful of the rise of other men at court, notably the queen's father, Earl Rivers, and brother, Anthony Woodville, Lord Scales. He especially resented William Herbert, the new Earl of Pembroke. Herbert was a rising star in the Yorkist firmament and his growing power in Wales set him against Warwick who had longstanding interests there.

Warwick also believed that Herbert was spreading malicious rumours – also going around the French court at the time – that the disaffected Warwick was now in league with the deposed Lancastrian queen, Margaret of Anjou. Privately, King Edward must have dismissed this notion as laughable, but he could not completely ignore it. When he asked Warwick to come to London to address the rumours, the earl was reluctant. In the end, early in 1468, he did so but only in the most grudging and unbending manner. Despite Warwick's unhelpful mood, the king continued to reward him with lands and income – as if Warwick was short of such things!

I have noted before that Edward IV preferred conciliation to confrontation with his leading subjects – sometimes at very great risk to himself. Here again we see the king trying hard to win over Warwick rather than drive him further away. But during 1468 it became increasingly obvious that Warwick would not accept being merely one of a number of royal advisers. The earl's pride would not let him buy into the concept of being 'first among equals.'

While his leading magnate was sulking, Edward had more pressing problems: there had been a notable increase in lawlessness during 1466, 1467 and into 1468. One of the most enduring planks of the Yorkist manifesto had been to reduce corruption and restore law and order, but it appeared to many folk that Edward was failing to do so. Part of the renewed unrest was also down to an increase in the activities of Lancastrian loyalists. It seemed that every time Edward thought he had restored control, new pockets of resistance popped up. While none of these was large-scale, taken together they were certainly worrying.

During 1468 Warwick returned to London and the documentary evidence tells us that he and his Neville brothers: George – lately removed as Chancellor – and John, now Earl of Northumberland, were all prominently involved in government. So, to judge from appearances, the Nevilles were back on board the good ship Edward. But all was not as it seemed...

By 1469, Warwick was actively pursuing two converging policies, which were both directed against Edward. The first of these was to cultivate an alliance with the Duke of Clarence through a marriage with his elder daughter, Isabel, for which Warwick still awaited a papal dispensation.

If you're wondering why Clarence went along with this, it was basically because Clarence was what we might call a bit 'flaky'. While he was handsome and charming like his brother, he lacked most of Edward's other, better, qualities. Despite the immense rewards showered upon him since the victory of 1461, he was forever dissatisfied. As an ambitious prince, he viewed a marriage to the elder Neville heiress as an excellent way of increasing his already very large landholdings and power.

At the same time as Warwick was wooing Clarence, he was also exploiting the growing disaffection of the commons against Edward's government. In the spring of 1469 he used his own men in the north to positively encourage rebellion. Though it is certain that the commons had legitimate grievances, it is unlikely they would have risen in such numbers without the promise of support from some local members of the gentry who just happened to be committed to the earl. Warwick also promoted his own image through propaganda – a favourite Yorkist weapon – and his generosity to all and sundry. Then – as now – folk were easily swayed by rich men who promised the poor better times.

Between April and July 1469 there were several uprisings in the north, but it is almost unbelievable how little we know about these revolts. Not only are the available sources sparse, but they are almost entirely contradictory. This has led to much confusion about the whole episode. We don't really know whether there was one rebellion or two – or even three!

What *do* we know? Well, the first rebellion – in the spring of 1469 – appears to have been motivated as much by a desire to restore the influence of the Percy family as any other grievance. Needless to say, John Neville, Lord Montagu – who of course was Warwick's brother – had no reservations about crushing any pro-Percy revolt. It seems unlikely therefore that Warwick had any role in encouraging that particular uprising.

However, we do know that Warwick was behind a larger revolt in the summer and even helped to direct its manifesto. Its apparent leader went by the name of Robin of Redesdale, but he was most likely one of Warwick's loyal retainers in the north. This summer revolt was much more dangerous for the king, but Edward reacted uncharacteristically slowly to the threat of rebellion, making a rather laboured progress to Nottingham to raise troops to counter the rebels.

While Edward was moving – albeit sluggishly – to deal with the revolt that Warwick had helped to promote, the earl himself was elsewhere. At the end of June 1469 the earl announced the Clarence–Neville marriage in a letter to his supporters in Coventry and, almost at once in early July, he departed with his brother, Archbishop George Neville, along with Clarence and Isabel, to Calais where the marriage took place.

With the vital marriage agreed, Warwick made his intentions crystal clear, directly associating himself with the northern rebels and issuing a rather sinister statement which compared the ills of the present regime with the failures of Edward II, Richard II and Henry VI – all of whom had of course been deposed. Having launched his propaganda campaign, Warwick then returned to England.

Meanwhile, the northern rebels swept southwards, bypassing the king, to arrive in the Midlands opposed only by the armies of William Herbert and, from Warwick's perspective, another upstart, Humphrey Stafford, Earl of Devon.

At this critical moment in his reign, Edward for once was too slow to grasp what was happening: betrayal by Warwick, but also by his own brother, must still have seemed unthinkable to him. The Lack of clear information did not help him. He did not know how many rebels there were, or that Warwick was hurrying to join them. So he assumed that his loyal earls, Herbert and Stafford, would have sufficient strength to suppress the revolt. He assumed, but he did not know for certain – and thus, England was back in crisis mode again.

Chapter 21

The Kingmaker Illusion

IN JULY 1469 Edward IV, who had been king for eight years, faced his first serious challenge since 1464. This time, it came not from the Lancastrians, but from those closest to him: his chief noble ally, Richard Neville, Earl of Warwick, and the heir presumptive, Edward's own brother, George, Duke of Clarence.

We have seen that both Warwick and Clarence were discontented – in my view with very limited justification – but there it was nonetheless.

With hindsight, we know that the Earl of Warwick was deliberately orchestrating the largest of the 1469 rebellions led by a shadowy figure known as 'Robin of Redesdale': almost certainly one of Warwick's northern clients.

With Edward raising an army at Nottingham, Warwick raced back from Calais in order to join up with the large rebel army which had swept southwards into the Midlands. Charged with defeating the rebels were two recently-elevated Yorkists: William Herbert, Earl of Pembroke, and Humphrey Stafford, Earl of Devon; their combined efforts would be required if they were to halt the rebel advance until the king arrived with reinforcements.

Unfortunately, on the eve of battle, Herbert and Stafford – both rather stubborn, bullish, men – managed to fall out spectacularly. The result was that on 26 July William Herbert was left to face the rebels alone on at the battle of Edgecote near Banbury in Oxfordshire. Stafford, with an army of several thousand archers, sulked nearby, and only decided to go to Herbert's aid when it was already too late. The fighting at Edgecote was fierce and many of Herbert's Welsh men were slaughtered. Even so, a rebel victory was only secured when Warwick's vanguard arrived to compensate for the rebels' own heavy losses.

William Herbert, and his brother Richard, were captured and immediately executed by Warwick. The Herberts were not the only ones to feel the earl's wrath. The queen's father, Richard Woodville, Earl Rivers and her brother John were also captured and executed. There had been executions before, of course, but it's worth bearing in mind that none of these men had broken any law and had only taken up arms to support their lawful king. Warwick's summary action – based not on any legal authority, but on jealousy and malice – was to set a very dark precedent.

Edward, deserted by some of his own men, then sent away his brother-in-law, Anthony Woodville, who, if caught, was very likely to be executed like his father. Edward then surrendered to George Neville, who took him first to Warwick Castle and later to the great northern Neville stronghold of Middleham. His younger brother, Richard of Gloucester, and his close adviser, William Hastings, were allowed to leave Nottingham unharmed.

Warwick, in the belief that he was now firmly in control, summoned a parliament – presumably to gain their approval for his actions – because of course, he was only acting for the common good... But he would also need parliament to sanction the elevation of Clarence over his older brother. By the middle of August 1469, Warwick appeared to be in command of both the king and the kingdom. In the blink of an eye, it seemed, the king had been deposed.

But in fact, he had not. Warwick has often been described as the 'Kingmaker', and he must have intended to make Clarence king. Surely that must have been Warwick's intention from the moment he plotted with Clarence. He must have promised him the throne; otherwise, what was the point of suggesting in the rebel manifesto that a king who had failed, such as Edward, should be deposed?

Yet, in the summer of 1469, George Duke of Clarence did not become king. Why not? Well, we don't really know. Perhaps Warwick's closer association with Clarence convinced him that the king's flawed brother was not the answer. For a time he seemed instead to want to try to rule with Edward as a sort of 'puppet king'. But anyone who had the first idea about Edward IV's character could have told Warwick he was making a huge mistake. Edward was intelligent, capable of conceding ground when circumstances did not favour him, and well able to seize the initiative if an opportunity arose.

Very soon, it didn't matter what Warwick thought anyway because his apparent control was shown to be an utter illusion. The great groundswell of popular support he had expected simply did not materialise. Though Warwick had some support in the north, hardly any of the ruling classes supported his coup. Among the nobility and members of the king's council, he was almost completely isolated. Without their support, parliament would be reluctant to take any extreme action such as crowning Clarence – especially when his older brother was still alive and well in Middleham Castle.

Warwick's early plans for a parliament were quickly shelved amid governmental chaos as well as a new Lancastrian rising. It did not help Warwick that there was even more disorder after he took over than before: local feuds abounded and the earl could offer no answer without the authority of a king.

Ironically, it was the new Lancastrian rising in the north which revealed Warwick's weakness, because, when he summoned men to suppress the revolt, he was ignored. He was thus forced to release Edward so that troops could be mustered to suppress the Lancastrian rising and thus restore confidence in the government.

By September, Edward was in York acting independently and, by October, he was back in London in the bosom of his allies. Publicly, he declared his goodwill towards both Warwick and Clarence, but no one was fooled. Though the king did not punish Warwick, he was unlikely to forget the earl's savage execution of his rivals, especially since two of them were close members of his wife's family. As I have said before, Edward was clever in dealing with people. He didn't always get it right, but he was subtle and measured in his political relationships.

So, while allowing the Nevilles to retain some pride, Edward began to limit their power and influence. In the north, Henry Percy, Edward's erstwhile enemy, was restored to his hereditary earldom of Northumberland, which John Neville had held for several years. Men such as Edward's youngest brother, Richard, Duke of Gloucester, Thomas, Lord Stanley and Henry Percy all gained greater roles at Neville expense. If Edward hoped for reconciliation, he did not expect it; and, while his brother George could perhaps be forgiven his lapse of loyalty, the Earl of Warwick would not.

Was Warwick right in his accusations against Edward? Had Edward failed to rule effectively? There were certainly some complaints about lawlessness, but the way things deteriorated when Warwick assumed control could not have given those with grievances much comfort. And were Warwick's rivals, in particular the Woodvilles, unusually rapacious in their appetite for wealth and power? I would suggest probably not, by 1469 at least. It was in the nature of all landed families to try to increase their holdings however and whenever they could. Warwick laying that charge against anyone else was rather the pot calling the kettle black.

The Woodville family as a whole was not as well established at the centre of power as it would be ten years later – and remember, Elizabeth Woodville had yet to provide the king with the essential male heir, so even she was probably on borrowed time.

What Edward was doing in the late 1460s was trying to balance the power of his original supporters, such as Warwick, with some new men whose advancement would depend upon Edward himself. This was eminently sensible because his father had discovered that the support of one faction alone – even one as strong as the Nevilles – did not guarantee stability. Men like William Herbert and Humphrey Stafford – whom Warwick had so savagely cut down – were supposed to provide Edward, along with the Woodvilles and his own brothers, with a new and broader powerbase for his kingship. Taken together with his clear preference for accommodating rather than executing his erstwhile opponents, I see this as a sensible policy which encouraged unity rather than division. I think it would have been very successful had it not been for the Earl of Warwick's outrageous ambition. Why outrageous? Because Warwick was not a man stripped of power by Edward; on the contrary, he was constantly showered with rewards by his king – even after his failed coup of 1469. Yet that was not enough for Warwick, who wanted to be the guiding hand behind the throne: the supreme councillor to the king. Well, it might have worked with Henry VI, but Edward IV – seriously? You begin to wonder whether Warwick knew that young man at all.

It was Warwick's naked ambition alone which destabilised Edward IV's regime. Over the winter of 1469–70, the earl chewed over his recent failure. True, he had achieved the advantageous marriage he coveted and had removed several of his prominent rivals, but at the cost of utterly destroying his relationship with Edward. Hence, his position in the state was now extremely perilous and, if anything, his potential enemies were more numerous and hostile than before. The Woodvilles were certainly not going to forget what he had done.

Even so, as long as the king had no son, Clarence remained as heir presumptive and, though Warwick had not appeared ready to crown his son-in-law in 1469, Clarence was still the only real alternative to Edward that Warwick had.

But 1469 had demonstrated that, unless Edward was actually deposed, Clarence was not likely to replace him. To do that, Warwick would need to engineer another crisis, but this time he would have to outmanoeuvre the king and bring a powerful force against him in the field. The king had to be seen to be defeated and deposed so that there could be no coming back.

Chapter 22

A Cunning Plan...

DURING THE WINTER of 1469–70, the Earl of Warwick had contrived to paper over the cracks in his relationship with Edward IV. When the dust settled after the failed coup of 1469, Warwick had retained all his lands and titles, and he had removed several of his worst enemies. Nor had the Duke of Clarence suffered from his involvement in the plot against his brother. So, if the two prominent rebel lords appeared to be no worse off for their daring little act of treason, why was Warwick contemplating open rebellion?

Well, though the king had not moved against him, Warwick knew that Edward would probably find it difficult to forget his betrayal. It was one thing to forgive an enemy who had fought honourably against you, but quite another to forgive betrayal by a friend. Edward, he assumed, was just biding his time until Warwick's position might be undermined by others, or until he could gradually reduce the earl's resources. Then Warwick would be in no position to survive the king's revenge.

If Warwick felt that he had no option but to rebel, then equally he must have seen that his only realistic hope of success lay in replacing Edward with the man who was still the heir, his new son-in-law, Clarence. But to stage a successful coup on such a scale, Warwick would need two things to happen: firstly, there must be a trigger to spark a rebellion and create an atmosphere of instability and fear; and secondly, he would need to have sufficient support from key nobles to back Clarence for the throne.

During the winter, Warwick found his trigger in a dispute in Lincolnshire between Sir Thomas Burgh – one of the king's household knights – and a rival landowner, Lord Welles. This particular dispute was a hot one, which led to Sir Thomas Burgh's house being robbed and destroyed by Lord Welles, his son, Sir Robert, and an assortment of their cronies. Such baronial feuds were always going on, but mostly they did not cause any more than local trouble because no nobleman of importance ever bothered to get involved. It would be far too risky. But by 1470, risky was Warwick's middle name...

King Edward clearly felt that he needed to support Sir Thomas Burgh, since he was a knight of his own household, and thus he declared in February 1470 that in March he would raise an army at Grantham in Lincolnshire. The purpose of this

1. Henry VI of England. (*Poems and Romances* (Shrewsbury book), illuminated by the Master of John Talbot, public domain, via Wikimedia Commons)

2. Edmund Beaufort and envoyés de Rouen. (Philippe de Mazerolles, public domain, via Wikimedia Commons)

3. Richard, Duke of York. (Copyright Derek Birks; the stained glass windows at St Laurence's Church, Ludlow)

4. Castle Inn, St Albans, marking the death of Edmund Beaufort, Duke of Somerset in 1455. (Spudgun67, CC BY-SA 4.0 <https://creativecommons.org/licenses/by-sa/4.0>, via Wikimedia Commons)

5. Margaret of Anjou. (Talbot Master (fl. in Rouen, c.1430–60), public domain, via Wikimedia Commons)

6. Cecily Neville. (http://www.thebookofdays.com/months/may/31.htm, public domain, via Wikimedia Commons)

7. Edward IV. (Ann Longmore-Etheridge, CC BY-SA 4.0 <https://creativecommons.org/licenses/by-sa/4.0>, via Wikimedia Commons)

8. Elizabeth Woodville. (Unidentified painter, public domain, via Wikimedia Commons)

9. Lady Margaret Beaufort. (Irrilyth, CC BY-SA 4.0 <https://creativecommons.org/licenses/by-sa/4.0>, via Wikimedia Commons)

10. Cock Beck from Old London Road. (Cock Beck c. by Ian S, CC BY-SA 2.0 <https://creativecommons.org/licenses/by-sa/2.0>, via Wikimedia Commons)

11. Cock Beck footbridge. (Footbridge over Cock Beck by Ian S, CC BY-SA 2.0 <https://creativecommons.org/licenses/by-sa/2.0>, via Wikimedia Commons)

12. George, Duke of Clarence. (Unidentified painter, public domain, via Wikimedia Commons)

13. Burying the Earl of Warwick. (M. & N. Hanhart Chromo Lith (floruit 1839–1865)[1], public domain, via Wikimedia Commons)

14. The Siege of London, 1471. (Unknown, possibly Jean Spifame, public domain, via Wikimedia Commons)

15. Rivers and Caxton Presenting a Book to Edward IV. (Lorenzo Lippi, public domain, via Wikimedia Commons)

16. Edward V and Arthur Tudor. (Copyright Derek Birks, taken at the stained glass windows at St Laurence's Church, Ludlow)

17. King Richard III. (Barthel ii, public domain, via Wikimedia Commons)

18. Richard III and Anne Neville. (VeteranMP, CC BY-SA 3.0 <https://creativecommons.org/licenses/by-sa/3.0>, via Wikimedia Commons)

19. Buckingham finds the Severn impassable. (James William Edmund Doyle, public domain, via Wikimedia Commons)

20. Elizabeth of York. (Elizabeth_and_Henry.jpg: Malden, Sarah, Countess of Essex (c.1761–1838) derivative work: Jappalang, public domain, via Wikimedia Commons)

21. Henry VII. (Unbekannter zeitgenössischer Maler/ unknown contemporary painter, public domain, via Wikimedia Commons)

22. Perkin Warbeck (Unknown source, public domain, via Wikimedia Commons)

A Cunning Plan...

announcement was probably to frighten the Welles family into submission, but if that was its purpose it failed miserably. The response of Lord Welles was not to tremble in his boots but to ask Warwick and Clarence for their support. Now, I think it's very unlikely that such a request came out of thin air – mainly because there seem to have been some connections between the Welles faction and some of those who rebelled under Warwick's leadership the year before.

By the end of February, it seemed that a deal was done. Welles would start the ball rolling and then Warwick and Clarence would join in to support him against the king. Warwick, as ever, was keen to stir up support among the common classes, putting it about that the royal army would be used to punish them for previous disturbances in Lincolnshire.

When the king began raising his army, it was a simple matter for Warwick and Clarence to claim that the men they were also mustering were to assist the king against Lord Welles and his rebels. While the king continued to gather his army, he summoned Lord Welles to London and was probably a little surprised when Lord Welles actually turned up. Since the lord appeared to be repentant, Edward decided to pardon him and the whole matter then seemed a little less urgent, so Edward took several days to meet his brother Clarence in London before eventually leaving for Grantham.

It's highly unlikely that Edward suspected his brother of any wrongdoing, or he would have acted against him in London. Instead, Edward rode north with a few lords and his ordnance while, unknown to him, Clarence waited in London to have a chat with Lord Welles – after which he rode north to meet the Earl of Warwick at Coventry.

Meanwhile, in Lincolnshire, Lord Welles's son, Sir Robert, was whipping up commons support, warning that the king was coming to destroy them. He circulated a proclamation to that effect to all the local churches – you see, there was fake news even then. Rumour had it that the rebels would have contingents from other parts of the land to enable them to put a very large army in the field.

Edward's immediate response was to send to London for the recently pardoned Lord Welles. When the king interrogated Lord Welles again, he confessed all, apart from the small matter of the involvement of Warwick and Clarence. At the same time, the Duke of Clarence wrote to Edward promising to come to his aid, with Warwick, as soon as he had sufficient soldiers.

Confused? You might well be...

Warwick's original plan went something like this: Sir Robert Welles would stir up the Lincolnshire rebels while the king was delayed from setting out by the submission of Lord Welles and the meeting with Clarence. Meanwhile, Warwick himself would raise troops, then join with Clarence and head for Leicester, while ostensibly promising to support the king. Sir Robert Welles would ignore the king's army at Grantham and instead bring his large army of rebels to Leicester to join forces with Warwick and Clarence. Warwick would arrange a rising in Yorkshire, which would prevent the king from calling upon his northern lords for aid when he eventually realised the scale of the forces ranged against him. The result of all this would be that the king would face an overwhelmingly superior enemy and would not be able to summon any support.

It truly sounds as if it might just have been a cunning enough plan to succeed – so what went wrong? Basically, Edward did not keep to the script – and for that matter, neither did Sir Robert Welles.

The king, annoyed that Sir Robert was still raising an army of rebels when his father had only just received a royal pardon, declared that if Sir Robert did not submit at once then his father, Lord Welles, would be executed as a traitor.

Sir Robert was therefore presented with a simple, though agonising, three-way choice: he could submit; he could abandon his father and continue on his way to meet Warwick at Leicester; or he could ignore Warwick completely and attack the king in the hope of releasing his father.

Sir Robert chose the third option and took his army to Empingham – only a few miles away from where the king's army was camped at Stamford. Edward interpreted this, rightly, as a sign that Sir Robert was not going to submit. Perhaps Sir Robert thought that Edward would not carry out his threat immediately, but he did and Lord Welles, as promised, was executed.

We are told that Sir Robert intended to attack Edward and overwhelm him with his superior numbers. Sir Robert had clearly not learned much about his king, for in the event it was Edward who attacked with the firepower of cannon, which the rebel army lacked. The rebels could either hold their ground and be destroyed by the king's ordnance, or they could advance. They chose to advance and, with some crying out the customary battle shouts of 'A Warwick! A Warwick!' or 'A Clarence! A Clarence!' they met the king's army head on.

What springs to mind, by way of comparison, is the infamous Charge of the Light Brigade, during the Crimean War. Already battered and dispirited by cannon fire, the rebel infantry was simply no match for the king's army. The fight was all too brief and, in a very short time, a retreat became a rout. Many divested themselves of Clarence's livery in their haste to escape, which led to the Battle of Empingham being forever known by the term: 'Lose-cote Field'.

If the cries of 'A Clarence! A Clarence!' had sown any seeds of doubt in Edward's mind about his brother's involvement in the revolt, the discovery of a box of letters that Clarence had written to Sir Robert Welles dispelled any remaining uncertainty. Yes, there was indeed a smoking gun.

It was hardly surprising that Edward immediately summoned Warwick and Clarence to him to explain what they were doing. But the two noblemen – perhaps equally unsurprisingly – prevaricated while they considered their options. The planned Yorkshire rising had already begun, so perhaps all was not yet lost. If enough of the northern lords were willing to support them, they might yet succeed in toppling the king.

A Cunning Plan...

In the middle of March, Warwick and Clarence, having told the king's envoy that they were going to disband their armies and answer his summons, instead kept their armies intact and travelled north. The rebel earl and duke were still protesting their loyalty, while at the same time they moved in search of allies. In Yorkshire, Warwick hoped for support from his brother John, and perhaps from some other prominent northern noblemen, such as Lord Thomas Stanley.

However, as Edward headed north, his position improved by the day as more lords joined him with their retinues. Messages flew to and fro. The king repeated his summons to the two renegade lords, promising them a fair hearing. Again they professed their loyalty, but asked for assurances of safe conduct, which the king refused. By 20 March a battle between the two forces still seemed likely, until news reached Warwick that his brother John – far from joining his rebellion – had in fact answered the king's call to suppress the Yorkshire rising.

As Warwick turned his dwindling army towards Manchester, his last hope lay with Lord Thomas Stanley, the most influential lord in the north-west. But Stanley became suddenly rather elusive, finding urgent matters to attend to elsewhere. Without at least Stanley's support, Warwick knew that his venture was doomed and headlong retreat was the only course open to him.

Fleeing south, Warwick and Clarence picked up their wives and families and managed – just – to evade the king's pursuing army. They headed for the south-west and, from Dartmouth, they boarded several ships to sail along the English Channel. After failing to gather more ships and men en route at Southampton, they sailed on to Calais. Warwick, of course, was still Captain of Calais and there he expected to find ample men and resources to enable him to regroup. But King Edward had already written to Warwick's deputy at Calais, and thus Warwick's ships were denied entry.

It was a miserable journey for the Nevilles and Clarence as Warwick's heavily pregnant daughter, Isabel, went into labour on board and subsequently lost her child.

Warwick had little choice but to hope for a warm welcome elsewhere in France. So, indulging in some gratuitous piracy against Burgundian vessels on the way, his ships continued their journey. Perhaps Warwick believed that acting against the Burgundians, who were enemies of France, would ease his entry into a French port. He probably thought it couldn't hurt his reputation with the French king, Louis XI, when he asked for his protection.

Condemned in England as a traitor, Warwick now faced an ignominious end to his illustrious career. As a controlling force in English political life, he was at last finished – or was he?

Chapter 23

The House of Cards, 1470

IN APRIL 1470, Richard Neville, Earl of Warwick, was finished; he was no longer a great player in the original English 'Game of Thrones'. He was washed up, but even the wily Louis XI of France must have been at least a little surprised at his exact location. Warwick arrived in France having carried out some serious piracy against Burgundian ships in the Channel after being denied entry to the port of Calais. It must have been music to Louis's ears when he heard that the earl had sailed into the French port of Honfleur with Flemish prizes in tow. Louis's chief continental enemy was his neighbour, the Duke of Burgundy, and the French king, a master of diplomacy and intrigue, saw at once how he might profit by means of the defeated and desperate Earl of Warwick.

The French king understood that Warwick was not simply some run-of-the-mill renegade Englishman – and there were quite a few of those in France already. No, Warwick was a man whose very name might still inspire support. But if Louis was to make full use of this diplomatic windfall, he would need to act fast – while Warwick's credibility was still high with many in England.

Louis knew from Warwick's diplomatic missions during the 1460s that the earl favoured a French alliance – a policy over which he fell out with King Edward. The latter had instead allied himself to Burgundy, France's enemy, and that was clearly an alliance dangerous to France. So Louis XI was desperate to break it.

It was clear to Louis, from Warwick's actions over the past twelve months, that he was trying to affect a regime change in England by his attempts to install the Duke of Clarence on the throne. While Louis was very keen on regime change, he did not want the Duke of Clarence – another Yorkist – to be the next king of England. He had a better idea, which would ensure that England would no longer be allied to his main continental enemy, Burgundy. He wanted to restore the House of Lancaster in the person of Henry VI. Burgundy had supported Edward IV and thus was no friend of Lancaster.

This might seem a rather forlorn idea, with King Henry lodged securely in the Tower of London, but remember that his wife, Queen Margaret of Anjou, and his son, Edward of Westminster, were in France. Even so, anyone who has followed the story of the Wars of the Roses so far must think that it would be a very tall order indeed to persuade Queen Margaret to join forces with her most implacable enemy, Richard, Earl of Warwick. But here Louis XI lived up to his nickname of 'the universal spider'. As an expert manipulator of people, he knew exactly which buttons to press to persuade these two intransigent foes into an unlikely alliance.

If Warwick had ever considered the possibility of a reconciliation with Queen Margaret, he must have viewed it as very much the last resort. But in May 1470 the last resort had been reached, and it is a measure of Warwick's utter desperation that he was willing to fling aside all previous loyalties to mount one last attempt at achieving power.

Thus, between May and July 1470, Louis was able to broker negotiations between Warwick and Margaret – and he could be very persuasive indeed. He would have emphasised to both parties that this opportunity was their last chance.

One potential stumbling block, however, was the Duke of Clarence, because, if Louis's plan succeeded, Clarence would no longer be the first taxi on the rank. Instead, he would, at best, be parked somewhere out of the way – in the worst case scenario he might find himself under a car park...

For all his numerous faults, we should not see Clarence as a mere cipher to be manipulated by others. He was a man who still had resources and influence in his own right – as will be made abundantly clear later in this sorry tale. For the time being though, Warwick's son-in-law would have to take a back seat.

Yet even if Warwick were willing, how could the former queen, Margaret, be persuaded to agree to a pact with the man she regarded as the prime architect of her family's demise? She must have regarded the earl as the devil incarnate. But Louis still had a joker to play: without support from him, neither Margaret nor her son would ever have power in England again. If she wanted to restore her husband Henry and the Lancastrian bloodline to the English throne, she would have to do it on Louis's terms, or not at all.

And Louis's terms were clear: a joint venture with the Earl of Warwick, cemented by a marriage between their children. If Warwick's remaining daughter, Anne Neville were to marry Prince Edward, the heir of Lancaster, it would give the alliance some genuine substance beyond mere promises.

Margaret must have been mightily reluctant, for the marriage was very unequal. If Anne Neville was marrying up, then Edward of Westminster must be marrying down. If he succeeded his father, Henry VI, as king, then a prestigious marriage to a foreign princess would be more appropriate than wedding a mere nobleman's daughter. But the reality was that her son had no chance of removing the House of York without the help of both Warwick and King Louis.

So, Margaret had to swallow her bile and come to terms: but she had no intention of making it easy for Warwick. At Angers on 22 July 1470, the two participated in an act of public reconciliation, during which Warwick spent a quarter of an hour on his knees saying sorry. Several days after this touching scene, Anne and Edward were betrothed. To say it was an uneasy alliance would be an understatement, for

Margaret certainly did not trust Warwick at all – and who could blame her? After all, this was a man who was willing to abandon not only his erstwhile friend and ally, Edward IV, but also the entire House of York's grip upon the English throne. And for what? For his own ambition and advancement. Yes, Queen Margaret was wise not to trust Warwick an inch, even though that lack of trust would prove her undoing.

When the plans were laid for this new Lancastrian invasion of England, Margaret refused to leave France until Warwick had demonstrated his commitment by overthrowing King Edward, nor would she allow her son to accompany Warwick. Against all the odds, Warwick succeeded in putting together a coalition of Edward's enemies, including not only Queen Margaret but also the renegade lords: Jasper Tudor, King Henry's half-brother, and John de Vere, Earl of Oxford, another exiled diehard Lancastrian.

Despite his new allies, Warwick would have known that his success in England – as ever – would depend upon the actions of several key men: his brother John Neville, Lord Thomas Stanley, Henry Percy, Earl of Northumberland and, not least, George, Duke of Clarence himself. How would all these individuals react in the crisis that Warwick was about to create?

John Neville's position was unusual. King Edward had frequently rewarded him for his loyalty, not least for suppressing Lancastrian pockets of resistance. In particular, he had given this prominent member of the House of Neville the Percy earldom of Northumberland. John, as a lifelong despiser of the rival Percy family, must have been ecstatic about that. Yet in March 1470, five years later, Edward returned the earldom to the Percy heir. He compensated John with extensive lands in the south-west, promotion to the rank of marquess and the betrothal of his son, newly created Duke of Bedford, to Edward's eldest daughter, Elizabeth. The latter, in particular, was no mean reward, since Edward still had no son. However, it seems that John Neville did not see these inducements as sufficient compensation for losing much of his northern lands and influence. As a man of the north, he felt slighted.

Another key magnate, Lord Thomas Stanley, is often viewed as untrustworthy, though much of that reputation refers to actions from 1470 onwards. There was no reason yet for Edward to doubt Stanley's loyalty. But what was constant about Thomas Stanley was that he always did what he thought was best for the survival and prosperity of the Stanley family.

During July and August 1470, Edward IV was in the north of England dispersing rebels who had been encouraged – again – to act by Warwick. Edward hoped that a blockade of French ports by his own ships, and those of his Burgundian allies, would keep Warwick trapped in France. Warwick's fortunes stood on a knife edge because soon even his own men refused to go anywhere until they were paid. Only Louis's assistance got him out of that bind, but then he had a stroke of luck. Storms scattered the blockading fleets for long enough to allow Warwick's invasion force to set sail for England in September.

The House of Cards, 1470

When he landed in the south-west in September 1470, Warwick proclaimed that he was coming to restore the rightful king, Henry VI. However dishonest one might feel that this claim seems now, there is no doubt that, at the time, it did resonate with some people. Bear in mind also that at this point Edward IV had no male heir, whereas Henry VI did. However unlikely it was, and whatever his motives, Warwick had put together what appeared to many to be an attractive political package.

Warwick, Clarence and Oxford headed north while Jasper Tudor diverted to Wales to gather support there. King Edward was still in the north stamping out Neville-backed risings, which was exactly where Warwick intended him to be. Though Edward was still confident that he could defeat Warwick, one by one his leading nobles joined the rebellion. These notably included Lord Stanley and the Earl of Shrewsbury – but also crucially, and at the very last minute, Warwick's brother, John Neville, who was still smarting from the loss of his earldom. For Edward, who expected that John Neville was bringing reinforcements, his defection was a body blow.

With Warwick advancing from the south and John close by in the north, the king had no choice but to disband his army and flee. In a matter of weeks, the whole Yorkist house of cards had fallen. Edward fled abroad with his brother Richard, the staunch Lord Hastings and a few other close companions, to his Burgundian ally, Duke Charles. Meanwhile, his pregnant wife, Elizabeth Woodville, took sanctuary with her daughters – not for last time – at Westminster Abbey.

A victorious Warwick headed for the capital to free the bemused Henry VI and set him on the throne while he awaited the return of Queen Margaret and her son, Edward – now married to Warwick's daughter, Anne.

Nevertheless, the earl still faced some tricky problems. The coalition of forces he had brought to bear against King Edward included some of his own most vociferous enemies. Once Queen Margaret did return, along with a few more bitter foes such as Edmund Beaufort, Duke of Somerset – younger brother of Henry, executed at Hexham – and Henry Holland, Duke of Exeter, Warwick must have feared what would happen. All that though lay in the future because Queen Margaret, beset by her own doubts about the wisdom of trusting Warwick, was still reluctant to take the leap of faith and return to England.

Thus, at the heart of Warwick's stellar alliance lay a good measure of animosity and mistrust. Even some of his friends were nervous: some supporters, notably the lords Stanley, Oxford and Shrewsbury, received little immediate reward for their vital support. His brother John, who had also risked all to support him, must have been uneasy about his rival in the north, Henry Percy, who still retained the restored earldom of Northumberland. If his allies harboured doubts about what they had done, those with no love at all for Warwick were just biding their time until Queen Margaret arrived in the hope that old scores might then be settled.

It is hardly surprising that there were quite a few supporters of the deposed Edward IV who believed that, if enough pressure was applied, Warwick's unholy, ragtag coalition would simply fall to pieces.

Chapter 24

Return of the King?

IN OCTOBER 1470, Yorkist England was effectively dead. Edward IV, with his brother, Richard, Duke of Gloucester, brother-in-law, Anthony Woodville, Earl Rivers and his old friend, William, Lord Hastings, was in Flanders under the protection of his erstwhile ally, Duke Charles of Burgundy – who was also his brother-in-law.

Edward's queen, Elizabeth Woodville, had retreated with her daughters to sanctuary in Westminster Abbey where, in November, she finally gave Edward a son – not that it seemed to matter quite as much by then.

Edward's journey to Flanders had been far from straightforward and a warm reception there was by no means guaranteed. In fact, Duke Charles would not see him at first because Edward's very presence created a problem for him. Just as Louis XI of France wanted England as an ally against Burgundy, Charles of Burgundy wanted England as an ally against France. While Edward IV was king, Charles had secured that alliance, but now he would need an alliance with the new English government, Warwick's Lancastrian regime. You may think that was rather disloyal of Charles, but he had to consider what was best for Burgundy: it would be hard for Burgundy to face an alliance of France and England and survive.

Fortunately for Edward, Warwick was not interested in an alliance with Burgundy because he was already heavily committed to France. It was no coincidence that Charles first met Edward in December 1470, shortly after Louis XI made his warlike intentions towards Burgundy crystal clear.

Charles then had no choice because his very survival depended upon supporting Edward. With the backing of Charles, Edward was able to acquire some ships for a significant invasion fleet, though we are not exactly talking about an armada here. Between January and March 1471, Edward continued his preparations to return to England, while Warwick used his fleet to make punitive attacks on Edward's allies: not only Burgundy, but also the Duchy of Brittany, which, like Burgundy, lived under the shadow of superior French power.

Breton ships played an important role in distracting the English fleet while Edward prepared to launch his invasion force. But where was the French fleet all that time? Well, they were idling at anchor as they waited to escort Queen Margaret and her son, Prince Edward, back to England. She was still in France, allowing her deep mistrust of Warwick to turn into a festering great sore. The delay would prove critical because the one really solid advantage the Lancastrians possessed was a male heir more or less old enough to take over from Henry VI. The sooner Margaret took her son to England, the more stable the new regime would be. Yet she remained dithering in France, still unwilling to believe that Warwick's defection to her cause was genuine.

Warwick himself, meanwhile, was making preparations in case Edward should evade his fleet and land in England. But the measures he took revealed a thick seam of distrust towards some of his most powerful new allies. This was demonstrated by the fact that only a small handful of men were given commissions of array: in other words, the legal authority to raise troops. Among the trusted few were his son-in-law, the Duke of Clarence, his brother John Neville, Jasper Tudor and John de Vere, Earl of Oxford – hardly a broad base of support. Usually commissions would be delegated to other local magnates, such as Lord Stanley and the Earl of Shrewsbury, both of whom had just supported Warwick's coup. But clearly Warwick was circling the wagons around several chosen men and any others who might conceivably support Edward were closely watched or imprisoned, such as John Mowbray, Duke of Norfolk.

On 11 March 1471, Edward IV attempted what must have seemed to most folk at the time an impossible task. He sailed from Burgundy with thirty-six ships and close to 2,000 men, including many mercenaries. And though it was a force which could not be ignored, Warwick was prepared. The two men had never actually fought against each other, and you get the sense that Warwick faced the threat of Edward with some confidence. But if he viewed the coming struggle as a master versus apprentice situation, he was in for a shock.

As so often in life – and certainly in this conflict – the weather now interfered with the well-laid plans of mere men, and not for the last time. Edward's fleet was hit by a savage storm in the North Sea which dispersed his ships, leaving him more or less on his own. Nevertheless, Edward landed on England's north-east coast at Ravenspur on the Humber estuary. Ravenspur had been ravaged by the sea for generations and not long after this period it disappeared under the waves entirely.

Several of Edward's other ships managed to land elsewhere along the coast and their men made every effort to join him. In the end, he probably had about 500 men – which was certainly not enough to retake a kingdom. There was an ironic precedent, however, for Edward to copy because Ravenspur was where Henry Bolingbroke, later to be crowned Henry IV – the first Lancastrian king – had landed in 1399. Edward, like Bolingbroke before him, had only a few men and thus, copying Bolingbroke, he decided to put the word out that he had returned to England only to claim his father's dukedom – in Edward's case, that of York.

Edward then headed for the city of York with his small force. Though several men warned him that he would not be welcomed there, Edward never lacked confidence in his own abilities and pressed on regardless. It was a huge gamble and his bid to regain power could have ended there, with him trapped in the city with only a handful of men. But Edward entered York professing publicly not only his loyalty to Henry VI, but also to the young Edward, Prince of Wales – who was still, incidentally, loitering with his mother in France. Soon the familiar Edwardian charm offensive won people over sufficiently for him to receive a night's hospitality.

Edward's low-key arrival in York added substance to his claim that he only wanted his dukedom, and so, when he left York again and headed south, he posed an awkward problem for those who could have opposed him. Two men in the north could have stopped Edward in his tracks, but neither did – possibly because they were rivals for power in the region. Henry Percy, Earl of Northumberland, perhaps recalling that it was Edward who had restored him, against the odds, to his earldom, did nothing and thus, astonishingly, no Percy hand would be raised against him.

This is bizarre in a way because it's not as if Edward was especially popular in the north – he wasn't at all. In fact, few men in the north had rallied to his cause since he landed – far fewer than Edward hoped. But it was one thing not to join him, and quite another to take up arms against him because who would go against him, if Northumberland had not? Thus Northumberland's initial inactivity was vital to Edward's survival.

But what about the other power in the north, Warwick's own trusted brother, John Neville, Marquess of Montagu? Why didn't he stop Edward? The problem for Montagu was that since no one else had yet opposed Edward, it was difficult for him to rally support for such a move.

Once Edward moved further south into the Midlands, a confusing game of cat and mouse began, with the fate of the kingdom at stake. At Nottingham he was joined for the first time by a substantial force of several hundred men. But not far away in Newark, the Earl of Oxford and the Duke of Exeter had a much larger Lancastrian force at their disposal. They, however, failed to act.

Now you see, this is what I like about Edward IV. Did he scurry away in the opposite direction from the superior force? No, he made straight for the enemy – and his decisive action threw them into a panic. Simply by marching towards them, Edward caused the Lancastrians to disintegrate.

By 25 March 1471, Edward had crossed the River Trent and arrived at Leicester where he finally received substantial reinforcements in the shape of 3,000 men raised by Lord Hastings. These were dangerous times for nobles and gentry in the Midlands because both sides were now writing letters to them calling for their support.

By 27 March, Warwick had assembled an army of perhaps 6,000 men, which could have taken Edward's smaller force head-on, but unusually for Warwick, he hesitated. Instead of taking the decisive action for which he was so renowned, Warwick withdrew to Coventry to await the arrival of the Duke of Clarence, the Marquess of Montagu, the Earl of Oxford and the Duke of Exeter. Warwick's course of action was sensible because he reasoned that such a massive combined force would be able to annihilate Edward. But in war, sensible actions do not always bring victory and Edward, still unopposed, advanced his own army to the nearby town of Warwick.

So, there we have it: Edward, encountering a force much larger than his own, faced imminent destruction… But, the thing we always know about the Wars of the Roses – possibly the only thing we know for certain – is that there was always another curveball coming… and the next one came on 3 April 1471.

Warwick's hesitation led some men to question, perhaps with some justification, whether he had the nerve for the fight. One of those was the Duke of Clarence who, as we have already noted, had no real place in the new Lancastrian regime. Clarence decided that blood was thicker than water, and so switched sides to re-join his brother. The pair met and were reconciled at once, though clearly this was not the work of a few minutes. Edward's whole family had been working hard to detach his brother George from Warwick for some time: especially his mother, Cecily Neville, his sisters and his brother Richard, of Gloucester.

Although Warwick was his father-in-law, Clarence had little reason to continue to support him since he no longer had any chance of being king in the new regime, whereas with Edward, who had only an infant son, there was still a much bigger role available. As the 'spare thumb' of Warwick's regime, Clarence was even more worried about his future than Warwick himself. Clarence's sudden defection to Edward, taking all his adherents with him, meant that Edward gained up to 4,000 men, which completely changed the military balance between the two sides. At Warwick, Edward set aside his ruse and declared that he was king again. With hindsight of course, the subterfuge seems pretty hard to believe, but at the time it created enough confusion to sow doubts about his intentions and paralyse his enemies.

So, by early April 1471, after a few weeks of confusion, when the dust had settled, there were two large armies facing each other: Edward's at Warwick and Warwick's in Coventry. Since neither was now large enough to destroy the other, they were locked in a deadly stalemate.

Chapter 25

The Fog of War

IN EARLY APRIL 1471, two large armies faced each other in the Midlands: Edward IV, attempting to retake his throne, was camped at Warwick, and he was opposed in Coventry by the man who had once been his staunchest ally: Richard Neville, Earl of Warwick. The earl had thrown in his lot – the very last lot in his pocket – with the Lancastrian Queen Margaret. But since she had not yet reached England, she was in no position to help her new ally.

Since neither force could dislodge the other, Edward and Warwick were locked in a stalemate. But it was a stalemate which could not last long because simply feeding so many men in such a small area was a tall order. Since they could not sit there indefinitely, Edward took a gamble and marched to London. If he got there before the Earl of Warwick, London would provide him with men, money, resources and legitimacy, for it was the seat of government. It also offered the chance to recapture Henry VI.

Such was the speed of Edward's advance that Warwick had no chance of catching him before he reached the capital. Warwick ordered the city of London to hold out until he arrived, while Edward told them to secure Henry VI and await his arrival.

Interestingly, at that critical moment, the most prominent Lancastrian in London, Edmund Beaufort, Duke of Somerset, decided to leave the city before either Warwick or Edward arrived. Why? Because he had received news that Margaret of Anjou and her son had finally sailed from France and were expected to arrive shortly on the south coast. It is an interesting indicator of Lancastrian priorities: Margaret was far more important to Somerset than Warwick. If Somerset had remained perhaps things would have been different, but probably not because Edward was advancing upon the city with a large army which no one in London had the means – or the will – to oppose. The city welcomed him in and the only leading member of the new regime left there, George Neville, Warwick's brother, could do nothing but submit, along with several other Lancastrians.

Edward had a brief and amiable chat with Henry VI, who seemed genuinely pleased to see him, and then got on with the business of organising his forces to stop Warwick. He hurried to Westminster – not only to greet his wife and new son, Edward (yes, another Edward, I'm afraid) – but also to be crowned king again.

It's difficult not to admire Edward's progress from Ravenspur to London; no one could have predicted how it came about, but the key was holding his nerve and that was one of the man's greatest attributes. However, so far nothing had been won: the enemy was still there and – with the imminent threat of Queen Margaret's arrival – Warwick's army would only get stronger. It was imperative that Edward did not allow the two forces to join up, so he had to defeat Warwick swiftly. In a matter of days, Warwick would be at the city gates, but Edward chose to ride out of London and meet him head-on in the field.

Warwick was heading south from St Albans when, on the afternoon of 13 April, Easter Saturday 1471, Edward set out from London with his army which, bolstered by new recruits, probably amounted to perhaps 10,000 men. All the sources agree that Warwick's army was larger, so the outcome was by no means certain and the odds did not favour the newly re-crowned king. With him, Edward had the usual suspects: his two brothers, his brother-in-law Earl Rivers, Lord Hastings and others, but he also had the old king, Henry VI. Since possession of the king was everything, Edward could not just leave him behind in London.

Not only was Warwick's army larger, but he also had far more cannon than Edward and two of the most reliable military commanders in England: his brother, John Neville, and the Earl of Oxford, John de Vere. It was going to take something rather special to defeat Warwick, and that's one way of describing the battle that followed.

As was usually the case with Edward, once he started moving an army, he did not stop until he was where he wanted to be – in this case, very close to the enemy. His vanguard encountered Warwick's patrols at Barnet on the Great North Road and drove them north through the town. There is some conjecture now about exactly where the battle was fought, including a suggestion that it was a little further north than has previously been thought. However, having walked the traditional site myself, I think it still makes a degree of sense.

In 1896 Sir Lonsdale Augustus Hale described something he called the 'fog of war' in his book of the same title. It was, he wrote: 'the state of ignorance in which commanders frequently find themselves as regards the real strength and position, not only of their foes, but also of their friends.' If ever one wanted a classic example of Hale's phrase 'the fog of war' then the battle of Barnet provides it.

When Edward's army pushed into Barnet and reached Warwick's main force under cover of darkness, that's where the fun began... In the dark, Edward was able – by moving his men quietly – to get very close to the enemy line. However, precisely because it was dark, they actually got much closer than they intended. Not only that, but they contrived – since they could not see where the enemy were – to set up their battle line so that it was not exactly aligned opposite Warwick's. Thus, Edward's right wing ended up extending well beyond Warwick's left flank, which it faced. And of course, at the other end, Edward's left flank was similarly overlapped by Warwick's right. In the night, all were blissfully unaware of this rather important development.

As soon as Warwick realised that Edward's army was within reach, he used the night hours to bombard the Yorkists with ferocious artillery fire, although the Lancastrians were firing blind. Edward had expected the barrage and because he had positioned his army so very close to Warwick's line, most of the cannon fire went over the heads of his men. They were under orders not to fire back lest they should give away their close proximity to the enemy.

One can only imagine the atmosphere on Easter Sunday morning, with the two battle lines littered with debris and screened by smoke from the cannon. To make matters worse, just before dawn, a thick fog descended upon them all. Edward planned a very early morning attack, which started with a brief salvo of fire by his archers and hand gunners, firing blind like Warwick's gunners during the night. Then Edward's men advanced on foot – as was the way in this period – and launched their attack.

The first point to make is that no one fighting on that field had the slightest idea what was happening elsewhere on the field. If one section of the battle line was advancing, their comrades quite close by had no inkling of it. There was so much noise: shouting, possibly sporadic gun or cannon fire, not to mention the metallic clash of arms. You might hear some shouts of triumph, but you had no idea whose shouts they were. All you could do in that situation was try to kill whoever was in front of you – and, obviously, try to avoid getting killed.

Normally on a battlefield, if one flank of an army is seen to be hopelessly overrun then most likely the whole army will be turned and routed. But the key word there is 'seen'. Because of the original misalignment of the two armies, when Warwick's right flank, commanded by the Earl of Oxford, advanced there was no one in front of them. Accordingly, they swung round and found Edward's left flank at a tangent, driving them back with heavy losses. So great was their impact that some of Edward's men fled into Barnet and others even as far as London itself, carrying with them news of Warwick's victory. Some of Oxford's men pursued the fleeing Yorkists into Barnet, where many then decided there were better things to do than return to a battle that was already won.

Oxford's total rout of Edward's left flank should have been decisive – except that no one else saw it. The rest kept on fighting as if it had not happened. And, of course, just as Oxford's men had overlapped on one end of the battle line, so Edward's overlapped on the other and his right flank drove Warwick's left in onto his centre. Even in a fog, King Edward must have been a formidable opponent – taller than most men, armed with a couple of poll axes and with the best quality armour available, he pounded into his enemies and drove them back.

One account tells us that the Earl of Oxford, realising that the battle had not yet been won, managed to gather some of his men and rejoin the fight. However, because the battle line had shifted around, his men ended up facing those of John Neville who, mistaking Oxford's Star banners for Edward's emblem of the Sun in Splendour, launched an attack against them. Believing they had been betrayed,

Oxford's men broke and fled. Whether the story is true or not, it certainly reflects the degree of confusion that existed that day.

After several hours of brutal, bloody, hand-to-hand fighting with mace, poll axe and sword, the battle was won. The two Neville brothers, Richard and John, who had played such a prominent role in English history, were both dead – along with perhaps a thousand more men on each side.

Edward had defeated the greatest challenge yet to his grip upon the English throne. Against the odds, and in possibly one of the most bizarre battles in English history, he had defeated his old friend and ally, Warwick. He could now return to London in triumph, except that only a few hours after his victory on Easter Sunday, Queen Margaret and her son, Prince Edward, landed at Weymouth in Dorset.

In a day or two, Edward IV would receive word of her landing, just as she would learn of the crushing defeat and death of Warwick and the destruction of his army.

What would she have thought about that, I wonder? I imagine that she shed few tears over the earl's death; she may have thought, as her Lancastrian advisers told her, that she was better off without him. Nevertheless, she did not have her husband, Henry VI, either – and it was in his name she was supposed to be fighting. In any case, how easy would it be to raise another army quickly? Surely there would be no more volunteers for another round of slaughter.

Chapter 26

Another Bloody Meadow...

ON EASTER SUNDAY, 14 April 1471, at Barnet, Edward IV emerged unscathed from yet another maelstrom of a battle. It had been bloody, it had been muddled, but it had also been decisive. His enemies, the Earl of Warwick and his brother, John were both dead and Edward was back in charge once more. Add to that the birth of a son to Queen Elizabeth and you have the foundation of a Yorkist dynasty.

But as we know, one problem remained and it was no small matter. Queen Margaret, wife of the imprisoned Henry VI, had landed at Weymouth on the Dorset coast within hours of Edward's victory – and she brought with her a son who could be the foundation of a dynasty for Lancaster. Not only that, but her son, Edward of Westminster, was far older than Edward IV's boy – and certainly old enough to rule should ill fate or malice strike down his father, Henry.

Now, if you are thinking that the arrival of Queen Margaret and her young son would pose a much less significant threat than the might of Warwick, then think again. What was Warwick? A mere earl with not a trace of royal blood in his veins. All the same, you might wonder: after so much turmoil and upheaval, during which Edward IV had occupied the throne for years, why would anyone want to restore a king like Henry VI who, at every turn, had shown himself incapable of ruling wisely?

The answer is in several parts really: firstly, Margaret was offering a clear alternative to York, with a return to the legitimate line of kings, the heirs of the warrior king, Henry V. Also, no man in fifteenth-century England was keen to be an oath-breaker – it was a convention by which men lived their lives. So, the habit of loyalty to a hereditary monarch was a strong incentive. Just consider how many men had already fought and died for Henry VI, despite his shortcomings.

Finally, Edward had promised a change for the better: good government, prosperity, unity and the rule of law. But he had clearly not delivered on all of that and some folk decided that perhaps God was giving them another chance to put matters right.

Warwick himself had profited – albeit temporarily – from a groundswell of support for the old Lancastrian regime. The challenge now for Margaret was to recapture that enthusiasm, having carelessly allowed it to wane while she dithered in France.

Hearing of Warwick's disastrous defeat would have come as a body blow to Margaret. Though she may have cared little what became of her new ally himself, she could ill afford to lose the massive resources and the momentum he had gathered in her husband's name.

Now she had a decision to make: fight or flee? To fight would be to risk all on one throw of the dice, but would she ever have a better chance of recovering her husband's throne? She knew in her heart that she would not. One of her key advisers was Edmund Beaufort, Duke of Somerset – an experienced military commander– and for him too this was a last chance to regain his lost prominence in the kingdom.

Margaret must have been encouraged by the positive reception she received in the south-west, but she was no fool and she knew she would need more than just the men of Dorset, Devon and Cornwall to get past Edward IV. The big question for her was how to defeat Edward, a man as yet undefeated on the field of battle and whose power was once again considerable. But though Edward had London and much support in the Midlands, his hold on other areas was less secure. In Kent – where Warwick had been perennially popular – and the north – where there was much latent Lancastrian support – his control was very tenuous.

Having joined at Exeter with the men raised in the far south-west, Margaret had to decide whether to head east to London to draw upon support from Kent and perhaps other southern counties, or to link up with Jasper Tudor in the Welsh Marches and then march north to the Lancastrian heartland.

While she formed her strategy, Edward IV could only gather as large an army as possible and try to work out where she was heading. You may wonder why it was so difficult to locate an army of several thousand men, but remember there were no aircraft, drones or satellite imaging, just plain old eyesight. Communication was as fast and reliable as a man could ride a horse. Hence, Edward had patrols and scouts everywhere, seeking a definitive indication of Margaret's intended route. She, on the other hand, sent out parties of men in various directions to deliberately mislead him. Thus, another game of cat and mouse developed. If Edward guessed wrong, Margaret would slip past him and, a little further down the line, he would encounter her again with a much greater force at her back.

Her decision made, Queen Margaret headed north and, as they say, the die was cast. Her army marched via Taunton, Wells and then Bristol – at each point feinting to go east to confuse Edward.

On 24 April, Edward went west to Windsor then north to Abingdon, where he pondered the possibilities for a day or so and awaited news. If Margaret was heading north then she would have to cross the River Severn before meeting up with Jasper Tudor's Welshmen. Once she was ahead of him, Edward would be unable to stop her progress northward. So Edward gambled again, and marched rapidly westwards; a march of thirty miles in a day brought him to Cirencester. Edward still hoped to stop Margaret near Cirencester and arrayed his army ready to do battle, even though he was still unsure where the Lancastrian army was.

By Wednesday 1 May Margaret's army was nowhere to be seen because it was still in Bristol. Somerset and Margaret were doing quite well in confusing Edward about their movements but, on Thursday 2 May, Edward decided to make for Bristol, hoping to encounter the Lancastrians on the way and force them to fight. Margaret's army, however, was racing north towards Gloucester where she hoped to cross the River Severn.

Outmanoeuvred, Edward IV could not now stop Margaret's army from reaching Gloucester, but he despatched riders ahead to the town and ordered the Governor of Gloucester, Sir Richard Beauchamp, to close the gates to Margaret's army.

All now hinged on Beauchamp and it would not be too much of an exaggeration to say that the fate of Edward's crown lay in that one man's hands. Which way would he jump? There is evidence that there was some support for Margaret in the city, but Beauchamp owed his appointment to Edward and thus decided to close the city gates. This made the Lancastrian position suddenly very dangerous. The Yorkist army was hard upon their heels, so they could not assault the city and instead had to hurry on to the next river crossing – the ford at Tewkesbury, which they reached late on Friday 3 May.

Edward, now that he knew where his opponents were, was driving his troops hard and catching up fast. They advanced for thirty miles arrayed in their three 'battles' as they were known: vanguard, centre and rear-guard – ready to engage the enemy at a moment's notice. But by the time they rolled up south of Tewkesbury and rested for the night, they were exhausted.

Though Margaret's army could not now escape the Yorkists – crossing the Severn while under attack would not be a great plan – she was actually in a strong position to fight. She could choose the battleground and it was well-chosen. To attack, Edward's men would have to advance through a warren of lanes and hedgerows and cross several streams, climbing all the while before they could reach their opponents.

For both sides, only one outcome would suffice: complete victory and the death of the opposing leaders. This is not the place for an extensive assessment of the battle, but here is what happened in a nutshell.

Edward, as we know, was not a commander who tended to wait very long once he saw his enemy. On Saturday morning, he arrayed his army and attacked. His vanguard, led by his younger brother, Richard of Gloucester, found the assault hard going, but they did have more guns and archers than the Duke of Somerset and were able to put his defensive line under great pressure. Somerset responded by launching a swift and powerful counterattack against Edward's centre. All hung in the balance as Gloucester was forced to turn and aid his brother. Gradually, Somerset's men were forced back towards their own lines and then a vital intervention came. Edward had positioned 200 men-at-arms in nearby parkland with a certain amount of licence as to what they should do during the battle. As it happened, they chose an excellent moment to intervene and made a massive

Another Bloody Meadow…

difference. The cream of Somerset's force was routed and mercilessly hacked down in what is still known as the Bloody Meadow.

Edward then pressed on with the jugular within his grasp. Though it seems that Prince Edward fought bravely, the second stage of the battle was all too brief. Along with many of his comrades, the 18-year-old prince – the last hope of Lancaster – was killed. A few others, such as the Duke of Somerset himself, sought sanctuary in nearby Tewkesbury Abbey. It did them little good, for Edward's soldiers simply dragged them out to face their punishment. Men like Somerset, who had already been pardoned once by Edward, could expect no mercy and a couple of days later they were executed.

Queen Margaret, who had fled the field and forded the River Severn to escape, was soon captured and the Lancastrian dream was over.

It wasn't quite the end, however, because there were reports of revolts in Kent and the north. So although Edward had won two crushing and politically decisive battles in the space of a few weeks, he now had to persuade his exhausted men to go on the campaign trail once more.

Chapter 27

Peace for Our Time...

IN MAY 1471, after two brutal campaigns within a month, there was still no respite for Edward IV. Although he had killed Edward, Prince of Wales, and captured the elusive Queen Margaret, there was news of unrest elsewhere. In Yorkist England 'elsewhere' usually meant in the north, the south-west or Kent. Though Edward's victory had more or less pacified the south-west, Edward now faced new challenges in both the north and in Kent – and he could not be in both places at once.

Unwilling to leave the north to fester, he headed there first, setting off for Coventry where he aimed to raise more troops. He needed to bolster the army which had fought so hard – and effectively – for him first at Barnet and then Tewkesbury. However, by mid-May, the Earl of Northumberland reported to Edward that the north was at peace. This was not that surprising because by then news of the catastrophe at Tewkesbury would have reached any potential rebels in the north. Edward was still not very popular in the north, but the destruction of the Neville family's power meant that they were in no position to lead a revolt and the restoration of Percy fortunes under Edward ensured the loyalty of Northumberland.

The settlement of affairs in the north meant that Edward was free to head back south to deal personally with the uprising in Kent which, because it threatened London itself, was a serious cause for concern. You may wonder why, when the House of Lancaster appeared to be dead and buried, anyone would continue the struggle. I mean, what was there left to fight for?

Well, firstly, it's important to know that the Kent uprising started before the Tewkesbury campaign. Its leader was known to contemporaries – and history – as Thomas, Bastard of Fauconberg. He was the illegitimate son (clue in his nickname!) of William Neville, Lord Fauconberg, who had fought for Edward IV at Towton. Thomas was therefore a cousin of the Earl of Warwick and joined his cousin in exile in 1470. Like his cousin, he enjoyed naval command and liked to indulge in a little piracy from time to time. When he returned with Warwick, he was employed in such activities and, as a result, developed a close association with Kent and the men of the Channel ports.

When Edward IV returned to England in the spring of 1471, Fauconberg went to Calais to bring back fresh troops for Warwick from the garrison there. However, he did not arrive in time to save Warwick. One imagines that this would have been a great blow to Thomas since he had committed his future to an alliance with his cousin. So, he decided to continue to support Queen Margaret and by early May he had amassed a sizeable force in Kent – perhaps as many as 10,000 men – though he claimed to have nearer to 15,000. His supporters, however, included few reliable soldiers – only really the contingent from the Calais garrison. The rest were ordinary working men for the most part: cloth-workers, farmers, and builders.

So, to return to my question: what was there left to fight for? Primarily, of course, there was the House of Lancaster, but, as we often find in popular revolts of all periods, men took part because of local grievances as much as anything else – for example, some dairymen of Essex joined the rising as a protest about the low income they received from the London buyers of their goods. Some no doubt also joined in the hope of partaking in the rich pickings of London if the rebels were able to enter the city.

Because the king had been entirely focussed upon the crisis in the west, Fauconberg was able to make a considerable advance across Kent towards London unchecked by anyone. He wanted to get to Edward, but London stood in his way, so he asked the city authorities to allow his army to pass through London and promised that there would be no pillaging. For the city fathers there were two issues to consider: firstly, their loyalty to the king – a rebel army, once in the city, might attempt to free Henry VI, which would only fan the flames of rebellion. But more of an issue for the mayor and aldermen of London was that Kent rebels had previous form when it came to trashing the city and their previous 'visits' had caused massive damage and loss of life. Many Londoners would have lived through the last such episode in 1450 during Jack Cade's rebellion, and it made sense to keep the rebel army outside the city. In declining Fauconberg's request they also took the trouble to inform the rebels that Edward IV had just annihilated the Lancastrian army at Tewkesbury.

If the authorities expected this news to disperse the rebel army, they were disappointed, as Fauconberg decided to press on and attack the city. Being a naval man, he brought his fleet up the Thames and moored it on the south bank close to the Tower, where of course Henry VI was still lodged. At the same time he launched an assault from Southwark on London Bridge. Although some of the south gate to the bridge was damaged, Fauconberg could not cross the river. Perhaps he had hoped for some defections from within the city, but nothing much materialised.

On 13 May, Fauconberg stopped attacking the bridge and, changing tack, marched along the Thames to the west, claiming that, having crossed the river at Kingston, he would head back along the north bank and sack Westminster before taking the city from the west. It probably would have been better not to tell everyone what he intended because this gave Anthony Woodville, Earl Rivers, who commanded at the Tower, the chance to send some of his men to Kingston by barge. However, before anyone had arrived at Kingston, Fauconberg decided to march back to Southwark again. The whole day was spent marching to and fro along the river to very little purpose.

Was Fauconberg indecisive, or had wiser counsels simply prevailed? Crossing the river further west was a dangerous move for an army which had its origins in the south-east. Furthermore, by then everyone knew that Edward IV was on his way. Though Fauconberg wanted to fight Edward, it was better that it should be at a place more familiar to his own men. So on the 14 May he reverted to plan A: a full-scale attack on the city.

This did not start well. Fauconberg positioned his guns on the south bank and there was an artillery exchange which showed that the city's cannon had more firepower than the rebels. Though the rebels were forced to retreat from their guns, they continued with the attack. Their ships took several thousand men across the Thames to the east of the city where they were joined by the men of Essex and attacked both Bishopsgate and Aldgate. At the same time there was another assault on London Bridge which managed to cross part way and set fire to some houses upon the bridge. But it was heavily defended and they could not break through. At Bishopsgate, the gate was also damaged but not breached. However, at Aldgate, the rebels came close to taking the gate and were only frustrated by the intervention of Earl Rivers, who sent out several hundred soldiers from the Tower to strike at the rebels from the rear. This, combined with a sally forth by the defenders at the gate, resulted in a rebel defeat.

So, after much expenditure of effort and blood, Fauconberg's three-pronged attack had failed and he retreated to Blackheath, south of London. Even so, he remained close to London until the advance guard of Edward's army appeared on the horizon. At that point the rebels voted with their feet and went home: Fauconberg's fleet of around forty ships sailed back to the south-east ports and the Calais garrison returned to Calais.

By the time Edward arrived back in London on 21 May, the revolt was over and the clearing up process began, which included a few executions. Fauconberg himself was initially pardoned which, as we have seen, was not an unusual act by Edward. However, by September Fauconberg had been executed – perhaps because he had rattled a few cages and Edward had had enough of him.

Some other rebels were punished too, but not the Calais garrison because, as we know, no one went out of their way to annoy the Calais garrison...

There remained then only one matter for Edward to decide upon: what was to be done with Henry VI? During the 1460s there had been every reason to keep Henry alive, since killing him would have meant that his son – free in France – could have claimed the throne as king, not simply the heir. Now his son was dead, Henry would once more become the focus of diehard Lancastrians' hopes. Quite simply, the problem would not go away until he died. The claim by a pro-Yorkist contemporary that Henry, having heard of the death of his son, died: 'of pure displeasure and melancholy' seems a trifle unlikely – even by Henry's standard of emotional frailty. More likely is that Edward ordered his death. Politically, of course, it was the right decision, though morally it could never be. Henry VI died, as he lived, as a mere symbol of kingship.

The only other Lancastrian supporter making trouble was Jasper Tudor, who had left Queen Margaret to raise troops in Wales. He could not, however, reach Tewkesbury in time to help her. After a few minor successes, he returned to France in September 1471 with his young nephew – a lad of little importance called Henry Tudor, Earl of Richmond. They never got to France and washed up at the court of Duke Francis of Brittany, where they remained for many years – but more of that a lot later…

The revival of Edward's fortunes was remarkable, but despite all his energy, charisma and military skill, it was only made possible because when he first landed in 1471 his enemies were indecisive. Some of the blame can be borne by Warwick himself, who seemed, when pitted against his protégé, to lack the drive that we are accustomed to seeing from him. But I think it is also reasonable to blame Margaret of Anjou for her endless reluctance to return to England. I understand that she was wary of trusting Warwick, but she gained nothing from delaying – especially once Edward had fled to Burgundy. From that moment the clock was ticking. Those were the months when she should have been in England establishing herself and her son. She only failed to regain the throne for her husband because she waited far too long. Can anyone imagine that even Edward could possibly have triumphed against Warwick and Lancaster? He could not have – but in the end he was gifted a situation in which he could pick off his enemies one by one.

After 1471 there would be twelve years of peace – a peace which almost all contemporaries would have seen as enduring. Edward had two sons, a loyal brother working in harmony in the north with the Earl of Northumberland and a stable government which embraced the vast majority of those who had once fought for Lancaster. What could possibly go wrong?

Part Four

The Crisis of 1483-7

Chapter 28

Peace, the Final Frontier...

MINDLESS REPETITION IN documentaries can be annoying but there is some value in stepping back from the chaos now and again to consider what has happened so far.

Quite early on in my examination of the Wars of the Roses, I suggested that the wars were not one long period of crisis, but a series of major and connected, but essentially separate, crises. We have waded through two of them so far and in order to understand the third seismic political crisis of the era, I think we ought first to look at the effects of the first two.

People these days talk about vested interests and fake news as if they are inventions of our time. Sadly, they aren't. Wherever there has been a government by man, there have been factions and vested interests, and so it was in Yorkist England. The existence of factions is not a problem in itself because factions are merely an expression of people's differing perspectives on life. People disagree so it is normal therefore for factions to disagree – I mean, if they didn't there would be no point in having factions.

The problems occur when factional strife goes unchecked and takes control of events. We saw that clearly enough during Henry VI's reign: both York and Somerset – and their predecessors for that matter – saw a king who wanted a quiet life. Henry VI was a king who wanted everyone to agree that peaceful coexistence was good for the soul. Had Henry removed either York or Somerset he might have kept his throne a bit longer – there was certainly ample justification for most kings to have removed York after his antics in 1452. But Henry did not – perhaps could not – do so. He made vacillation into something of an art form.

But how is that relevant to the 1470s and the final crisis which occurred in 1483?

It's relevant because Edward IV faced the same problem as his predecessor – or any other medieval king – which was to balance the influence of his most powerful subjects. In his first reign, Edward was inclined to pardon his enemies in an effort to bring them into the fold – to foster a spirit of unity, if you like. While that seemed to make sense after a period of conflict, many of those who had supported Edward IV – indeed had shed quite a few pints of blood on his behalf – were reluctant to share any of the spoils of victory with their defeated enemies. Very few of them had actually fought for a change of king because they thought the House of York had been cruelly robbed of its royal birthright in the previous century. They fought because they wanted more power, wealth and influence for themselves and their families. It was pretty obvious that if the leaders of the losing faction kept their lands, for example, then there would be less to hand out as rewards to the victors.

Edward tried to be even-handed: rewarding his supporters, but trying also to build bridges with his previous opponents. We have seen that there were problems with this policy which allowed former enemies – such as the Duke of Somerset – to keep not only their freedom, but also in many cases their lands and titles. We have also seen that it was the dissatisfied victors – men like Richard Neville, Earl of Warwick and George, Duke of Clarence – who were entirely responsible for creating the second crisis of the period.

How then did Edward IV approach his second attempt at ruling England, and, in particular, how did he try to control his most powerful subjects?

One big advantage Edward had was that there was really no feasible alternative to him after 1471. The House of Lancaster – bar a few minor relatives – was extinct. This was, of course, very important, but before we get too carried away, remember that the origins of the crisis of 1469–71 came not from Lancaster, but from within the Yorkist faction itself. Edward IV was no fool and he knew that his future success would depend on how well he could hold together the sometimes warring forces that had restored him to the throne.

Let's begin then by taking a look at the key political heavyweights in England in the 1470s, because we can say, with absolute certainty, that whatever caused the crisis at the end of Edward's second reign, these were the people who brought it about.

I think it is useful to divide these individuals into two groups: not necessarily opposing groups. One group derived their influence directly from Edward IV himself, whereas the power and position of the other group pre-dated Edward IV.

The first group includes the queen, Elizabeth Woodville, and her numerous family members, the two most important politically being her brother, Anthony Woodville, Earl Rivers and her elder son from her first marriage, Thomas Grey, shortly to be made Marquess of Dorset.

This group also included the king's two brothers, George, Duke of Clarence and Richard, Duke of Gloucester. Both had supported their brother's campaigns in 1471 and, though Clarence came late to the party, without him it would have been a wake.

The group also included William, Lord Hastings, Edward's most trusted personal friend and ally. Edward had made him what he was, and Hastings remained a faithful servant.

There were, no doubt, a host of others, right down to the plethora of knights and officials in the country as a whole – and it's always best not to forget them, because, as we shall discover, they could still have an important role to play.

Then there was the second group: largely members of the nobility whose families had been ennobled long before Edward's time. Their immense landholdings meant that they were effectively kings in their own parts of England where they controlled the lives of their clients and servants.

Foremost among these men were: Henry Percy, Earl of Northumberland, restored to prominence in the north after the catastrophic demise of the Nevilles, and Thomas, Lord Stanley, a power in the north-west, who had tried to ensure in the previous crises that he was on the winning side. History has not been kind to him, but he was not acting for his reputation hundreds of years in the future but rather to ensure his family's prosperity in the present and near future. You'd have to say that his policy had so far appeared to work rather better than, shall we say, that of the recently deceased John Neville, Marquess of Montagu.

There was also Henry Stafford, Duke of Buckingham, who had enormous landholdings in the west of England and the Welsh borders. There was a trickle of royal blood in his veins since he could claim descent from Edward III and, like most such descendants, it was not something he was inclined to forget.

Until 1476 another important nobleman was John Mowbray, Duke of Norfolk, who held extensive lands in East Anglia.

These were the chief suspects, and I can tell you now that it was these men who were responsible for the demise of the Yorkist government.

So, what resources did Edward IV have to work with to keep all these powerful people happy?

Well, firstly, he had a lot of land, confiscated from his defeated enemies, in particular Warwick's vast estates, to spread around his allies. He also had goodwill, because as I've said there was no real alternative. What about Clarence? I think that horse had already had a run out and gained very few backers. So, anyone who wanted advancement simply had to work for the current regime. In the second half of his reign, many local men became deeply invested in Edward IV's government. These were the people often forgotten in history: the knights and officials who enforced the laws, collected the taxes, served on judicial commissions of all sorts, mustered men-at-arms when required, and so on. Anyone studying the crisis of 1483–85 will know that these people played a pivotal role in how events unfolded.

So Edward had lands, he had goodwill and commitment, but most importantly, he had a son and heir, Prince Edward – and by 1473 he had a spare: Prince Richard. That meant that there was a direct male line of succession for the House of York.

Finally, Edward had the continuing support of the merchant community – especially in London – who believed that he would provide stable government and prosperity. And, by and large, he did.

During the next twelve years, Edward did all he could to strengthen his hold on the kingdom and provide a secure succession for his son. However, only weeks after his death his legacy began to fall apart because his son, Edward, was only

Peace, the Final Frontier...

12 years old, and those charged with the responsibility for his minority government failed to unite around him. So what went wrong?

Despite the enormous amount that has been written about the crisis of 1483, there is no consensus about why it occurred – or, to be more specific, who was to blame. I find it astonishing that the antics of Richard, Duke of Gloucester and his contemporaries can still excite so much emotive argument after more than 530 years. The main reason for all this often very acrimonious discussion is of course that we lack the evidence to be certain of what happened and why. Yet there are many other occasions in history where we don't know those things, so what is different about 1483?

Quite simply, the difference is Richard, Duke of Gloucester, King Edward's loyal younger brother. The personality cult which surrounds him today is quite remarkable and its power was amply demonstrated when his corpse was discovered and unearthed a few years ago. So, how are we to make any sense of a crisis which is still charged with such energy so many centuries later?

My own method has always been to examine the individuals involved and as far as possible determine the motives behind their actions. Words like 'blame', 'fault', 'guilt' and 'innocence', which are frequently bandied about, for me have no place in this sort of discussion. I don't seek to apportion blame, merely to try to ascertain what happened and why.

So, where do we start? Clearly, for things to go wrong so soon after Edward IV's death, the problems must have begun a lot earlier than 1483. And they did, because the epic tragedy of the 1480s was born in the 1470s.

Chapter 29

A Surfeit of Brothers...

IN HENRY VI, England had a king who, despite all his faults, had been anointed by God. In our very secular age, it is easy to dismiss the importance of that fact.

The problem with seizing the throne by force of arms was that, if you were successful, you demonstrated to others that it was possible to achieve. Though Edward IV claimed the throne by right, not enough of the established nobility or gentry of England truly agreed with him. When Edward wrestled the throne from Henry, he did so with the aid of the very powerful and ambitious Richard Neville, Earl of Warwick. We have seen how Warwick, in causing the crisis of 1469–71, attempted to supplant his earlier protégé, Edward, with another in George, Duke of Clarence. Ultimately, Warwick failed to be the 'kingmaker' that history so regularly insists that he was, but much blood was spilt in his attempts to replace the monarch by force.

In 1471 Clarence returned to the Yorkist fold, re-joining his brother to help crush Warwick and then Lancaster too. But what lessons did the three surviving York brothers draw from what had happened in 1471? The answers to this question are, I think, the key to what happened after Edward's death in 1483.

Edward IV, for his part, learned that you couldn't really trust anyone – and in particular, you couldn't trust anyone with a claim to the throne. You might say that's pretty obvious, but before 1460 having a claim to the throne was not in itself a reason to rebel against the established king. Otherwise, there would have been endless wars of succession in England throughout the Middle Ages. When medieval English kings were overthrown, it was not just because someone else thought they had a better claim. When Edward II, for example, was deposed, the line of succession continued unbroken with his son. Richard II was deposed because he alienated too many of his leading subjects. When Henry VI became king, he was an infant with several uncles who could easily have swept him aside if they chose to do so; but they didn't.

By 1471, however, things had changed. Edward had seized the throne, Warwick had taken it back in Henry's name and then, improbably, Edward IV had regained it. That sequence of events was unprecedented, so Edward knew that he would need to build his dynasty with great care if it was to survive him. Though he continued to be lenient to former opponents, he needed to ensure that it would be difficult for them to act against him. He had to build up the strength of those who were most loyal to his regime so that the greatest power in the realm would be concentrated in the hands of a few trusted magnates. His youngest brother, Richard Duke of Gloucester, a paragon of loyalty, was among that group – but George, Duke of Clarence, despite his vital change of heart in 1471, was not.

Having said that, Edward had to reward Clarence for what he had done, so he gave him extensive lands in the south-west, which were handily available because of the prominent Courtenay family's support of Lancaster. But was this great wedge of additional land enough to satisfy Clarence? It was not.

Clarence had drawn his own lessons from the events of 1471. You might think he would be thanking his lucky stars that he was still alive, but no. The lessons he took from the crisis were rather different: firstly, he learned that, without him, Edward IV would have lost. Also, since Edward's heir was only a small child, Clarence was still in the line of succession. Thus he saw himself – as ever – as a very important man. And as such he should be appropriately rewarded.

Even before 1471, Clarence had extensive landholdings, but the demise of the Earl of Warwick meant that one of the largest legacies of the Middle Ages was now up for grabs and Clarence – as the husband of Warwick's elder daughter, let's not forget – wanted it all for himself.

The Warwick legacy was therefore a big and complex issue in 1471, but it was not just a simple matter of the king giving the lands Warwick had once held to someone else. Critically, though the king could dispose of some of the Neville lands Warwick held, others he could not. Also much of Warwick's holding derived from his wife's inheritance and was in theory still held by his widow, Anne Beauchamp, Countess of Warwick. The Countess – inconveniently – was still alive and in sanctuary at Beaulieu Abbey. She petitioned the king – and virtually everyone else she could think of – to keep her lands.

In 1471, Edward rewarded his brother Richard, Duke of Gloucester, with Warwick's Yorkshire lands around Middleham and Sheriff Hutton – a Neville heartland – as well as some other northern lands of the Nevilles. He also gave him the lands of the defeated Lancastrian Earl of Oxford, John de Vere, and several other rebels. These lands gave Gloucester a presence in the north and east of the country.

Clarence could not have been happy about the loss of the Neville lands to his younger brother, but he was even less happy when Gloucester set his sights on marrying Anne Neville, widow of the Lancastrian Edward, Prince of Wales, but more significantly the co-heiress to the Earl of Warwick, with her sister Isabel – who, of course, was Clarence's wife. If Gloucester married Anne Neville then he would undoubtedly contest Clarence every step of the way as he tried to gain control of the entire Warwick inheritance.

Fiction writers like to suggest a long-standing romantic relationship between Richard and Anne because of Richard's presence in her father's household in the mid-1460s. But for me, that's a long stretch, though not impossible. More likely is that, for any nobleman, Anne Neville was clearly the best catch in England: sixteen years old and a major heiress – what's not to like?

From Anne's perspective, Gloucester was the perfect choice because he was just about the only man in England who could pursue her inheritance against Clarence with any hope of success. It's quite possible that Edward himself encouraged the marriage because he would certainly rather that his loyal brother shared the Warwick inheritance than that his suspect brother got all of it.

Clarence actively tried to prevent Gloucester's marriage and during the winter of 1471–2 relations between the two brothers were, shall we say, rather tense. To get his bride, Gloucester was obliged to carry her off in February 1472 and deposit her in the sanctuary of St Martin le Grand in London. She stayed there until she married Gloucester, most likely in July 1472. Events, as they say, had moved quickly – and certainly far too quickly for Clarence's liking. The final settlement of Warwick's legacy took rather longer.

The two brothers put their rival claims to the king's council. Warwick's widow, Anne, tried to fight her corner too. The dispute dragged on. In June 1473, Gloucester took his mother-in-law Anne, Countess of Warwick, out of sanctuary, which prompted fears by Clarence that she would give her lands to Richard. But only in 1474 was the dispute settled when parliament did as it was told by Edward and confirmed that the Countess of Warwick's lands would be dealt with as if she was dead – a wholly unusual and deeply unpleasant measure. In order to broker a deal between his two warring brothers, Edward IV had cut the Gordian Knot. So Clarence and Gloucester shared their wives' inheritance between them – though the titles of the earls of Warwick and Salisbury would descend through Clarence's bloodline rather than Gloucester's.

None of the brothers emerged from this mess with much credit, with Edward himself being forced to sacrifice principle and legal precedents in order to solve the dispute. Yet here is a clear example of how he differed from Henry VI. Edward, ever the pragmatist, found a way to keep the peace between his two brothers. It wasn't pretty, but it was effective – at least for a time.

So what of Richard, Duke of Gloucester? It's fair to say that Richard had remained quite reasonable throughout the whole sorry process, but, like Clarence, he was determined to get his share and equally indifferent to the fact that his mother-in-law might suffer as a result – because being declared legally dead when you were still very much alive must have been a real slap in the face for the Countess of Warwick.

Over the next year or two, Gloucester's dominance in the north was established, though he shared control of that important and dangerous region with Henry Percy, Earl of Northumberland. While Percy remained independent of Gloucester, the two men cooperated, when required, to ensure a degree of harmony. So, for most of Edward's reign, Gloucester was powerful in the north; but not by any means all powerful.

Clarence was, of course, never happy. He had not secured the whole Warwick inheritance that he coveted and his unwillingness to compromise throughout was the chief reason why the dispute was so acrimonious and long-lived. His attitude did not win him much favour from either Edward – who felt that Clarence had pushed him into a corner – or Gloucester, who resented the lengths he had to go to receive his share.

In 1476, Clarence's wife Isabel died after a difficult childbirth. It is hard not to feel some sympathy for Isabel Neville, for life had thrown her a succession of curveballs. Her death meant that Clarence was back in the marriage market, which did not bode well, given his frequent errors of judgement in the past. But Clarence, like every other nobleman of his time, saw marriage as a means of advancement, so he was keen to act fast. His sister Margaret, the widow of Duke Charles of Burgundy, suggested a marriage with her stepdaughter Mary, the sole heir to Edward's key foreign ally, the Duchy of Burgundy. Edward would not allow it, nor another suggested match with the sister of James III, king of Scotland. Let's be honest, Edward would have been a fool to allow any marriage which might enhance Clarence's power or resources – and he was not a fool.

Needless to say, Clarence reacted with his usual petulance, withdrawing from court to sulk. It's possible that he started to circulate stories that his elder brother was a bastard and should not be king. We have no evidence that he plotted against Edward, but it seems highly likely. He was not a man to sit and contemplate his troubles for long without attempting to do something about them.

In May 1477 Edward, tired of Clarence's plotting, gave him fair warning by prosecuting to the fullest degree several men – one of whom was in Clarence's household – who were inciting others to treason. The object of the exercise was to persuade Clarence to shut up and toe the line. It backfired because Clarence was always slow to take a hint. Far from submitting, he decided to weigh in and declare his support for the very men who had already been condemned and executed.

This was clearly an act of folly, but no one should be surprised. The result was that, by the end of June 1477, Clarence was in the Tower awaiting charges of treason. In January 1478 parliament met to hear a case of attainder against Clarence, which was introduced by Edward himself. Given Edward's customary willingness to forgive even some of his most hardened enemies, it speaks volumes that he was prepared to lead the condemnation of his own brother.

In his speech to parliament Edward stressed that, despite the duke's former treason, he would have been prepared to forgive his brother except that his brother did not know when to stop. In other words, Edward could not see how he could continue to trust him. In a case of attainder, there was often no proper trial or examination of evidence. A man was simply accused of treason, some justifications were provided, and usually parliament agreed.

Clarence was executed privately to reduce the fallout from the death of a royal duke – whether that was by being drowned in a barrel of wine, as was put about at the time, we shall never know. But it's difficult to feel much sympathy for Clarence because he seemed hell-bent on achieving self-aggrandisement or self-destruction.

Once again, Edward had shown himself to be a strong king capable of the most unpleasant of deeds to maintain his authority and the peace of the kingdom. Some historians have suggested that it was an example of Edward losing his grip in his later years – I'd say it was exactly the opposite. He did what was necessary to secure his throne, no more and no less. The removal of Clarence meant that no one now threatened Edward's throne. Well, that's good to know…

Chapter 30

Trouble with the In-Laws

A WHILE BACK in our journey through the Wars of the Roses, I examined the king's marriage to Elizabeth Woodville in 1464. I pointed out that the marriage raised to prominence the entire Woodville family, including Elizabeth's two sons from her first marriage and her numerous brothers and sisters. A lot of judgements have been made about the Woodvilles, both by historians and many others interested in this period. Mostly those comments have been negative and mostly they were based on almost no contemporary evidence at all. Despite the prominent part this family played in the events of the period, we only have sketchy knowledge about most of them, except perhaps the queen herself.

The notion persists that the Woodvilles were a 'problem' in the reign of Edward IV – and that they helped to cause the crisis which occurred immediately after Edward's death. I remain unconvinced about that, partly because lumping all members of the family together as if they were some kind of political party is an anachronistic and unhelpful approach. That is the problem with much modern comment about the Woodvilles: it tends to treat them as if they were an entity but, if we are to accurately assess their role in the crisis at the end of Edward's reign, we need to look at them as individuals, not as members of a faction.

Clearly Edward's queen, Elizabeth, was the most prominent Woodville. I've said a little about her already: she was a beautiful widow with two young children who was elevated, in the blink of an eye, to the status of a Hollywood superstar. Elizabeth showed on numerous occasions that she had a mind of her own. It seems pretty clear to me that then – as now – a strong-minded woman, ready and willing to stand up for herself, was often resented by men used to getting their own way. Contemporary evidence suggests that Elizabeth was determined to make the most of her position, defending her rights and property whenever necessary. And of course, if your husband was the most powerful man in the country, few dared to argue openly against you.

Elizabeth's determination to look after her siblings and her sons has also earned her much condemnation. One of the many charges laid at the door of the Woodvilles concerns their marriages. The queen had five brothers and six sisters. Suitable marriages had to be arranged for her sisters, though only one of her brothers, John, gained a marriage as a result of his new royal connection.

John's marriage, though, was a corker and one which, shall we say, excited some comment at the time. John was aged twenty when he married the Duchess of Norfolk, Katharine Neville, who was in her sixties. The large Norfolk inheritance was complicated and several heirs were already jockeying for position; the intervention of a young male Woodville was something which none of those heirs would have welcomed. We don't know what Katherine thought about it – was she appalled, or did she welcome a toy boy? Certainly, although she had a reputation as a formidable lady, she does not seem to have protested too much, so my guess is that the resentment came from others.

Elizabeth's sisters, it is said, flooded the marriage market and snapped up most of the eligible noble heirs. I think that is probably true to a degree, and certainly the marriages gave the newly-elevated Woodville family connections with many noble houses. But was that so bad? Noble heirs had to marry someone, and, from the king's perspective, it was better that they married someone within his own sphere of influence. There is no actual evidence that the grooms of the Woodville sisters resented their marriages. Why would they? True, their new wives came from a family whose status was lower than their own, but they had just married into the royal family and could expect some benefit to accrue from that.

Much is made, in particular, of the marriage of the queen's youngest sister, Katherine Woodville, to Henry Stafford, Duke of Buckingham. They were most likely married in 1465 or 1466 when she was about seven and he was eleven years old. There was nothing terribly unusual about that in medieval times. Later it was claimed that Buckingham – a man of royal descent – resented the marriage to the queen's sister and was therefore hostile to the Woodvilles in general. Though that may be true, there is no evidence of that resentment before 1483; rather you would think that Buckingham – like his fellow bridegrooms – might have viewed his marriage as a means of advancement at court.

However, there is a little conundrum here, because the fact is that, of all his leading peers, Edward used the Duke of Buckingham least. He was wheeled out frequently enough in ceremonial roles, but Edward never gave him any important command or responsibility. Why did Edward ignore Buckingham? From the glimpses we have of the man in his brief time in power in 1483, it seems likely that Edward neither trusted him nor rated his abilities. Now you have a cause for resentment which makes a lot more sense than being married to the queen's sister. His lack of influence in Edward's reign must, above all, have rankled for a man who prized his royal lineage so highly.

Aside from the queen herself, the most prominent member of the family was her brother, Anthony Woodville, Earl Rivers. Rivers was a great deal more than just the queen's brother. In November 1473, Edward gave him the important position of Governor of his heir, young Edward, Prince of Wales. I have seen it written that this was a poor decision on Edward's part, but I can't for the life of me see why. Rivers had everything to recommend him for the post: he was a cultured and well-educated man – his patronage of the printer William Caxton singles him out from his peers. He was also an excellent soldier and a man solidly loyal to the king. Though Rivers was not solely responsible for the guidance of the prince, he was clearly a key influence on young Edward.

Rivers was not a saint. Like every other successful magnate, he did not get where he was without jealously safeguarding his rights and also having a keen eye for how he might obtain more land. I doubt you will find a powerful man of the period who did not do so. Gloucester, Clarence, Neville, Herbert, Percy, Beaufort, Stafford... that was what they all did. There is plenty of contemporary evidence that Rivers was respected by his peers and – lest you think that was merely because he was the queen's brother – let us not forget that Clarence, who was the king's brother, did not inspire similar confidence.

Rivers was undoubtedly in a strong position to influence the next reign because of his close connection to the heir. His concern would be to ensure a smooth succession, but in the 1470s and even in 1483, Rivers – like everyone else – could not have foreseen that the succession was going to happen quite so soon.

Another prominent Woodville was, confusingly, a Grey. Thomas Grey was Elizabeth's elder son by her first husband, John Grey. Thomas was promoted to high noble rank during the 1470s and in 1475 was made Marquess of Dorset. Later, on the eve of Edward IV's death, Dorset would also be given a role in charge of the Tower of London.

Dorset and his brother, Richard Grey, both played important roles in the events of Edward's reign. Richard Grey was based in Ludlow with his uncle, Earl Rivers, at the heart of the household of young Edward, Prince of Wales.

At this point we must focus on a very important factor in the later years of the reign: the relationship between the Woodvilles and Edward's close friend and most loyal courtier, William, Lord Hastings.

In view of what was to happen in 1483, the evident rivalry between Hastings and certainly one – perhaps several – members of the Woodville family must be seen as of critical importance. However, so much has this issue been embellished over the centuries that it is almost impossible now to tell fact from fiction.

One thing we can be certain of: Hastings and Dorset were enemies. That much can be gathered from the simple fact that in April 1483 the dying King Edward tried to reconcile the two men. The cause was of their mutual hostility is more difficult to determine, though it appears to have its origins in rivalry over mistresses. Really? Well, allegedly. Perhaps, though, there is also the fact that Dorset saw himself as one of the up and coming courtiers and might have viewed Hastings as yesterday's man. But Hastings, in his early fifties by 1483, probably felt that he still had a key role to play in the state for many years to come.

Was Hastings also at odds with other members of the Woodville family, such as Antony Woodville, Earl Rivers? It is difficult to tell. There is talk in some of the primary sources of Rivers resenting the fact that Hastings was appointed to the prestigious and strategic role of Lieutenant of Calais. Anthony had held the post before Edward's temporary deposition in 1470, and despite his heroics in saving London in 1471, he somehow incurred Edward's displeasure shortly afterwards. Let's not forget that Calais had the kingdom's only standing army and was therefore a vitally important post. But rivalry over influential or lucrative posts was a fact of life at any court and Edward's was no exception. It would thus be very misleading to represent every such rivalry as a deadly feud.

There is also talk of Queen Elizabeth resenting Hastings' continued encouragement of her husband taking mistresses. Perhaps she did see Hastings as a bad influence on her husband, but we know that Edward rarely did anything he did not want to do – and Elizabeth must have known that better than most. It seems unlikely to me that Elizabeth Woodville would want to make Hastings an enemy, unless of course she was taking her son Dorset's part in their personal quarrel.

Whether there was any truth in these various stories is almost immaterial. The fact was that by April 1483, for whatever reasons, Hastings genuinely regarded the Woodville influence in the council and over the new young king as far too strong. How that opinion was reached and over how long a time is lost with much else in the fog of the fifteenth century, but it does not really affect our analysis of the crisis which occurred in 1483.

What about the rest of the Woodville family?

Well, I am averse to giving lists, but let me summarise: Elizabeth's brothers included Edward Woodville, who became a prominent and very capable soldier; Lionel Woodville, a churchman who, among other posts, held the see of Bishop of Salisbury; Richard Woodville, the most obscure of the brothers; and finally, John – married to the elderly Duchess of Norfolk – who was executed with his father in 1469 during the attempted coup by Warwick.

In the fifteenth century, the fortunes of every noble and baronial family depended upon their social and political connections both with their peers and their inferiors. The Woodvilles were no different in that respect. By the mid-1470s they were powerful courtiers individually, but there's very little evidence that they were any more grasping or rapacious than other major families at court.

By 1483 several members of the Woodville family held positions of importance in the kingdom, but they did not have any sort of overwhelming power. Other men held positions which arguably gave them far more resources than the Woodvilles. We have already mentioned that Lord Hastings was Lieutenant of Calais and he was also Lord Chamberlain of the King's Household – a post which enabled him to control access to the king. In the north – still something of a foreign land to southerners – the king's surviving brother, Richard, Duke of Gloucester and Henry Percy, Earl of Northumberland, held sway. From 1471 onwards, Lord Thomas

Stanley controlled a vast area of the north-west of the kingdom and was the Lord Steward of the King's Household. Other magnates too exercised control in their various spheres of influence, notably Henry Stafford, Duke of Buckingham in the Welsh marches and John Howard in East Anglia.

It is often casually asserted that by 1483 the Woodvilles were too powerful, but based on what happened next, I would argue the opposite: they were not anywhere near powerful enough...

Chapter 31

Richard, Duke of Gloucester

RICHARD, DUKE OF Gloucester, was Edward IV's youngest brother, but in historical terms he has become a figure of immense proportions. Everyone has a view about him and the power of his historical presence was amply demonstrated in 2012 when his body was discovered in Leicester and excavated. The world's press gathered and the interest was truly global.

Everyone that has written or spoken about Gloucester since 1483 is mindful of the dramatic events of April to July 1483, when he went from being the late king's loyal brother to being king in his own right. But if we are to have any hope of teasing out what this man was like – and why he acted as he did in 1483 – then we need to strip away all the hype and see him as his contemporaries did.

During Edward IV's reign, no one – not a single person in the whole of Christendom – could have told you that Gloucester, within months of his brother's death, would seize the throne from his young nephew. We need to adopt this same viewpoint at the start of our analysis and therefore we must not regard Gloucester either as a saint or a monster. We have to look at the events as they unfolded and shut out hindsight. Hindsight is actually not that helpful when reliable knowledge of events in the fifteenth century is so hard to come by.

Let's start by looking at what Gloucester was up to during Edward's second reign during the 1470s and early 1480s.

We have already seen that in the early 1470s Gloucester was preoccupied with a long-running and sometimes bitter dispute with his elder brother, George, Duke of Clarence. This dispute was about two things: Gloucester's marriage and the Warwick inheritance. Surely it's all the same thing, isn't it? Didn't the marriage give him the inheritance? Well, only to a limited extent.

Gloucester's marriage was, in itself, an important event. For any nobleman – as we have seen – marriage mattered a great deal. Gloucester rightly saw Anne Neville, the younger of Warwick's two daughters and co-heiress to his estates, as the best match available. She was 16 years old and already a widow, having been married, albeit briefly, to Edward of Westminster, the Lancastrian Prince of Wales killed at Tewkesbury.

A marriage to Anne would bring Gloucester some lands but, more than that, she was a Neville and for many folk in the north, Neville blood was worth a lot more than Plantagenet blood. Marrying Anne put Gloucester at the head of the Neville affinity in the north. Clarence, of course, did his best to prevent the marriage, but, as we have seen, he failed.

So, what about the lands he gained? If the king had simply attainted Warwick and his brother John Neville after their deaths at Barnet in 1471, all their lands from whatever source would have gone to the Crown. They would then have been in the gift of the king so he could distribute them as he pleased. However, since Clarence was already married to the elder heiress, Isabel Neville, he did not want the lands to go to the Crown at all. He wanted them to go to him. If that happened then he would not be dependent upon the king's favour to keep his lands in the future. Gloucester did not want the lands to go to the Crown for the same reason – that is, he wanted his share.

As I've already explained, the Neville inheritance was complicated. Half of the lands were still held by Warwick's widow, Anne Beauchamp. Remember it was by his marriage to her that Warwick gained such a spectacular array of lands to start with. Only when she died would that part of the inheritance go to her daughters and their husbands. You may recall that Edward, to pacify his brothers, came up with a rather grubby little solution to this problem by having parliament declare that the widow's lands should be dealt with as if she was already dead.

Though this freed up Anne's lands, it did not settle possession of Warwick's other Neville estates, many of which had to be inherited through the male line of descent. His daughters – and therefore their husbands – actually had no claim upon those Neville lands at all. There were male descendants of the Neville family who still had rights to such lands, notably John Neville's son, George. Since George was only six years old, Gloucester had been given temporary charge of his lands. As part of the solution to the brothers' quarrel in the mid-1470s, parliament also decided to disinherit George Neville because of his father's treason and give his lands to Gloucester.

The upshot of all this manoeuvring and intrigue was that Clarence kept much of Warwick's lands in the south and Gloucester received most of those in the north. For Gloucester, these lands were the bedrock of his position of dominance in the north and thus of vital importance to him. If that all sounds pretty straightforward, it wasn't: there was a bit of a catch to Gloucester's gains.

If you've drifted off while I've been explaining some of the intricacies of inheritance, now is the time to tune back in. The catch was that Gloucester and his male heirs would continue to enjoy the Neville estates only as long as the disinherited George Neville or his male heirs were still living. If George were to die with no male heir, then Gloucester would only have those lands for life and after his death other Neville heirs could claim them. Though you may think this arrangement overly complicated, the purpose of it was to punish John Neville's descendants for his treason, but not to punish other members of the Neville family who might be entitled to inherit his lands if he had no heirs.

What did this mean in practice? Gloucester's hold over a vast area of land was at best tenuous and dependent upon two factors: the life of George Neville and the continued favour of the king.

In his dispute with Clarence, Gloucester had shown that he was determined to assert his position and carve out an area of influence for himself in the north. I should stress that, in that regard, he was no different from Clarence or indeed any other powerful lord in England. Marriages and sharp dealing were often used to gain both influence and landed estates.

Gloucester received other lands too, mainly those of the attainted Lancastrian, John de Vere, Earl of Oxford. It is interesting to note that Gloucester also forced Oxford's elderly mother to relinquish her estates to him, in tactics which were not too dissimilar to the treatment of his mother-in-law, Anne Beauchamp. This action, and others in building his portfolio of lands, shows us that he had a bit of a ruthless streak when it came to securing his own interests.

Gloucester's establishment of a power base in the north was only partly to do with land ownership. It was also achieved by making connections with those men previously of Warwick's affinity, such as the Conyers, Metcalfes and Harringtons. Much of this was done during the 1470s when he also recruited men of lesser rank, such as Robert Brackenbury and Richard Ratcliffe, who would serve him to the end. There was nothing remotely sinister about any of that; it was how society worked. Great lords had retainers who served them and whose interests were in turn promoted by their lords.

After the fall of the Nevilles in 1471, it was by no means inevitable that Gloucester would become the dominant power in the north, because several other men also had designs on that prize. Henry Percy, Earl of Northumberland, who you will recall was restored to his estates by Edward IV, expected that after the fall of Warwick he would dominate the north, as his ancestors had in centuries past. Thomas, Lord Stanley, also believed that he would be able to extend his already powerful position in the north-west of the region.

The most obvious conflict, though, was likely to be between the Percys and Gloucester's new Neville allies. And we know where Percys and Nevilles at each other's throats in the north can lead – and so did Edward IV. Clearly unrest in the north was the very last thing he wanted, so who better to place there than his loyal brother, Gloucester. Stability there was crucial to his rule, but planting Gloucester there was likely to provoke disappointment from both Percy and Stanley. It took several years to establish Gloucester's influence in the north and not until 1474 were disputes between Gloucester and the two northern heavyweights settled. Compromises were made, but two things were very clear: firstly, Gloucester could pull rank over both Stanley and Northumberland; they might work together in the main, but Gloucester had precedence over the other two. Secondly, Gloucester's supremacy was still very much subject to the will and pleasure of his brother, the king.

Once Gloucester's position was firmly established – so after about 1475 – tensions in the north calmed significantly. Gloucester seemed easy to work with and collaborated well for the most part with his fellow northern lords. Since Gloucester was mainly resident in the north, he began to consolidate his many land-holdings there, effectively swapping some southern estates for some more northern ones. Over the years he was a great patron of religious houses and buildings in the north. His influence stretched over a wider area of the north than even Warwick's had done: Cumbria, Northumberland, Yorkshire and Durham were his domain.

His domination effectively buried – at least for a time – the old northern rivalries such as that between the Percys and the Nevilles. He was, in many respects, a force for good in the north, at a time when the economy of the region was taking quite a hit. This then was exactly the outcome that his brother had hoped for: Gloucester was keeping peaceful control of the region by settling disputes between lesser lords and maintaining the rule of law. It's clear that Gloucester took this duty seriously, sometimes even to the extent of supporting those who had been wronged by one of his own clients. He earned a deserved reputation as a man who promoted justice in the north.

However, what is equally clear from Gloucester's actions throughout is that, where his own personal rights were concerned, he was prepared to bend the law to the point of breaking it. Nonetheless, that does not detract from what he achieved from 1475 to 1483.

As the king's chief magnate in the north, it was also Gloucester's responsibility to coordinate the defence of the kingdom's northern border with Scotland – a frequent source of trouble in the past. You may recall that in the 1460s Queen Margaret tried to use Scotland in her attempts to put her husband, Henry VI, back on the throne. Though she was unsuccessful, one of her bargains had involved ceding possession of the border town of Berwick to the Scots.

The loss of Berwick was strategically important to England since it controlled Scottish access to the north-east. But Edward IV, ever the pragmatist, had been keen to build bridges with the Scots rather than tear any more down. Although in 1474 a truce was agreed by the treaty of Edinburgh, the treaty only lasted till 1480 when the two countries went to war again. Why? Basically, because the border Scots and the border English wanted war not peace and, like his northern colleagues, Gloucester also favoured war.

King Edward saw Scotland as merely one part of his whole diplomatic strategy and he wanted stable relations with the Scots given the need to commit resources to support his ally, Burgundy, against the wily Louis XI of France. Gloucester's view, however, was entirely parochial. As hereditary Warden of the West March, Scotland was a threat to his domain and needed to be dealt with and it's clear that Edward felt obliged to back his brother on this. In 1480 he appointed Gloucester as

Lieutenant-General and again in 1482, to wage war against the Scots on his behalf. Gloucester was successful in taming the Scots and recapturing Berwick in 1482. He was rewarded in February 1483 by the creation of a county palatinate for him – a sort of independent domain within the kingdom. This palatinate would include Cumberland and an adjacent part of south-west Scotland, the only slight drawback being that Gloucester hadn't yet conquered that bit of Scotland!

Nevertheless, in 1483 Gloucester could look forward to a bright future in the north where he had made himself indispensable to his brother.

Though he was patently a man of the north, there is a lot of nonsense talked about Gloucester's relationship with the court in London. Yes, he was rarely in the south after the death of Clarence in 1478, but that was not because of any mysterious hostility or rift. He attended important state occasions and was a vital part of the government. His place was in the north because that was where he was needed and that was also where he could exercise most influence. Compare him with Warwick, who spent less and less time in his northern heartland as he became more embroiled in national politics. Gloucester, by contrast, was exactly where Edward wanted him to be with his finger firmly on the northern pulse.

We are told that there was animosity between Gloucester and the queen, but there is absolutely no evidence of it at all before the cataclysmic events of 1483. Nor is there any evidence of a rift with Anthony Woodville, Earl Rivers – indeed, as late as March 1483, Rivers was actually asking Gloucester to arbitrate in a dispute he was involved in. You don't invite someone you don't trust to judge a dispute in which you are a party.

Only after the death of Edward IV did anyone refer to any hostility between Gloucester and any of the Woodvilles. If you doubt this, ask yourself why on earth Gloucester would worry about the Woodvilles when he had such immense power in the north – far more power than all of them put together?

Always remember, however, that Gloucester, like everyone else, did not expect his brother to die so soon. Though Gloucester was doing well, he depended, like everyone else, on the favour of the king. So if his brother were to suddenly die, and there was a new king, then all bets would be off…

Chapter 32

Edward, Prince of Wales

IN THE LAST years of Edward IV's reign, his grip upon the kingdom was secure and he faced few, if any, serious threats. In the defence of the realm and the ruling of the kingdom, he relied heavily on certain key individuals: his brother, Gloucester; his brother-in-law, Anthony Woodville, Earl Rivers; Henry Percy, Earl of Northumberland; Thomas, Lord Stanley; Thomas Grey, Marquess of Dorset, the queen's son; William, Lord Hastings and John, Lord Howard. These men held considerable power and had a vested interest in the continuation of their privileged positions. Such is the way of the world that when a new reign beckons, we often find some men gravitating towards the heir, to prepare the way not just for his smooth succession, but theirs as well.

The essential problem with 1483 is that a new reign was not beckoning; it was not even thinking about beckoning. The beckoning hand was still firmly stuffed into its pocket.

The heir to the throne, Edward, Prince of Wales, was a twelve-year-old who spent most of his time at Ludlow, except for the odd state occasion and, of course, weddings and funerals. If you have a twelve-year-old nephew – or niece – who you only come across at family weddings and funerals, you might think how little you actually know about that child.

Prince Edward was really quite isolated, which I am sure his father saw as generally a good thing. He did not want every Tom, Dick and courtier trying to insinuate themselves into the young heir's life beyond those carefully chosen few who held office in the boy's household and council. However, this isolation and young Edward's close association with Rivers and his half-brother, Richard Grey, was to backfire spectacularly later in 1483. But I'm getting ahead of myself.

It's time to take a closer look at young Edward – a figure who is ignored far too often. How Edward reacted to the crisis of 1483 would have a considerable bearing on how events turned out. His reign would be very short – indeed his whole life was pretty short – and thus few words are expended upon him. What's the point, it might be asked, when he had such little impact on life and politics in fifteenth-century England? After all, there were plenty of others who were more interesting and influential than young Edward. The only aspect of Edward's life that has been endlessly debated is the abrupt end to it. But in my view, that is not the most important thing Edward has to tell us.

Anyone who has ever brought up a child and seen them through their formative years knows that it is not always an easy task. It was not any easier in medieval times, especially when you were raising a future king. The man given responsibility for this great task was Earl Rivers. I have discussed his appointment before and it seems to me a very sensible one.

If we are to judge Rivers on how well he carried out the task he was given then there is enough contemporary evidence to indicate that young Edward was well-educated, responsible and in possession of both a strong personality and an independent mind. In short, Rivers did a pretty good job. Actually, as we'll see, he did rather too good a job.

How are we to form any sort of impression about this boy? I expect that if you ask most people who Edward was, without mentioning that phrase of doom: 'the princes in the Tower', they would be hard-pressed to identify him at all, let alone tell you anything specific about him. But if they do have any impression of him at all, it will probably be that he was a poor, innocent child – a pawn in the hands of others. The most enduring image of Edward comes from the Victorian artist, John Everett Millais, and depicts a young, innocent and vulnerable boy. As I see it, this timid image is a travesty which serves only to obscure further the nature of a boy who has made little enough of an imprint on history as it is. It's a romantic Victorian representation of the young prince that obscures the true Edward and is a very unhelpful image for anyone trying to get to know this boy.

When I began to research the life of Prince Edward, I found only a handful of mentions from the time he was born in the sanctuary of Westminster Abbey in December 1470 until his accession in 1483. I reckon I could list those mentions on a postage stamp – perhaps a large postage stamp. If we want to know what the boy was actually like, or how he developed, we need to look at the evidence relating to the one place where he spent almost his entire life: his household at Ludlow.

Here I must give much credit to Nicholas Orme, a scholar who has shed much light upon the limited information we have about Edward's household. Only when I stumbled across Nicholas Orme's informative work on Edward's upbringing in his paper: 'The Education of Edward V', did I begin to get a clearer picture of what the boy Edward, Prince of Wales, might have been like.

Edward's household was established and governed by a set of ordinances – or rules, if you like – issued in 1473 before the prince was even three years old. These ordinances basically laid out how Edward would be raised: his activities, his worship and his studies. The boy's day was closely regulated by the hour in a daily timetable.

An entire household was created for Edward, led by several key Yorkist figures. Anthony Woodville, Earl Rivers, as mentioned earlier, was to be the prince's governor – a new term for the role. John Alcock, Bishop of Rochester, was to be Edward's spiritual guide and teacher as well as president of his council, and Sir Thomas Vaughan, a staunch supporter of Edward IV, was his chamberlain – the man who controlled access to the prince. It is worth mentioning that these same key personnel were still around ten years later when Edward IV died.

So what does all this tell us? Prince Edward's first ten years were closely regulated. Now while that might have worked quite well in his early years, it seems to me that, as the lad got older, he might have started to resent the relentless rigour of his day. I ask myself whether the son of the strong-willed and passionate Edward IV and the equally strong-willed Elizabeth Woodville might not have found this strict regimen a little irritating?

But is there any actual evidence that young Edward rebelled against this regime as he neared his teens? Well yes, there is. In February 1483, a revised set of ordinances was issued by Edward IV. Now you might think that sounds sensible enough because clearly, the rules for a 3-year-old would not be appropriate for a twelve-year-old. But a closer look at the new ordinances reveals some rules that might fit very well into the instructions given by a modern parent to a teenager they have just 'grounded'.

For example, the prince was to be accompanied by at least two appropriate people all day every day; he could not give any orders without the approval of Earl Rivers, Bishop Alcock, or his half-brother, Richard Grey. In addition, his servants were given strict instructions not to encourage the prince to act against the ordinances – i.e. to break the rules. If the prince did break the rules, or acted in what is described as an 'unprincely' manner, then these three men were to give him a warning and, if he persisted, they were to tell his parents as soon as possible.

The new ordinances also tightened up access not only to the prince himself, but also to his household offices and the men who ran them. In addition, accounting for expenses was also made more rigorous. There was perhaps a concern that the prince had been rubbing shoulders here and there with some untrustworthy folk and that the household had become a little too comfortable for its officials.

It seems to me, that it can only have been necessary to make the rules stricter if there had already been instances of the young prince breaking the old rules.

What? A twelve-year-old boy bucking the system? Surely not.

It is fascinating, of course, to read between the lines of such regulations and we must be wary of drawing firm conclusions from such tiny fragments of evidence. Yet these ordinances – unlike almost every other tantalising fragment of evidence in the fifteenth century – are no one's opinion and possess no bias.

What then do the new ordinances tell us about the prince in 1483?

For me, they confirm my opinion of the young lad. Not a pathetic little boy, but one on the verge of manhood, with strong views and an independent mind – like both his parents. Why does that matter? Because Edward's personality was to be a vital factor in the events of April to July 1483.

I have often pondered the question – as I'm sure many others have – that if young Edward was such a pathetic little boy, why did Richard of Gloucester bother to take the throne at all? Surely he could have simply ruled through the child?

The reality was that this was a son of Edward IV – a youth who did not want to be ruled by his uncle Gloucester, or anyone else.

There are, of course, many other factors to take into account, as we head towards the train crash that was April 1483; but one we must not overlook is the nature and personality of young Edward V.

Chapter 33

Crisis? What Crisis?

IN APRIL 1483, Edward IV died. It was most unexpected, but not quite as unexpected as its consequences... But, well, it happens... kings, like everyone else, die – and some, like Edward IV, die earlier than anticipated.

The immediate problem of course was that the heir to the throne was only twelve years old – well, so what? Henry VI was less than a year old when he became king, yet he succeeded peacefully enough. So, what was different about the accession of Edward V?

Well, let's get a few things clear to start with. Firstly, whatever anyone says about the events of 1483 – be they an eminent historian or simply an interested student of the period – we are all hamstrung by the lack of clear evidence about the motives, and in some instances the actions, of those who played a leading part. We are forced to draw conclusions and attribute motivation on the basis of a few scraps of evidence.

Perhaps as a consequence of this fact, I have often heard it said – or seen it written, especially online – that we can't be certain of anything in 1483, so therefore any interpretation of the events is possible.

This is complete nonsense because despite the deficiencies of the evidence, there is a great deal that we *do* know about the events of 1483.

The problem for all of us studying the period revolves around several key issues which are impossible now to fathom, despite the valiant attempts of many to do so. One of these imponderables is the death of the 'princes in the Tower' as they are known: Edward V and his younger brother, Richard. We don't know who killed them – or even if they were killed – but I am not sure it actually matters that much in terms of analysing what took place beforehand. I know, it's heresy isn't it? But for me, the issue of the fate of the 'princes in the Tower' is a rather glorious distraction from the crisis that occurred when Edward IV died. So I shall ignore the demise of the princes for now, and concentrate instead on what happened first.

There are so many ridiculous ideas put forward about the period immediately after King Edward's death that it's difficult to know where to start. Let me say it again: the king's illness and subsequent death were a shock. No one was prepared. If anyone tells you that the Woodvilles poisoned him to seize control, they are deluded. The Woodvilles were far stronger with Edward IV alive than dead. As it was, they were very much on the back foot, along with everyone else.

When Edward IV died, no one was really ready for a new king. It was a bit like the railway service after a week of snow: the rolling stock and the drivers were all in the wrong place. In the spring of 1483, neither of the two main players, the new king Edward V and the old king's brother, Richard of Gloucester, who was most likely to be named protector, was in the right place. Both were far from the centre of power in London where the late king's council had to attempt to thrash out a programme for what should happen next. They were doing so without knowing the wishes of either the most powerful man in the kingdom, or the new young king himself.

But in the absence of the king, and the absence of his son and heir, and the absence of the likely protector, someone had to make some decisions about what should happen next. This awkward task fell to the late king's councillors – who were still empowered to act until a new authority was put in place.

The difficulty lay in the fact that, among the councillors, there was a clear division between those who thought that the new king's affinity with his Woodville relations might cause problems for the realm and those who did not see it that way.

The leading members of the Woodville family in the capital were Queen Elizabeth and her son Thomas, Marquess of Dorset. Neither was especially humble, and their annoying confidence in their position certainly unnerved the Lord Chamberlain and Captain of Calais, William Hastings. His bitter rival, Dorset, who commanded the Tower of London and Hastings, worried that Earl Rivers would escort the new king from Ludlow to London with a large army at his back, and threatened to withdraw to Calais where he had a readymade army of his own.

After some probably quite heated discussion, the council agreed that Rivers would limit the force escorting the king to no more than 2,000 men and that the date of the coronation would be 4 May. The sooner Edward was crowned, the more influence the queen expected to have over affairs of state; conversely, the less influence the likes of Gloucester and Hastings would have.

It is small wonder then that Hastings wrote to the Duke of Gloucester, urging him to come south with all possible speed, lest he lose control of events. By the way, although Hastings was in a bit of a panic, he was not inviting Richard to hurry south to depose his nephew!

Another nobleman, Henry Stafford, Duke of Buckingham, also appeared to be in communication with Gloucester in April 1483. He too, we are later told by chroniclers, hated the Woodvilles and feared they would take over.

But hang on, let's take a step back, shall we? What is this supposed Woodville takeover bid based upon? Well, Earl Rivers had the king, Dorset had the Tower and Sir Edward Woodville, the queen's brother, commanded the fleet. The apparent strength of Woodville power is, however, an illusion which has been used to justify the events that followed – but don't be fooled.

Did the Woodvilles expect to have great influence under Edward V? Yes, of course they did. Would they aim to reduce Gloucester's influence? More than likely. But were they planning any sort of military coup? No, not at all. There is no credible evidence at all for that.

If Earl Rivers intended to seize control of the government he would have been racing to London with the young king and his 2,000 men. But was he? Nope. Rivers wasn't racing anywhere. In fact, it seemed to take forever for young king Edward to even set off from Ludlow, let alone get to London. Rivers was in such a hurry he even agreed to make a detour to meet the dukes of Gloucester and Buckingham en route.

Rivers was a confident and capable leader, but everything we know about him suggests that he would have preferred to work with Gloucester rather than against him. We have already established that there was no history of bad blood between the two men – which is exactly why Rivers was quite relaxed about meeting Gloucester on April 29 1483 at Northampton. He neither feared nor distrusted the duke.

Indeed, the idea that Rivers – of all people – was plotting a coup is laughable.

If we assume that Rivers was not part of a coup against Gloucester, then the whole idea of a Woodville plot immediately becomes ridiculous, because he was the only member of the family in a position to do so. The queen's inability to raise any forces herself was amply demonstrated by her swift flight into sanctuary when she heard of her brother's arrest.

That leaves us with Edward Woodville – who was blissfully unaware there was any sort of a crisis at all until after Gloucester had seized control. And, of course, there was the man that Hastings disliked so much, the Marquess of Dorset. Frankly, I can quite understand why anyone would dislike Dorset but, on his own, Dorset was a vain and unreliable nothing – a fact he proved time after time in the years to come.

The idea of a Woodville conspiracy was only concocted later to justify their arrest and the few wagonloads of old weapons exhibited in May as evidence of their warlike intent were, even at the time, regarded as window dressing.

So if there was no actual military coup planned to destroy Gloucester, why then did he seize power?

First of all, let's dispense with the 'he was a monster' argument. Clearly, he was not a monster because the whole of his life up to 1483 tells us otherwise. But that same life story also tells us very clearly that when his own interests were threatened, Gloucester would use any means – outside the law if necessary – to defend them. This is not a matter of opinion, but fact. It did not make him a monster but it did mean that he believed that his own interests trumped all other considerations. I see a great parallel between his actions and those of his ever-disappointed father, Richard, Duke of York.

Egged on by Hastings, who feared the influence of the ambitious Dorset, Gloucester did indeed hurry south, meeting up with Henry of Buckingham on the way. We've said a little about Buckingham before – he was the invisible nobleman of Edward IV's England. Since Edward had given him almost no political influence at all, he was also a frustrated invisible nobleman, whose pride and royal lineage made certain that he would not forgive the slight. The historian Desmond Seward describes Buckingham as being 'clever' and possessing 'genuine personal magnetism'; well, that is a Buckingham I simply don't recognise from his actions. If he was clever then it was a form of low cunning; a bit more intelligence might have helped him to impress Edward IV. And personal magnetism? Compared to whom? Gloucester, like his father – and unlike his older brothers – had no such magnetism, so perhaps Buckingham impressed him. But I doubt it. Gloucester was a shrewd judge of men and I'm sure he regarded Buckingham as a willing, and rather gullible, ally.

Some have suggested that the arrest of Rivers and his nephew, Richard Grey, at Northampton was Buckingham's idea. It's certainly possible, because it's just the sort of spiteful and provocative act you might expect of a man so long out in the cold and anxious to punish anyone he saw as responsible. But even so, I can't quite see it.

Either Gloucester already intended to seize Rivers before he arrived at Northampton, or he took an opportunity that presented itself. I suspect it was the latter, because Gloucester could not have known how few men Rivers would bring with him. But in the end, whoever first had the idea, Gloucester must have sanctioned it. In my view, the train of events after that arrest was almost inevitable. The arrest was a provocative act; it radically changed the political situation in the kingdom and raised worrying questions for all about what might happen next.

But let's not get too far ahead of ourselves – though it's so easy to do in 1483.

Why did Gloucester arrest Rivers? Surely, since the two men appeared to get on well enough during their evening together, they could have worked together under the new king – as other royal dukes had before them. It might not have been easy, but it would surely have been possible. So why was Richard, who had used conciliation before in his dealings with other nobles, not prepared to attempt conciliation in this case?

There are several strands to this answer. At a very simple political level, you could argue that Hastings' warning against the Woodville 'threat' gave Gloucester genuine cause for concern. And the absence of a Woodville plot in 1483 does not, of course, mean that they would not have threatened Gloucester's position and interests later in the reign.

But how might they have done so? What was it that Gloucester was so afraid of? Surely Gloucester was a great power in the north – even his own brother had not curtailed his power. His excellent working relationship with both Northumberland and Stanley made him virtually unassailable. His power and resources far outweighed those of all the Woodvilles put together – so how could they possibly threaten him?

Crisis? What Crisis?

Well, if you've been paying attention, you'll already know. You will recall that much of Gloucester's land was not his outright. Some was in the gift of the king – and now there was a new king. Some of his other lands could be claimed by members of the Neville family after Gloucester's death, threatening the security of his family and especially his son.

So, what might appear to be Gloucester's unassailable position would depend heavily upon his nephew, Edward V. These weighty matters, which affected Gloucester so deeply, would soon be in the hands of a twelve-year-old boy and his chief advisers. Even if Gloucester was among those advisers, he might not be able to prevent the others from stripping away some of his landholdings. At fifteen – in less than three years' time – the new king would come of age and Gloucester's fate would be entirely in his nephew's hands. Better perhaps to remove some potential rivals while he could, even if doing so threatened his future working relationship with the young king.

Clearly, Gloucester feared those around the prince because when, having already arrested Rivers and Grey, he arrived at Stony Stratford to meet the young king, he proceeded to arrest his aged chamberlain, Sir Thomas Vaughan – a faithful Yorkist who was then in his seventies.

It is worth noting at this point that we can deduce from the various accounts of Gloucester's first meeting with the new king, that young Edward made a spirited protest about the arrest of the close advisers who had managed his household for the previous ten years.

The queen, hearing the news of the arrest of her brother and son, fled to sanctuary at Westminster Abbey. Dorset also fled into hiding – possibly at Westminster, possibly elsewhere. With the queen in sanctuary, Dorset on the run and Rivers arrested, you might assume that Gloucester felt relatively safe. But the story of 1483 is that he clearly did not feel safe.

Who was there left to fear? The only reasonable answer is Edward V himself. The youth, like his father, might respect his opponent's temporary advantage, but he would wait for his moment to regain the initiative. I suspect that Gloucester feared this and knew what would happen in a few years' time when the king ended his minority.

I think it is helpful to understand that everything that happened next had nothing to do with the Woodvilles at all. It was all to do with the young king himself and his relationship with his uncle, Richard of Gloucester.

Chapter 34

Off with his Head!

ON 4 MAY 1483, Richard, Duke of Gloucester escorted his nephew, young King Edward V, into London, accompanied by his new best friend Henry, Duke of Buckingham. He displayed wagon loads of weapons to give credence to his assertion that the Woodvilles had been plotting against him. For many in the council it was enough that the dukes of Gloucester and Buckingham said there was a plot – even though we can be pretty certain that no such plot existed.

The council, shorn of its Woodville members, was sympathetic to Gloucester, and Lord Hastings positively glowed about how well the duke had managed events. But the council was not simply going to hand over complete control to Gloucester, even though they expected him to be heavily involved both in the plans for the king's coronation and in the shaping of the new regime. The council always intended that Edward would be crowned swiftly and in that case there would be no need for a protector at all. However, as we have seen, that arrangement was not in Gloucester's interests, so he postponed the coronation of Edward V until 22 June on the grounds that it could not be properly organised any sooner. Most councillors probably agreed with him that some delay was sensible.

In the ensuing weeks, the councillors worked in two groups: one discussed arrangements for the coronation, while another met separately with Gloucester. You could argue that this made some sense so that important council business was not swamped by the minutiae of coronation planning. Yet it was not exactly common practice, and what little evidence we have hints that this division of the council caused mutterings amongst some of its members.

What, some wondered, was Gloucester discussing with his small group of councillors? Though such thoughts do not constitute opposition to the protector, they do at least suggest a little early unease.

Again, let's pause to take stock. We have dismissed the 'Gloucester was a monster' theory and so far, Gloucester had acted in what many thought was a reasonable manner – but only if his claim about a Woodville plot was true. His actions thus far, however, would have consequences: the council expected that Rivers and the other prisoners, already sent north to Gloucester's strongholds, would be tried and evidence of guilt supplied. This was, after all, not the Wild

West where a hanging judge could just decide to 'top' people without just cause. The problem for Gloucester was that he did not have just cause, because, as he very well knew, Earl Rivers had not been plotting against him. The trouble with making a pre-emptive strike was that he could not then prove Rivers' guilt – or even his intent.

A decade or more earlier, the Earl of Warwick had set an uncomfortable precedent when, in 1469, he executed Rivers' father and William Herbert, Earl of Pembroke, when both were basically following the orders of their king. In 1483 Gloucester found himself in a similar position to Warwick because Earl Rivers had committed no crime. Having taken the plunge and arrested Rivers, he had nothing to justify his actions if Rivers went on trial before the council. Worse still, if Rivers was then acquitted, it would be a political disaster for Gloucester. So Rivers and the other captives had to remain under lock and key in the north.

However, the queen did still hold one significant card: with her in sanctuary she had King Edward's younger brother, Richard, Duke of York – the presumed heir should anything happen to his elder brother. Gloucester began to work to persuade the queen to allow her younger son out of sanctuary to live with his brother. Though it is difficult to see how the boy presented any threat to Gloucester in early June, events were to move swiftly in that particular month.

In London, councillors would have seen no evidence of any Woodville threat since the queen was in sanctuary at Westminster with little opportunity and zero resources to challenge Gloucester. The council was keen to heal the growing breach at the heart of government by getting the new king crowned and bringing back a degree of stability. They would therefore have been very surprised to learn that, by 11 June, Gloucester was sending his man, Sir Richard Ratcliffe, north with letters calling for the urgent despatch of troops to London. These letters were sent to various northern lords, including the Earl of Northumberland, as well as to the city of York.

So, what was the urgent need for these additional forces?

If we are to believe the explanation offered afterwards, Gloucester faced a new plot by not only the Woodvilles, but also William Hastings. As we have seen, with the key Woodville players already neutralised, they simply could not have put together a coherent plot in June 1483. It was more or less impossible.

What about Lord Hastings then? Why on earth would Lord Hastings, who had congratulated Gloucester on all that he had done so far, be plotting against him? And with the Woodvilles of all people, when Dorset was his most bitter opponent? It seems very unlikely – well, not only unlikely but, in practice, virtually impossible, since Hastings' main military power, the Calais garrison, was still where it was supposed to be: in Calais.

Even assuming such a plot was practically possible, what possible motive could Hastings have had for joining with the Woodvilles, against whom he himself had warned Gloucester in the first place? Not personal ambition or malice against

Gloucester, because we know that it could not have been either of those. There was surely only one cause that could conceivably have united Hastings with the queen and Rivers – let alone Dorset: a threat to the young King Edward himself. As the closest friend of the boy's father, Hastings would certainly not have countenanced any action which threatened the boy.

Though there is no evidence of a plot against Gloucester in June, we have been here before – in April at Northampton. To Gloucester, if several nobles had secret conversations in dark passageways, it meant a plot. He was not going to hang about waiting for a smoking gun, or in his case perhaps, a dripping dagger. Gloucester was a pragmatist and, if his interests were threatened – as we have seen several times already – he did not hesitate to act. Hence his actions in the middle of June: first, the urgent letters north, and then, one of the most singular events of the Wars of the Roses – and that's saying something!

On 13 June 1483, Lord Hastings, loyal stalwart of the previous regime, and declared ally of Richard, Duke of Gloucester, was dragged from the council chamber and brutally beheaded. Even by medieval standards, it was a shocking event. The summary execution of a leading councillor in London was almost unprecedented and it sent a shockwave through the political establishment which would have very serious and ongoing effects.

There are two questions here: first, why was Hastings arrested and second, why was he executed without any delay? No imprisonment, no trial and no evidence.

The answer to the first question is clearly that Gloucester believed that Hastings was a threat – of that we can be certain. What is less certain, of course, is why the loyal Hastings was suddenly seen as a threat. It might have been because he suspected Gloucester was considering taking the throne from his young nephew; but equally it might just have been that Hastings opposed the use of force to prise the king's brother out of sanctuary. Most likely, we'll never know. You might wonder why though, if Hastings had actually known of Gloucester's intention to seize the throne, he would put himself at great risk by attending a council meeting. Why didn't he just flee to Calais and bring back the troops? It can only be because he believed that he was safe at a council meeting. So, perhaps he had only been generally sounded out by Gloucester, or perhaps Buckingham or some other intermediary. Whatever Gloucester intended at that point in mid-June, he had clearly decided that Hastings was an obstacle to it.

Why then the immediate execution of Hastings? This, I think, is a more interesting question. It could not have been a spur-of-the-moment overreaction by Gloucester, since he had clearly arranged in advance for his men to be ready outside the council chamber. Why could Hastings not just be locked up, like Rivers? Was he that dangerous? Well, he was influential and he could call upon the Calais garrison, but even so, why did it have to be done that minute, with not even a few hours delay? That firmly suggests that whatever Hastings knew – or Gloucester thought he knew – about his plans, he could not be given the opportunity to pass on his concerns to anyone else, let alone be given a trial.

We can see how worried Gloucester was at that moment because, at the same time as Hastings was taken, John Morton, Bishop of Ely and Lord Thomas Stanley, among others, were also arrested. Lord Stanley was, like Hastings, a key figure in the kingdom and not to be trifled with. By contrast with Hastings, Stanley had a broad and powerful base of support in England which might, if provoked, cause chaos for Gloucester in the north-west. Gloucester would need to be very careful how he handled Thomas Stanley.

The execution of Hastings was the pivotal event of the summer of 1483. Why? Because if William Hastings, staunch Yorkist and the man who more than any other had brought Gloucester to his present position of power, could be treated thus, then no man could feel safe. Now I know that many readers will admire Gloucester, but, from 13 June onwards, it was blindingly obvious at the time – and should be since! – that he intended to ruthlessly eradicate any opposition to his domination of the kingdom.

From that moment on, there was an atmosphere of uncertainty, suspicion and fear at court. The arrest of Rivers and Grey at Northampton was one thing, but the execution of Hastings and the arrest of Stanley in the council chamber was quite another. There were only about half a dozen seriously powerful magnates in England and we might usefully reflect on the fact that, since the death of Edward IV, Gloucester had imprisoned or executed three of them: Rivers, Stanley and Hastings, and made a fourth, Henry, Duke of Buckingham, his most trusted ally.

What conclusion would any experienced courtier draw from that?

It was quite simply a coup d'état and when it became known that Gloucester had sent for a northern army, it only accentuated the sense of alarm in London. We can be pretty certain that the question on everyone's mind at court was: what was Gloucester going to do next?

Well, one of the things he did next was release Thomas Stanley. Given Stanley's powerbase in the north-west, Gloucester was rightly wary of alienating him. He was released on good behaviour – as they say – but you would have to think that, whatever views the wily Lord Stanley, and his many clients, held about Gloucester before 13 June, they were unlikely to trust him quite so much afterwards.

All this, remember, was before there was any open suggestion of Gloucester taking the throne.

However, Gloucester's actions were beginning to create a power vacuum around him and he knew that without substantial noble allies he could not hope to retain control of the kingdom. Thus Stanley had to be released and placated; others, like Northumberland, had to be brought into the fold and new men, such as John Howard, had to be recruited with the promise of advancement.

What was in Gloucester's mind at that point, we don't know, but his next step was perhaps a hint. On 16 June, frustrated that the king's ten-year-old brother Richard was still in sanctuary, Gloucester sent more soldiers to Westminster and the queen was given no choice: either she handed her son over, or the soldiers would violate sanctuary and take him. Young Richard was then taken to the Tower to be with his brother. Let's be clear: they were not in a dungeon, but they had little freedom of movement. The young king's coronation was due to take place on Sunday 22 June, but remember that the moment Edward V was crowned, Gloucester could not rely upon keeping his powerful position.

It must have been crystal clear to Gloucester by June how the new king would view his actions thus far, and soon the coronation was postponed again, this time until November. Plans for calling the first parliament of the new reign were also shelved. When the coronation was postponed for a second time, and for so many months, it caused consternation and confusion. While the first postponement had seemed sensible, the second seemed not only odd, but also rather worrying.

On Sunday 22 June the growing uncertainty came to an abrupt end when Ralph Shaw delivered a sermon at St Paul's Cross in London, where he put forward for the first time the suggestion that Richard, Duke of Gloucester, was in fact – contrary to popular belief – the only true and legitimate heir of York.

The cat was now well and truly out of the bag.

Chapter 35

When Is a King Not a King?

IN THE LAST few chapters, I have been trying to make sense of something that doesn't seem to make much sense. For centuries, historians and students of history have wrestled with this conundrum: how was it that a man known for his loyalty, his sense of justice, his good lordship and indeed, his all-round common sense, ended up seizing the throne from his own 12-year-old nephew?

For many contemporaries, it was such a sudden and shocking event that they too struggled to come to terms with it. Even today, many just cannot believe that loyal Gloucester could possibly have done it – but the reality is that he did seize power. And what everyone studying this period has to accept is that Richard's seizure of power, leading to his coronation on 6 July 1483, was not an accident, or an act of God, nor was it the fault of others. It was the end product of a series of steps that Richard himself took between April and July.

That sequence of steps, remember, began with the arrest of Rivers, Grey and Vaughan in April, which caught everyone out. According to Richard, he was attempting to prevent a crisis and his explanation was generally taken at face value because of his reputation. But, as we have seen, it is doubtful that Richard's suggested Woodville plot ever existed. If it did, it was certainly over by the time Rivers was in prison and Queen Elizabeth was in sanctuary.

Yet only a month and a half later, in mid-June, Richard was sending secret and urgent letters north asking for more troops. Shortly afterwards came the summary execution of Hastings and the arrest of Lord Stanley, followed a few days later by the acquisition of Edward V's younger brother, Richard, from sanctuary in Westminster. For those at court, these events were worrying and unsettling in themselves, but then came a second, much longer, postponement of Edward V's coronation, followed by the shock announcement that neither King Edward V, nor his brother Richard, were in fact the legitimate heirs.

Blimey! Who saw that coming? Hardly anyone, it seems.

The revelation that the new king was illegitimate came out of the blue on 22 June. It has always seemed to many – me included – ridiculously convenient that this evidence came to light at the very moment that Richard needed some justification for removing his nephews from the succession. Of course, it could have been a complete coincidence – stranger things have happened – but I just can't believe it and nor could his contemporaries.

People at court were not stupid. Influenced by rumour and self-interest, yes, but not stupid. The fact that these allegations surfaced only days after Hastings' execution was not lost on anyone. Let us not forget that there were far more men of influence in London than usual because of Edward's impending coronation. Such men wrote letters to their relatives and clients in the country and those that survive support the conclusion that opinion about Gloucester was shifting. Where there had been confidence in a 'safe pair of hands', now there was at best confusion and at worst suspicion.

But let's take a look at the allegations: there is some evidence that, at first, the suggestion was made that Edward IV himself was illegitimate and therefore so were his sons. Aside from the fact that this called into question the honour of Richard's still-living mother, Cecily Neville, it was a weak argument because there was no evidence to back it up. That horse would not run, so a better idea was needed – and Richard found one thanks to Bishop Robert Stillington.

According to Stillington, it was Edward V and his brother Richard who were illegitimate because their father, Edward IV, had entered into a pre-contract of marriage with someone else – Lady Eleanor Butler – before the marriage to Elizabeth Woodville.

Now, in case you don't know, a pre-contract was binding under canon – that is, church – law. So, as far as the church was concerned, if there had been such a pre-contract, then Edward IV could not legally marry anyone else. It didn't matter that the said Eleanor Butler was dead – any children of Edward's second marriage would still be viewed as illegitimate.

Now, a lot of hot air and ink has been expended on the existence of this pre-contract. Edward's reputation with women suggested that it was not impossible. The secrecy of his later Woodville marriage muddied the waters further. But how reliable was Stillington? The whole question has been argued into oblivion.

Let's go wild for a moment and assume that it was true – that there was indeed evidence of a pre-contract that would make the two princes illegitimate under canon law. What should have happened was as follows: a church court should have heard the evidence in June/July 1483 and made a decision on the case. However, even if that court confirmed the illegitimacy, there was nothing to dictate that Edward V had to be deposed. Parliament, for example, simply had to declare that Edward was the rightful king and that by law he was legitimate. Once crowned king, and anointed by God, his illegitimacy became irrelevant.

The whole pre-contract argument is therefore a waste of breath and energy because, even if true, it did not mean that Edward V had to be removed from the succession.

So, folks, here's the nub of it, and it's a point which is far too often glossed over: had the king's uncle, Richard of Gloucester, chosen to, he could easily have enabled Edward V to succeed to the throne. Richard was the man with all the power at that moment; what happened was entirely in his hands. But instead of endorsing his nephew, he decided to take the throne himself.

He had a choice and he chose to remove Edward, which means that the revelation of the pre-contract – whether genuine or not – must simply have been the means he devised to depose his nephew.

So, back we go to the conundrum. Why?

It's been said by some historians that Richard's actions were proactive, not reactive; in other words, he retained the initiative throughout the crisis. It's certainly true that his actions put everyone else on the back foot, but for me, his actions do not appear well planned, and more often than not they came as reactions to the turn of events. In fact, so many of his actions were unplanned that you have to dismiss the notion that he always intended to claim the throne.

If we examine carefully the steps Richard took to the throne, it's quite clear that he could not have intended all of them before he left York in April 1483. This argument could apply to most of the steps, but is particularly obvious in the case of Hastings. Richard would not have intended, or indeed expected, to execute Hastings who – in the event of a Woodville plot – should have been Richard's chief ally since he was the man who warned Richard about the possibility in the first place.

Secondly, why did he wait until mid-June to call for extra men if he already intended to take the throne? Given that he cited a Woodville plot as justification, he surely would have had reinforcements closer than Yorkshire.

Richard had shown in the past that he could be single-minded, thoughtful and organised; but the train of events from April to July 1483 shows little evidence of forward planning. In the summer of 1483, Richard was making it up as he went along. As I see it, Richard's actions only make sense if we see them as unplanned and reactive. It was 'back of the envelope' stuff.

So let's assume that was the case. It reads like this: Richard, fearing Woodville influence with the new king, lashed out to remove the leading Woodvilles (Rivers and others). Though the council supported Richard, they wanted to press ahead with Edward's coronation and since the boy was already only a couple of years from maturity, a protector would not be required. It would have become clear to Richard very early in May that once the young king was crowned he would not be able to control him. He would not be protector but merely one of many voices in the council. So he delayed the coronation till later in June to give himself more time – not much opposition to that.

But fresh alarm bells would have been ringing for Richard when he heard that George Neville had died on 4 May. Remember that if George died childless – as he had – Richard's Neville estates would not necessarily go to his own son, but to other Neville heirs. His whole position as the greatest northern magnate would then depend upon the whim of Edward V – a youth he had already alienated beyond repair.

So, what was he to do about it? Remember how ruthless Richard had already been in the past where his own landed interests were concerned. For a man who was capable of browbeating old women into giving him their lands, was it so different to take a child's inheritance to protect his own? I don't think so. I believe that at some point during May – or at the very latest, early June – Richard decided that to preserve himself and his inheritance, the young Edward V would have to go.

From then on, there was some evidence of planning: what, he asked himself, would need to happen if he was to take the throne from his nephew?

You could probably come up with the to-do list yourself.

1. Send home for more men in case of opposition.
2. Informally sound out Buckingham, Hastings, Thomas Stanley, Lord Howard to see how they might react – whoops, Hastings could be a problem... maybe even Stanley...
3. Remove any potential opponents quickly, e.g. Hastings, who, as Captain of Calais, might present a genuine obstacle... Oh, and execute Rivers & co.
4. Get Prince Richard out of sanctuary; otherwise he could claim the throne when his brother, Edward V was deposed.
5. Postpone the coronation again and come up with a good reason why neither Edward nor his brother should be king... that could be a tricky one...
6. Get crowned ASAP.

Of course, it all worked out perfectly and Richard's potential opponents fell like dominoes.

By the time Richard's additional soldiers from the north began to arrive in London in early July, he scarcely needed them. His own coronation was only days away and so, on 6 July 1483, England had a new king. The trouble was that the previous one, Edward V, was still alive.

Although Richard of Gloucester was 'invited' to become king by a group of lords and commons, that group – reminiscent of those who acclaimed his brother Edward IV in 1461 – had no legal authority. Edward V had not been deposed by parliament – or any other legitimate body – but had simply been shouldered aside by a more powerful man. If you recall, after his acclamation in 1461 Edward IV still had a great deal to do to secure his kingdom, including a great battle to win at Towton.

No one could have known better than Richard how fragile his position now was. He was king, but the suddenness of it all meant that he still had a job to do if he was to establish himself firmly upon the throne. There were still a few loose ends to be tied up...

Chapter 36

Richard III... King Slayer?

HERE WE ARE, after thirty-five chapters, and finally, we get to that little matter of the fate of the princes in the Tower. This would be a great place to stop, but having got this far I have to see it through. And do you know, I reckon that's exactly what Richard III said to himself in the summer of 1483.

So let's not pussyfoot about: for what it's worth, as I see it, the death – or I suppose, conceivably, the disappearance – of the princes lies at the door of Richard III. Now I know that there are those who just don't want to believe it, but the arguments for anyone else being ultimately responsible are very weak. For the most part they stem from a firm belief that it couldn't possibly have been Richard because he was a fine fellow.

My answer to that view is to ask who knows what anyone is capable of doing when he is under the most severe pressure? For me, he remains the most likely suspect in a murder that will never be solved. Everything I've said about Richard so far is completely consistent with a man who would go to great lengths to avoid allowing his core interests to be compromised. Advocates of Richard tend to compare him a lot with his father, Richard, Duke of York – and I would agree that he shared several traits of character with his father. In particular, like the Duke of York, he convinced himself of the absolute 'rightness' of his cause. But as we have seen with his father – and we will see with the son – he was less successful at convincing others of that right.

I don't believe for a moment that Richard set out from York in April 1483 with the idea of killing his nephews. But each step he took toward the throne also took him closer to a decision about the fate of the two boys. It's perfectly possible that he believed such action would not be necessary, that such would be the popular groundswell of support for his kingship that the boys would simply be relegated to being young men of no political consequence – perhaps given positions at court to keep them on side and under close scrutiny – but no threat to Richard. That is quite possible.

Unfortunately for all concerned, it didn't quite work out like that – and if Richard had an ounce of political common sense he must have realised from the start that there might be a problem further down the line with his nephews. But here's the difficulty: like his father, he deluded himself into believing he was a popular choice as king. His ability to delude himself was gargantuan. His brother Edward, for all his many faults, had been a pretty popular king. I don't mean with the vast majority of common folk – most of whom never saw him, never knew him and probably cared little about him. But among the men who counted – the gentry and minor nobles who basically administered the entire country and the merchant community, who paid for it – Edward had ticked a lot of the right boxes, including providing two healthy male heirs.

With such influential people, Edward was therefore popular. Those folk wanted stability above all, and eventually, Edward IV gave it to them. Richard, of course, understood that – he had lived through it after all – and he thought that, as Edward's loyal brother, he could offer the same stability: a far better option than a boy king. Well, he was wrong – badly wrong. He should perhaps have listened more closely to the experienced Hastings and Stanley rather than the pompous Buckingham and the rapacious Howard. In a way you can understand Richard's growing optimism during June and July because everything he tried came off. But still, the warning signs were there.

Many wondered about the reason for Hastings' death – few at court could have taken seriously the allegation that he was plotting with the queen against Richard. They watched Richard take the throne and they joined the dots. The idea that the discovery of the princes' illegitimacy just happened to occur when it did, fooled no one.

A lot of the discussion on this matter can only be conjecture – it has to be because we only know one thing for certain about the fate of the princes: they disappeared from view. That much is certain; what is uncertain is everything else – when, how and why. We all have our pet theories but expounding them does not help so I'm not going to do that. Read my fiction if you want to know what I suspect, but there is no place for that here.

The princes disappeared from view in the summer of 1483 and the few contemporary sources – bless their cotton socks – are not very clear about when. It could have been any time between June and September. If it was early on, the suspicion must be that Richard took action before or just after his coronation on 6 July. If he acted later, he might have been persuaded to do so by the groundswell of opposition in the south, including quite possibly an attempt to free the princes at the end of July. You might think that because there appeared to be such an attempt at that time, the princes must still have been alive at that point. But their own servants had been dismissed and basically no one outside the Tower of London seemed to know whether they were alive or dead.

We could argue about this forever and get nowhere, so, let's just go with that single fact: the princes disappeared. The crucial thing is that it was not known at the time what had happened to them. Richard said nothing about it and his silence appeared deafening. Those who had benefitted from Edward IV's rule wanted to know – not surprisingly, I think – what had happened to his sons. The silence left by Richard was filled by plenty of others: Woodville supporters were up for a bit of stirring, but the queen clearly did not know her sons' fate or she would have made damned sure that everyone else knew about it.

But might the villain of the piece have been someone else? Some have suggested the Duke of Buckingham. If you have been following what I have said you will know my opinion of Buckingham. He was both ineffectual and vacillating; in fact, it is hard to imagine anyone less capable of organising, let alone carrying out, a secret and well-planned assassination. He couldn't even manage his own clandestine escape in November 1483! As a master of crime he should be well down the list of suspects.

Others have been thrown under the bus in a desperate attempt to exonerate Richard: Margaret Beaufort, Henry Tudor and so on. But the endless arguments about Richard's guilt or innocence rather miss the point – like so much of the frenetic discussion about this period. Even before foul play was suspected in respect of the princes, many had their doubts about Richard. So it matters little now – as it mattered little then – whether Richard was guilty of killing his nephews or not. What did matter was that enough men of substance were incensed by the events of the summer of 1483 and by the likelihood – unproven, of course – that the sons of Edward IV were dead.

There were rumblings of discontent quite early on from the very classes that Richard assumed would support him. Of course, many of those folk did nothing, preferring – in the light of bitter past experience – to see where events took them. After all, if a prominent man like Hastings could be killed then what could lesser men do? But there were others who wanted action and very likely it was a distraught and embittered dowager queen, Elizabeth Woodville, who fanned the flames.

Put yourself in her shoes: a mother trapped with her daughters in sanctuary, not knowing the fate of her two youngest sons but certainly aware of the fate of her brother, Earl Rivers, and an older son, Richard Grey – both executed. I think, if I were her, I might be bitter, and I would also fear the worst.

But Elizabeth Woodville's was not the only hand at work in the summer of 1483 – the other key player was Margaret Beaufort, Countess of Richmond and wife of Lord Thomas Stanley. My goodness, poor old Margaret Beaufort – if it wasn't enough that she had a very difficult life, she has been repeatedly vilified and eviscerated by generations of historians, fiction writers and virtually all advocates of Richard III. Get a grip, people! So much rubbish is spouted about this woman, it beggars belief at times. But more of that later when I've had a lie down!

My point is that there were several people who influenced opinion and Margaret was one – another was the Bishop of Ely, John Morton, who was among those arrested when Hastings was executed and thus became a 'house guest' of the Duke of Buckingham.

Some will tell you that Elizabeth Woodville and Margaret Beaufort between them engendered a revolt against Richard – well, quite honestly, that's a load of old cobblers. If there had been no groundswell of opposition to Richard, those two ladies did not have the influence, let alone the popularity, to generate it. They might well have facilitated opposition to Richard, but they did not create it out of nothing.

Who then were these opponents of Richard in the south? They were not dissidents, nor were they desperate, powerless men in the last chance saloon. They were the haves, not the have-nots – the very men that Richard wanted to carry on doing their work in the counties and boroughs of England. The fact that so many of these solid citizens were hostile to his rule simply cannot be ignored.

The very fact that responsible gentlemen, with everything to lose, were prepared to support a man like Henry Tudor, tells us that Richard's coup was deeply unpopular. I mean, who on earth was Henry Tudor? No one had a clue, yet they were prepared to support him against Edward IV's own brother. Henry could have been a village idiot for all they knew, yet they preferred him to the tried and tested Richard. It seems unbelievable, but that's what happened. Out of the chaos of 1483, it is one of the few clear outcomes of which we can be completely certain.

But why did it happen?

Throughout my analysis of this crisis, I have tried to explain the motives that lay behind the sometimes extreme actions that Richard took. The prime motive I believe was self-preservation. Though he seemed to be a very powerful man with vast landholdings and influence, I have shown that his lands would depend on the new king. And what influence would he retain with his two powerful northern rivals, Northumberland and Stanley, if many of his lands were stripped from him? None at all. They would happily capitalise on his weakness.

Richard's position therefore was not strong at all; in fact, it was fragile. He had few reliable allies and the opposition to him from many in the ruling classes bears this out. I mean, if you have to execute your chief advocate then your position must be dire. This was the one thing that Richard saw clearly in 1483 and what happened subsequently proved him absolutely – and tragically – correct.

In the southern counties and the Midlands, support for Richard was lukewarm at best. But, although it is often suggested that opinion hostile to Richard was confined to the southern counties where the October rebellion would soon break out, let us not forget that the power base of Lord Thomas Stanley – released by Gloucester on good behaviour, remember – was in the north-west. The Percy Earl of Northumberland too had always been a rival of Richard's rather than an ally. He coexisted with Richard when it was in his interests to do so – and because Edward IV had insisted that he did. But Edward IV was dead and all previous bets were off. In 1483, Northumberland waited to see how events would play out, but it was certainly not in his interests to see most of the old Neville lands remain in the hands of one man or family.

We would do well to keep in mind that it was not the men of the south that destroyed Richard two years later, but those of the north for, as G.R.R. Martin might have put it: 'the North remembered'…

Chapter 37

An Autumn Storm

IN JULY 1483, not long after his coronation, Richard III began a progress through the Midlands and the north of England. Rightly, he thought that people needed to see him and pay their respects. It was a way of impressing upon the governing classes that normal service had been restored after a short hiatus. His message to the shires was that there was no cause for alarm – except, of course, there was. Because, while Richard was attempting to woo the Midlands and the north, a significant opposition was growing against him in the south. It was almost exclusively led by local knights and gentlemen loyal to the memory of Edward IV and fearful that his two young sons had come to some harm. Their concerns were encouraged by the dowager queen, Elizabeth Woodville, and her unlikely ally, Lady Margaret Beaufort. While Lady Margaret's husband, Lord Thomas Stanley, accompanied the new king on his progress, she was in touch with not only the queen, but also John Morton, Bishop of Ely – still at that point a prisoner, in theory, of the Duke of Buckingham. She was also communicating with her son, Henry Tudor, who was languishing in exile in Brittany. Though Margaret did not create the opposition to Richard, she certainly played a significant role in organising it – significant, but not terribly effective.

What did Margaret Beaufort actually want in 1483? It's getting harder and harder to see beyond the vitriol and mythology that has been peddled about her. What is clear is that Margaret had been working for the return of her son to England for years – but certainly not as king. She was no fool and she saw that by the second half of Edward IV's reign, political stability had been restored. In such circumstances, no one was remotely interested in crowning her son. Edward IV – as we have seen – was always inclined to reconciliation with his enemies, often to his own cost. It is therefore perfectly logical that he should bring Henry Tudor back into the fold if possible. And it was possible because Henry posed a very, very, small threat to Edward. It seems highly likely that Margaret's negotiations with Edward to get her son home would have been successful given a little more time.

Even after Edward's death, such a return was still possible. Then... kapow! Richard took over. But did that change Margaret's aim? No, not immediately; in fact, you could argue – with the benefit of hindsight, of course – that Richard's greatest mistake was not sanctioning Henry's immediate return as Earl of Richmond. Doing so would have stopped in its tracks the autumn rebellion because there would be no alternative figurehead for it to focus upon. But he didn't do that, and the moment Margaret saw that her son could not return while Richard remained king, she must have begun to work on a different plan. This, of course, is why the adherents of Richard III have pointed the finger at her about the fate of the princes. But I think it is clear, from what little evidence we have of correspondence during the summer, that rumours about the princes started very early on – probably in July soon after Richard's coronation and perhaps even before that.

The reason those rumours persisted throughout the summer was quite simple: no one provided an explanation. The supporters of the late king, Edward IV, were gathering strength during the summer with the aim of freeing young Edward V and restoring him as king. Margaret Beaufort was committed to this and the claims which are endlessly and mindlessly repeated online and in fiction – that she had been plotting to put her son on the throne for ages – are simply nonsense. She saw a golden opportunity to get her son back as a key figure in a newly restored regime and she went for it. But, sometime in the summer, the focus of the opposition to Richard appeared to sharpen.

My own view – though I can't prove it – is that Margaret, always well-informed like her husband, Lord Stanley, got a whisper that the princes had been killed. Quite honestly, it would make no sense for Margaret to encourage her son to claim the throne unless she knew that the princes were dead. It would only cause confusion and division among those who might support an alternative to Richard. So Margaret's increasingly energetic fostering both of domestic opposition and her son's claim only really makes sense if she was certain the princes were dead.

What few historians have ever focussed on is the fact that the opposition seemed to accept word of the princes' death very easily. I cannot believe that experienced political operators would have switched allegiance from Edward V and his brother so suddenly and completely unless they were convinced of their deaths. How that occurred we don't know, but surely it had to be more substantial than Margaret Beaufort scribbling them a note to say: 'oh, by the way the Yorkist princes are dead – what about having my son as king?'

What is certain is that rebels stopped talking about Edward V as anything other than a victim and started talking about the Earl of Richmond as a possible king – and let's face it, they knew more about their horse than they did Richmond. Nevertheless, rebellion was stirring in the south of England and Henry Tudor became its focus. We'll never know for sure who was the brains behind the rebellion in the autumn of 1483, but it must have been Margaret, or Elizabeth Woodville, or John Morton – or, more likely, a combination of all three. One thing I'm pretty certain about is that the man who gave his name to the rebellion – Henry Stafford, Duke of Buckingham – contributed only confusion and chaos to the mix.

The question has been asked many times: why did Buckingham rebel against Richard III having been his chief ally in the seizure of power? It's been suggested that he was 'turned from the dark side' as it were by his prisoner, the wily Bishop John Morton. This view asks us to believe that the duke, searching his soul, found that he regretted supporting Richard and especially perhaps the death of Edward IV's sons. Well, I'm not buying that. Cast your minds back to Edward IV – a king who was prepared to forgive and employ even his worst enemies for the sake of unity and a quiet life. Henry Stafford was one of the foremost nobles of his day, yet Edward only wheeled him out on ceremonial occasions of state. He was given no governmental position or responsibility to match his status. Why not? Well, it can only be because he was incompetent – which he was – or because Edward did not trust him, and remember, Edward trusted most men until they proved thoroughly untrustworthy.

Richard, close to his brother, must have known why he avoided relying on Buckingham, but in the council Richard knew he would need noble support to balance Woodville influence. Who better to do that than a disaffected and powerful duke? The trouble is that such a man remained untrustworthy. One suggestion – from the near contemporary, Polydor Vergil – was that Buckingham had been promised the lands of the extensive Bohun family inheritance and was disenchanted that Richard had not fulfilled his promise. Yet the evidence suggests that Richard was in the process of doing so when Buckingham rebelled, so that idea makes little sense.

But if it wasn't remorse or greed that persuaded Buckingham to rebel, what was it? I suspect it was ambition. Always delusional about his own worth and full of his own importance, Buckingham himself had a claim to the throne as one of the ubiquitous spawn of the bloodline of Edward III. Did he believe that he could create chaos and emerge from it as king? It's possible, but also highly fanciful, as we shall see. He certainly managed to create chaos, but not in a good way, and I would suggest that Buckingham's contribution was less than helpful to the rebellion's chances of success.

So, let's look at how the rebellion played out...

It was actually several rebellions and, when that happens, the key to success is effective coordination. Sadly, these rebellions lacked cohesion. In so far as there was an overall plan, it was this: spontaneous risings in southern England would be joined by the Duke of Buckingham who would cross the Severn with his sizeable retinue. At the same time, Henry Tudor – backed by support from the Duke of Brittany – would cross the Channel with an invasion fleet, land somewhere on the south coast and join up with the rebels. The rebel army would then take London, defeat Richard and enthrone Henry – no doubt they would have a stab at achieving world peace while they were about it. As cunning plans go, this was not exactly that cunning.

Richard was sitting in the north, still making friends, shaking hands and no doubt kissing a few babies. He clearly knew about the outbreaks of revolt in the south, though initially he would not have been aware of Buckingham's involvement. Wisely, however, he did not rush about like the proverbial headless chicken; instead, he waited to see what would unfold. We should not underestimate this tactic; it wasn't easy for Richard to wait, but it proved to be a very sensible policy.

Had Richard raced south himself to do some immediate fire-fighting, he might have been vulnerable to other threats, notably from Thomas Stanley, who surely must have been aware of what his wife was doing. And let's not forget that in every political crisis since 1459, potential rebels had sought Thomas Stanley's support – and when they got it, for the most part, they were successful. It seems to me highly likely that Stanley was poised to intervene on the side of the rebels in 1483, if Richard appeared to be wobbling. He surely could not have forgotten his imprisonment only a few months earlier in July and thus had no great love for Richard.

When Buckingham popped up to oppose Richard, Stanley decided not to intervene. Were these two ideas connected? Did Stanley fear that a successful rebellion would benefit Buckingham if he was perceived to be leading it? Quite possibly, because Stanley's powerbase in the north-west was adjacent to Buckingham's in Wales. Never forget that Thomas would support whichever royal candidate promised to enhance his family's fortunes and status. In the autumn of 1483, Richard III was better placed to do that than Henry Tudor, even though Henry was Stanley's step-son. As ever, Stanley's support was vital.

On or around 10 October 1483, the rebellion began in Kent – frequently a hotbed of revolt in medieval and Tudor times. Simultaneous revolts might have gathered more momentum, but that didn't happen; instead revolt spread only as far as Wiltshire by the middle of the month and did not really take off in the south-west until November. By that time, the Johnny-come-lately Buckingham had already shot his bolt. Unable to raise much support for rebellion in Wales, he found that the elements were also against him.

It was a stormy autumn in more ways than one, for savage storms had an impact on the fortunes of the rebels. One effect was that Buckingham was unable to cross the flooded River Severn and join the other rebels – his much-vaunted retinue never materialised and he was obliged to flee in disguise almost alone. Even that he was unable to carry out effectively and was captured. It was a telling failure, for how often have we heard that only a rebel lord's household knights stayed with him to the end – yet Buckingham, with all his power and wealth, did not engender such loyalty. That was the pale shadow of a man that Edward IV rightly spurned.

By the time Richard arrived to execute Buckingham at Salisbury on 2 November, the revolt in the south-west had scarcely started and the Duke of Norfolk and his son, the Earl of Surrey, were busily mopping up the Kent rebels. Richard then headed for the only remaining centre of revolt: Exeter. But where was Henry Tudor with his invasion fleet? The truth is that we don't actually know. It's not clear when he sailed from Brittany or when he arrived on the English coast – you'll be astonished to discover that the contemporary sources are not very helpful. Where was he intending to land? Poole? Plymouth? Exeter? Somewhere else? We don't know, though my suggestion would be Poole – a large natural harbour, well-positioned between the various revolts. One account suggests that Henry's ships appeared off the coast at Poole but found little support and fled. However, as usual, the dates don't quite fit, so it remains a mystery.

What isn't a mystery is that Henry's fleet – so vital to the rebellion – was also a victim of the weather. Scattered by storms at sea, Henry found only one other ship with him when he reached the English coast and was thus in no position to support the rebellion. Discouraged by news of several defeats for the other rebels – and perhaps he learned of the death of Buckingham – Henry had little option but to return to Brittany with his hopes of kingship in tatters. By early November, the rest of the rebels at Exeter had been defeated and the revolt was over. But it remained to be seen whether the causes of the revolt would go away anytime soon.

Richard must have expected some opposition at the start – though perhaps not from Buckingham – and he dealt with it very effectively. Yet it was opposition that was not well coordinated or led, and not therefore much of a challenge, especially since Buckingham and Richmond were the only peers involved. That was the key point: to unseat a king they needed more noble support, and they did not have it. Notably, Lord Stanley had sided with the king.

Henry Tudor, after thinking that he was about to write a new chapter in English history, was forced to flee in the knowledge that he would still be just a casual footnote in the chapter entitled Richard III. Richard would now hunt him down in Brittany and put an end to any hope of the establishment of a new Tudor dynasty on the throne of England. Well, he could try at least…

Chapter 38

The Waiting Game

IN THE WINTER of 1483, Henry Tudor appeared to be exactly what King Richard said he was: a man of no importance who possessed neither a serious claim to the throne, nor any support. Ignored by the vast majority of Englishmen in the autumn, Henry had fled back to his Brittany bolthole with his tail firmly between his legs. He was, it seemed, a hapless, pathetic figure with nothing to offer England at all.

By contrast, King Richard appeared to have steadied the ship and shown the sort of decisive leadership that subjects might expect from their king. But, as history teaches us so frequently, appearances can be deceptive.

In the aftermath of the October rebellion, Richard's priority was to secure control of the troublesome south. While he had crushed the rebellion, he would need to stamp his authority on the region if he was to prevent further unrest. He could ill afford a repeat dose of what had occurred in the autumn. If there was a next time, then things might be different: the rebels might be better organised and led; Henry's invasion fleet might remain intact and actually effect a landing; the weather too might not be his friend next time. So he had to be certain of the south's loyalty – or if not loyalty, then, at the very least, acceptance of his rule.

Part of the process took place in January 1484 when almost a hundred rebels were attainted by parliament. But even before that, Richard had begun to appoint men he trusted to posts of authority in the south. They would be responsible for local order, serve as Justices of the Peace, take charge of strategically important castles and have commissions of array permitting them to raise troops if Richard required them.

Richard's modern critics have made much of this policy: the so-called 'plantation' of northerners in the south, it is claimed, was unpopular and only increased resentment towards him. But I think some perspective is needed on this issue. Firstly, after any regime change, some men gained lands and others lost – that was perfectly normal and indeed to be expected. It certainly happened under Richard's brother, Edward IV, and Richard's northern appointees were only ever a minority within the governing elite of the south. Nor were they all from the north, as some hailed from the Midlands or East Anglia. We are talking about fewer than forty appointments, so what is all the fuss about?

Well, even thirty-plus appointments was quite a lot – certainly enough to be noticed – and it went against the established order of things. It is hard for us to grasp in our global society of the twenty-first century, but in the fifteenth century local society was everything – from the highest lord down to the lowest peasant. The obligations that one family owed to another were the bedrock of late medieval life. That emphasis on identifying with a particular locality also meant that outsiders stuck out like the proverbial sore thumb. When a new northern lord also brought with him a northern retinue it had an impact at all levels of local society and disrupted traditional loyalties.

Let's not forget, however, that the vast majority of the southern ruling classes accepted the new regime – some enthusiastically and others no doubt with great reluctance – but nevertheless they accepted Richard's authority and played their expected part in local government and law enforcement. As always, it's helpful to put from one's mind what we know happened next: without Henry Tudor, Richard III's reign would likely have continued and, for all we know, prospered, underpinned by the local governing classes across the country, including the south.

The problem for Richard was that when he needed to replace disaffected men with those he trusted, there was not an infinite supply of them. As his reign continued, the reservoir of trusted men he had at his disposal began to evaporate.

It's quite possible that Richard saw the new appointments as purely a short-term policy while Henry Tudor remained a threat; but there is no doubt that where such men were employed during 1483–5 they often did cause resentment. Though that probably did not prompt many additional men to oppose their king outright, it might have persuaded a few more to go into voluntary exile with Henry, and more importantly it might have made a few more reluctant to fight for Richard when the critical moment came.

In January 1484 parliament met and endorsed several pieces of legislation which obviously included the Act of Attainder against the October rebels. But there was also another measure, referred to as 'Titulus Regius' – in other words, an act confirming Richard's right to the throne. Much is made of this confirmation by Ricardians, but it was not unusual for parliament to enshrine in law a political *fait accompli* about which they could do nothing anyway. Parliament was used throughout the Wars of the Roses to punish the losers and honour the victors. As a yardstick of what was 'right', therefore, it was utterly meaningless.

In this case, it's likely that the new parliament would have contained many who favoured Richard – especially since some who would have been eligible to become MPs were already attainted or abroad. The fact that one of Richard's closest associates, the lawyer William Catesby, was elected Speaker of the Commons, certainly suggests that. Those who had any doubts about the legality of Richard's seizure of power probably – in the light of all the attainders – wisely kept those doubts to themselves.

Apart from clarifying the right of Richard to be king, Titulus Regius was also a crushing indictment of the morality of his late brother, Edward IV, and his methods of government. A stark contrast was made with Richard's own pure and just qualities. The parliament of 1484 was also the first of a number of occasions when Richard required the key movers and shakers in society to swear loyalty to his regime and to his heir. He repeated the exercise with the heads of the London merchant companies – the merchants who were required to bankroll any regime. All these oaths were a little worrying: a king who required men to keep swearing oaths of allegiance was a king who suspected that many harboured doubts about the legitimacy of his kingship. It was a good way, though, of making men reconsider their commitment. I suspect that, for those who had to repeat their oaths, the experience might have been rather more unsettling than Richard realised.

Richard must have thought that he could count on the support of the leading magnates of the realm – after all, they could have rebelled against him in October 1483 along with the Duke of Buckingham, but chose not to. Men such as John Howard, newly-created Duke of Norfolk and his son Thomas, Earl of Surrey, quickly became the pillars of his regime. That was hardly surprising since they owed their meteoric advancement to him alone. Similarly Francis, Viscount Lovell, was a long-time friend whose loyalty was unquestionable. After the fall of Buckingham, increased influence was given to William Herbert, Earl of Huntingdon, who had married Richard's illegitimate daughter Katherine. Significantly, Richard's young nephew, John de la Pole, Earl of Lincoln, was given increasing responsibility. But if all these men were well and truly on side, what about the two great northern magnates without whom no king was safe: Thomas, Lord Stanley and Henry Percy, Earl of Northumberland? Both had been promised much in return for their support in 1483, but they would want to see how far their rewards stretched before they committed permanently to Richard.

There is an element of genuine tragedy about Richard III, which I suspect is why he garners so much sympathy even today. There's a sense that – although he was the architect of his own downfall – he was also unfortunate. An excellent example of this occurred in 1484 when Richard required all the lords and bishops to swear an oath to his son and sole heir, Edward of Middleham. Very soon after; in March, Edward of Middleham died. This was a body blow to Richard's regime. A king without an heir was a king who was always nervously looking over his shoulder.

Nevertheless, despite that setback, by the summer of 1484 Richard had restored his control of the country – at least for the time being. The continued presence of Henry Tudor was an ongoing problem, but one which it seemed Richard might need to solve with his foreign, rather than domestic, policy.

Henry Tudor was still in Brittany where, before the disastrous October rebellion, he had been joined in exile by a growing number of ex-courtiers of Edward IV. By December 1483, although he had been defeated, Henry actually had even more such supporters, their numbers swelled in part by the very failure of the recent revolts whose leaders were therefore obliged to flee the wrath of Richard III. It was the presence of such manifestly Yorkist exiles that required a change in Henry's approach. Previously he had been presented very much as the heir of Lancaster and therefore a threat – albeit a latent one – to the line of Yorkist kings. Given that most of his new supporters had supported the Yorkist Edward IV, such a wholly Lancastrian stance was no longer either tenable or desirable. Despite the reservations of diehard Lancastrians such as his loyal uncle, Jasper Tudor, Henry knew that he now had to appeal to a much broader base of support.

In the autumn of 1483, to attract support from disaffected Yorkists, Henry had promised the prospect of unity by means of a marriage to a daughter of the late King Edward IV. But if he wanted to be taken seriously by Yorkists, Henry had to give real substance to that promise. Accordingly, on Christmas Day 1483, he took an oath in the cathedral at Rennes in Brittany that he would marry Edward's eldest daughter, Elizabeth of York, as soon as he became king.

Though some recalcitrant Lancastrians remained unconvinced, this was a critical commitment as far as the Yorkists were concerned. Henry's court in exile must have been a rather uncomfortable place at times – a potentially toxic blend of erstwhile opponents. Yet his supporters all had one thing in common: they had no other alternative to Henry. So, if they wanted to oppose Richard III, they must bury their old differences. What united them therefore was not a common set of aims or even aspirations, let alone any admiration for Henry, but a shared enmity against Richard III.

But who were these Yorkists? Well, the previous queen's brother, Sir Edward Woodville, was there, as was her son, Thomas Grey, Marquess of Dorset, and members of the influential West Country noble family, the Courtenays. But there were no other Yorkist nobles; the rest were knights and gentry and it was upon such men that Henry Tudor pinned his hopes.

Despite Henry's commitment to the Yorkists, he was still in a very weak position: his claim – notwithstanding the oath to marry into the Yorkist line – remained as tenuous as ever. Not only was his descent via John of Gaunt's illegitimate descendants, the Beauforts, but he was claiming inheritance via a woman, his mother Margaret Beaufort. Henry also had no money, and it was always possible that some of his new allies would turn their backs upon him and betray him to Richard.

At this point, it is helpful to consider the state of Europe at that time. Remember that France was England's most powerful neighbour, but it was not the France of today. It was a France which included neither Brittany nor Burgundy, and much of French policy throughout the Wars of the Roses was directed at acquiring and absorbing both territories into France. Not surprisingly, those two duchies wanted to retain their independence. But, coincident with the emergence of Henry Tudor, there were also political developments in both Brittany and France.

In the summer of 1483, the French king, Louis XI – a master diplomat and schemer – had died leaving a minor, Charles VIII, as king under a regency council.

This meant that French policy over the next few years tended to vacillate depending upon which faction dominated the regency council at any given time.

Brittany, conversely, was ruled by the ageing Duke Francis whose only heir was his daughter, Anne. He feared, rightly, that it would be difficult to maintain the duchy's independence unless Anne married someone who had an interest in preserving the state intact. While Duke Francis had supported Henry Tudor in his 1483 rebellion, he might find it difficult to sustain that support if he came under pressure from Richard III's England – because he really needed English support to stave off French hostility.

So Henry Tudor, claimant to the English throne, has to be seen in the context of western European diplomacy. He was something of a trump card for any country which might be hostile to England – a means of prompting a regime change in England. Although in 1483 it was Duke Francis of Brittany who held that card, he was very reluctant to play it.

In the winter of 1483–4, Richard III put pressure on Brittany by waging war at sea against Breton shipping. It was a rather blunt attempt to force Duke Francis to hand over Henry. Once it became clear that the French regency council would continue the previous policy against Brittany, the duke had little option but to make an agreement with Richard III. In June 1484 such an agreement was reached – possibly at a point when Duke Francis himself was very ill and others prevailed at the Breton court – but, either way, the agreement spelt doom for Henry Tudor. Richard promised 1,000 archers to help Brittany against France in return for Henry Tudor.

Some sources tell an exciting story of Henry being tipped off by his mother, Margaret Beaufort, via the exiled Bishop John Morton – who was actually in Burgundy – that he would soon be arrested. Henry, we are told, abandoned his supporters, dashed across the frontier from Brittany into France with only a few close advisers and only narrowly escaped capture. Well, that story could be true, though the first actual evidence that Henry was in France came several months later in October 1484.

There is no doubt that, in hindsight, this was a critical moment, though it could not have seemed very auspicious to Henry at the time. One suspects that, for the young pretender, leaving the protection of the Duke of Brittany was a bit like removing his life jacket before jumping into the sea. Yet the move of Henry to France – though forced – changed everything. France was unlikely to become England's ally any time soon and would thus have no incentive at all to hand over Henry to Richard. Prising Henry out of Brittany might have been achievable for Richard, but getting him out of France was near impossible. France now had the means of destabilising Richard's hold on England should it wish to do so. France also possessed far greater resources to back a Tudor invasion than beleaguered Brittany.

Henry, mindful of the difficulties of keeping his rather unholy coalition of dissidents together, was desperate to invade in 1484, but France was not prepared

The Waiting Game

to provide the necessary resources and so he was forced to remain in France. But by the end of 1484, he received another boost in the arrival in France of John de Vere, Earl of Oxford. De Vere, like Jasper Tudor, was a Lancastrian zealot who had never submitted to Yorkist rule, preferring instead to be imprisoned for ten years. This is the same Earl of Oxford who was so successful in the fog at the Battle of Barnet in 1471, though his side was ultimately vanquished. He was one of the most competent military commanders of his day and a real boost for Henry's chances of success in the field against Richard – should he ever get to England! How Oxford managed to escape from Calais is a story in itself, but a good clue is that he brought his captor, James Blount, with him.

So, as 1484 ended, Richard knew that there could be no invasion by Henry Tudor until the spring or summer of 1485. He also knew that such an invasion was now almost inevitable. Indeed, his spies told him that it was certain that Henry would invade in the summer; and I think that in some ways that must have been a relief to Richard. The longer he had to keep the kingdom in a state of readiness to face an attack, the more difficult it became and the more the loyalty of his supporters was tested. At last, it seemed Richard would have an opportunity to crush his one remaining opponent once and for all.

Chapter 39

Fake News

I THINK IT'S fair to say that up to the parliament of 1484, everything had gone well for Richard: successful seizure of power, successful elimination of political rivals, successful suppression of rebellion and punishment of rebels and the approval of parliament for the validity of his regime. It was all going swimmingly until the spring of 1484, but from then on, Richard faced a series of setbacks beginning in March with the death of his only legitimate son, Edward of Middleham. From that moment on he was on the back foot.

There was a steady stream of gentlemen going to join Henry Tudor in exile, and there can be little doubt that for every man who made the dangerous decision to defect, there must have been others who sympathised but shied away from such an extreme course of action, which might threaten the fortunes of their families, possibly for decades to come.

Henry's enforced move to France in October 1484 helped his situation considerably, while the escape of the Earl of Oxford from royal captivity near the vital outpost of Calais only served to undermine the king's faith in his Calais commanders. A very capable general, Oxford immediately became a key member of Henry's company.

When Richard became king, England was technically at war with Scotland and in spring 1484 Richard planned a summer invasion of Scotland, perhaps hoping that the old ploy of uniting people in a foreign war would reduce opposition to him in England. However, whether because of a lack of resources, or grief at his son's death, or simply the distraction of having to prepare for an invasion by Henry Tudor, Richard did not carry through the Scottish attack and, by September, he had been forced to negotiate a peace with the Scots.

By Christmas 1484, Richard III knew that – one way or another – by the summer of 1485 his troubles would be over.

Persuading the former queen, Elizabeth Woodville, to emerge from the sanctuary of Westminster Abbey with her daughters, was something of a coup and Richard needed to do all he could to keep the Woodvilles on side. In doing so he could split the Woodville–Tudor alliance, which had tried to overthrow him in 1483. He almost succeeded in getting Elizabeth's son, Thomas Grey, Marquess of Dorset, to return to the fold, but his escape was foiled by Henry's men. Let it be said though that whatever side Dorset was on, he was unreliable and likely to be a liability.

Henry's public oath to marry Elizabeth of York when he became king meant that she too presented a threat to Richard. One way of neutralising that potential threat would be to marry her to someone else… Richard, now childless, must have at least considered setting aside his wife in the hope of having sons by another woman. He would not have been the first king to do so, but we must not forget that Queen Anne was Warwick's daughter and a heroine of the Neville north, which constituted a great swathe of Richard's powerbase. If he offended those Neville supporters, then Henry Tudor would be the least of his worries. He would be cutting off his own right arm.

So at Christmas 1484 much fuss was made at court of the young Elizabeth of York – we are told that she and Queen Anne even exchanged clothes. Contemporaries remarked upon it, so it obviously attracted some attention; but what are we to make of it? Well, at the simplest level, it may have been the king and queen trying to show that Elizabeth of York – Henry Tudor's intended – was one of the family and full-square behind the king. On the other hand, it might have been to raise Elizabeth's status at court prior to Richard marrying her himself.

All the same, cosying up to the Woodvilles was a dangerous policy. By removing her brood from sanctuary, Elizabeth probably thought she was bowing to the inevitable. But do we really believe that she was ever going to forget – or forgive – the deaths of her brother Rivers and her son Richard Grey? While it could not be proven that Richard had ordered the death of her two youngest sons, there was absolutely no doubt about Rivers and Grey.

Let's have a look at the whole issue of Richard and Elizabeth of York. The first thing is to dispense with all the frippery and nonsense that historical fiction writers – and historians who should know better – have dumped on us. Some would have us believe that Elizabeth of York, knowing that her uncle Richard had killed several of her closest relatives, was in fact in love with him. Spare me! He might be from the north but he's not exactly Jon Snow, is he?

Elizabeth of York would have been well aware of Henry Tudor's oath – and indeed he was probably involved in discussions with her mother about a marriage as early as the late summer of 1483. We have to remember that, in the fifteenth century, ladies such as Elizabeth were born to marry, not swan about and do as they pleased. While that might offend our modern sensibilities, there's no point in pretending it wasn't the case. I imagine though that being at King Richard's court at Christmas 1484 was a hell of a lot better than being cooped up in sanctuary the previous Christmas with only her mother and sisters for company! I dare say any young girl would have welcomed the attention and improvement in her fortunes.

What of Richard then? The idea of marrying his niece had some attractions for him, but I've already explained that the fierce loyalty to Anne Neville in the north meant that he had to be careful about how he treated her. Divorce was thus out of the question. But in March Anne became ill and she died fairly shortly afterwards. This – in conjunction with the possibility that Richard planned to marry Elizabeth – has led to suspicions both at the time and since that Richard poisoned Anne. It was noted that when she was ill he was rarely with her – but hey, who likes visiting a sick person? Just because he didn't fancy sharing a bed with his sick wife doesn't mean he actually killed her. Having said that, for a king who desperately needed a male heir, her death was very convenient. But we can draw no more conclusions about it than that.

If Richard believed that Anne's death would clear the way for a Woodville marriage, he was wrong. When he spelt out his cunning plan to the council soon after Anne's death, several key men were very hostile to the idea. Why? Surely it would remove one of Henry Tudor's most potent ways of gaining support. Well, the arguments put forward against the marriage were not as significant as the people who were putting them forward. As mentioned before, one argument advanced was the possibility of a hostile reaction from the Nevilles in the north – a fair point. But there was also a moral argument.

Now, call me an old cynic, but whenever someone puts forward a moral argument as a vehicle to stop something, I want to look under the vehicle's bonnet to see what's really going on. Richard was told that he should not marry his niece because their close kinship meant that it was more or less incest. Of course, at that time, such a close affinity would be seen by the church as a problem – though such marriages did happen from time to time, usually when powerful men, such as Richard, requested them.

As I said, it's more helpful to look at who opposed the marriage: key men such as William Catesby and Sir Richard Ratcliffe, who were among the king's closest advisers. They had committed themselves wholeheartedly to his cause and had benefitted a great deal as a result. A Woodville marriage, though it would undoubtedly hurt Henry Tudor, would also cause political problems in England. Some Yorkists who were rebels might decide to return, pardons would have to be given and perhaps lands and offices already handed out would need to be restored. Not only that, but a resurgence of Woodville influence would surely not be to the benefit of those most responsible for their demise – such as, er, Catesby and Ratcliffe.

Elizabeth Woodville had several great qualities but I don't think forgiveness was very high on the list. Catesby, Ratcliffe – and others – had ample reason therefore to persuade Richard to look elsewhere for a bride. It is a measure of how important their counsel was to him that he acquiesced.

However, during March 1485, fake news was running amok and on 3 April Richard was obliged to deny that he had ever had any intention of marrying Elizabeth of York. Despite his denial, the rumours continued. Elizabeth herself was packed off to Richard's castle at Sheriff Hutton in Yorkshire where she remained until matters were finally resolved in August.

The problem for Richard was always that his power base was too narrow. His reliance on ex-Neville retainers worked for a time, but he needed more widespread support. He had tried many policies to prise support away from Henry, yet in one way or another they all seemed to come to nought. For example, in his parliament of 1484 he tried to create the image of a just king to broaden his appeal and hence abolished the unpopular practice – employed by Edward IV – of raising income by means of benevolences. A benevolence was a sort of gift from a wealthy subject to his king – the sort of gift you make when your arm is twisted up behind your back. But then, as Richard's resources were depleted by the costs of keeping England ready to face an invasion, he too resorted to loans which were not exactly freely given.

To persuade the uncommitted, the propaganda war was ramped up to full throttle. Henry Tudor, Richard reiterated, came from a bastard line of descent and did not have a valid claim to the throne. The Earl of Richmond's followers were: 'murderers, adulterers and extortioners'. Though in general Richard adopted a high moral tone, for example in his condemnation of his late brother's licentious court, he seemed unable to carry it off. Because, fake news or not, it was quite clear that many of his subjects could not see beyond the allegations made against Richard: the death of his nephews, the poisoning of his wife and the proposed marriage to his niece. For a king who presented himself as just and God-fearing, it didn't look good.

One of the things it is important to grasp about these rumours is that it did not matter at the time whether they were true or not. All the trees felled to argue about whether Richard was guilty of these charges or not make no difference. The fact is that at the time many were simply not convinced of his innocence; as a consequence, it was very hard for those people to commit themselves to his cause.

What characterised the last six months of Richard's reign was desperation. On the surface, his position appeared strong: he had the support of his magnates, his bishops and he possessed the means of raising a very large army to counter Henry. Yet beneath that veneer of strength lay serial weaknesses, not least a suspicion that he could not entirely trust some of his magnates. Hence, when he went to Nottingham in June 1485, ready to face Henry Tudor wherever he might land, he took with him – as a hostage – Lord Thomas Stanley's eldest son and heir, Lord Strange. Some of his most dependable men were instructed to watch others for signs of betrayal.

With, he hoped, his key men in the right positions, Richard was as ready as he could be and just had to wait. Throughout June and July, he was still waiting; so were his subjects and, while they waited, they weighed their options. In almost every case, their motivation would have been their own survival and the continued prosperity of their families. That is what would determine which way they jumped when Henry actually arrived – if of course, they jumped at all...

Chapter 40

A Welshman Comes Calling

THE AIR OF desperation which seemed to drive all Richard's actions in the last few months of his reign, especially the suspicions he harboured about the loyalty of some of his key allies, was not just paranoia. Richard was right to be suspicious of them since their loyalty was only skin deep. The trouble was that there was nothing more that Richard could do about that. There were only so many hostages he could take to ensure compliance, and there was a limit to how many of his retainers he could task with watching those he did not trust.

It's been said to me, only recently, how foolish it was of Richard to put his trust in Thomas Stanley, Henry's father-in-law. But what choice did he have? There was no great pool of replacement lords to choose from. And in any case, trying to remove Lord Stanley would only have precipitated chaos in the north-west where his heir, Lord Strange, would have simply taken his father's place. What was Richard to do? Exterminate whole noble families? He went as far as he dared by holding Stanley's son hostage, and he could not be sure that even that would be enough to ensure Stanley's loyalty.

As I've said elsewhere, Richard's power base was far too narrow and the doubts which dogged his regime throughout the reign just would not go away. He could call Henry Tudor by any name he liked, but it did not improve his own standing. Rightly or wrongly, he did not inspire trust – and that alone would cost him his throne. But if you look at the situation on the eve of Henry's arrival in 1485 from Richard's point of view, he had done everything he could to strengthen his position. His armies were mustering, whether reluctantly or not, and all was in place to meet the pretender head-on.

So, let's examine Henry's mindset as he prepared to invade England for the second time. In the forefront of his mind would have been the reasons for failure in the autumn of 1483: basically insufficient support from the men who mattered most. Hence, it was vital for Henry to try to ensure that more noble support was in place this time. Clearly, he was in close touch with the Stanley brothers, Thomas and William. While I have hardly mentioned the younger Stanley, William, who was a power in North Wales, his role in the Bosworth campaign was to be vitally important. Henry's choice of landing place had much to do with his expectation of

Stanley support. He knew very well that he could not overthrow Richard with only a few thousand foreign mercenaries at his disposal.

During secret negotiations, it seems that Henry had received encouragement not only from the Stanleys, but also from a member of the influential Talbot family, who was also the Stanley brothers' nephew: Sir John Savage. In South Wales, a prominent landowner, Rhys Ap Thomas, also promised his help. Henry expected that his uncle, Jasper Tudor, as former Earl of Pembroke, would be able to raise significant support in South Wales. Taking all these pledges together, it is easy to understand why Henry made his first landing in Wales. That was where his likely support lay: Wales and Cheshire.

Henry would have known that persuading the likes of the Duke of Norfolk to join his cause was a waste of effort, but he must have hoped for Northumberland's support. As we already know, Northumberland was no friend to King Richard, but he would not act against him unless the odds were in his favour.

Anxious to keep his fragile coalition together – the flaky Marquess of Dorset had already tried to leg it – Henry moved as fast as he could and set sail with a fleet of thirty ships from the French port of Harfleur on 1 August 1485.

The core of his invasion force was several hundred English and Welsh exiles, but they were bolstered by mercenaries, including perhaps 2,000 Normans under the command of Philibert de Chandée. These had been provided by the French king, Charles VIII, and no contemporary description of them is very complimentary. I think, if you imagine the Dirty Dozen (you might have to look it up online) in the film of that name, that probably gives you some idea of what Henry's mercenaries were like – only there were a lot more than a dozen. With them was a small force of Scottish mercenaries under Sir Alexander Bruce – perhaps almost 1,000 strong.

This motley invasion force landed late in the day on 7 August 1485 at Milford Haven in Pembrokeshire. By the following day Henry had received support from some of his uncle Jasper's adherents, but other news was less encouraging: Sir John Savage and Rhys Ap Thomas appeared to be taking up a position to oppose his advance rather than join it. Morale in Henry's camp must have been low, for they expected at any moment to come under attack. Support was uncertain whereas opposition was inevitable.

It did not help that the Welsh and French contingents seemed to be forever at each other's throats and had to be separated. Indeed, the hostility of Rhys Ap Thomas towards the French might well have been why the Welshman did not immediately declare for Henry. A lot is airy-fairily said now about Welsh support for Henry Tudor, but at the time, if such support existed, it was invisible. Remember how little enthusiasm there was for the would-be Tudor king in the rebellion of October 1483.

Henry skirted the coast, unwilling to risk being trapped inland. At Cardigan he issued a declaration to his subjects exhorting them to come to his aid; in that letter, he played upon Welsh nationalism and presented himself as something of a representative for Wales. He also promised dire punishment for any who failed to support him – so Richard was not alone in that!

Henry's plan – communicated to the Stanleys and others – was to cross the Severn at Shrewsbury, and the idea was that his supporters would rally to join him there. However, if the likes of Rhys Ap Thomas now opposed him, Henry's invasion would be dead and buried because he would not even get as far as Shrewsbury. Fortunately for him, after some bargaining, Rhys joined Henry probably with about 2,000 men just before Shrewsbury. But even then Rhys hedged his bets by leaving two brothers and 500 men behind – just in case things went badly with Henry.

Welsh support alone though, was not enough: Henry needed the Stanleys. Though William Stanley arrived, it was not at the head of a large army, for it turned out that he had come only to talk. We are told that he reassured Henry that – when the moment came – the Stanleys would support him. But how confident could Henry have been that these nobles, whom he did not know at all, would keep their secret promises? He must have feared that they could easily change their minds at any point. Even so, the capitulation of Shrewsbury, enabling Henry to cross the Severn, could only have occurred because the Stanleys urged it. When he heard of it, Richard was very angry because the River Severn was an effective barrier to stop Henry going wherever he pleased. Now the pretender could do exactly that.

The position of the Stanleys was complicated and the movements of the two Stanley brothers during August bear this out. Before Henry landed, Thomas Stanley left the court at Nottingham, but was only allowed to do so by leaving his son, Lord Strange, as surety for his actions. When, by 10 or at the latest 11 August, the king learned of Henry's arrival, he recalled Thomas. The latter pleaded illness – a dangerous new disease had begun to occur at this time, called the sweating sickness, but I think it's unlikely Thomas had it. I think he was probably offering an excuse to gain manoeuvring time, and this is supported by an attempted escape by Lord Strange. It was unsuccessful and Strange, when interrogated, implicated his uncle William in treason, but not his father. He then wrote to his father urging him to bring all his force to join Richard, but he may have been coerced to do so and he probably knew his father well enough to know that he would do what he thought was best regardless of anything his son said.

Once William was, as it were, outed as a traitor, Lord Thomas needed to be very careful indeed – but as we know, he rarely showed his hand. Although he led his forces towards Leicester where the royal army was to gather, was he returning to the royal fold, or not? Who was he trying to reassure: Richard, or Henry? The importance of Thomas Stanley cannot be overstated: his lack of support for Henry in 1483 had destroyed the revolt. Would he do the same again?

Henry, for his part, could only hope for the best, so he advanced from Shrewsbury through Stafford to Lichfield and then to Tamworth. He then made a crucial decision to head for Leicester and try to bring the king to battle before all the royal armies arrived. On the way he was joined by several more of Edward IV's household men who, though pardoned by Richard for their part in the 1483 revolt, had never received all their lands back. There is that motive again: land. The student of this period ignores it at their peril.

As Henry advanced, Thomas Stanley, with his force of about 5,000 men, retreated, keeping close but not treasonably close. Then at an abbey near Atherstone, not far from Lichfield and close to Watling Street – the road to London – Henry met both the Stanley brothers and it seems likely that they reaffirmed their intention to support him. This was Henry's first face-to-face meeting with Thomas and I can't help thinking that it was significant, both symbolically and practically. After all, why would Thomas take the risk of meeting his son-in-law in person if his intention to support him was not serious? At the same time, Stanley's nephew, Sir John Savage, at last arrived with his retinue – and since he was part of the extended Stanley family, this was also a clear sign that they were committed to Henry.

So, after all the extensive preparation and waiting, Henry Tudor was at last poised to face Richard III in battle. He was heavily outnumbered so his fate would hang upon the decisions of others. However, there was nothing more he could do, except perhaps pray – which I am certain he did.

Richard – we are told – expressed delight when hearing of Henry's approach. But a few days later, in mid-August, he was stunned to receive a delegation from the loyal citizens of York enquiring what arrangements had been made to muster their men. It appeared that the Earl of Northumberland had issued no instructions, which did not augur well for the likely arrival of the northern troops. It must have seemed to Richard that Northumberland was dragging his feet deliberately – which, of course, he was.

This brings me to an important general point about noble loyalties. I get sick and tired of folk these days – half a millennium later – lamenting how fickle some of the nobles were in their loyalty. Put yourself in the position of the Earl of Northumberland, whose actions in 1485 have often been criticised. Scarcely a generation before, his father had been killed – along with many, many others of his clients and tenants – loyally supporting Henry VI. He himself had been stripped of his title and imprisoned for years – you don't forget something like that in a hurry.

But never mind the earl himself, how keen would his men be to enter into another brutal contest, which would bring them little gain and possible death? The earl's concern was the welfare of the Percy family, which in turn meant the welfare of all those who served them. What did Northumberland owe Richard – a man who had usurped much of the power in the north that he had expected to have for himself and who was now a king dogged by doubt and suspicion?

I think it is perfectly possible to argue that Northumberland owed Richard nothing at all. Yes, some will bang on about Richard being his anointed king, but we're talking about actual death and destruction here – not just of one man, but many of his affinity. For the men of the time, it was not some academic exercise. Anyway, brief rant over...

Aside from Northumberland's sluggish response to the call to arms, another factor must have given Richard pause for thought: the very fact that Henry had managed to cross the country from the Welsh coast to the heart of England unopposed. Why had no one resisted him at a point when his army was very small? Why indeed?

Nevertheless, when Richard set out from Nottingham on about 20 August to join his mustering army at Leicester, he could console himself with the news that John Howard, Duke of Norfolk, and his son Thomas, Earl of Surrey, were on their way. And although not all the other nobles answered his call, he could reassure himself that battles could be won without them. However, the evidence we have suggests that it was not only the nobility who stayed away, but many of the gentry too. Richard's army was – we are told – still significantly larger than that of Henry, and I see no reason to doubt that. Especially when, on 21 August, Northumberland's tardy army eventually arrived.

Richard, confident in his own ability as a general and a soldier, would have been pretty bullish as he awaited the battle. He had seen battle many times before and had participated in the most brutal fighting, whereas his opponent Henry knew nothing of battle at all. Richard would have known that if he could kill Henry, then loyalty to his own cause would suddenly become very solid indeed. He probably still hoped that both Stanleys would see him gaining the upper hand and throw their weight behind him. This is not so far-fetched because – notwithstanding their promises to Henry – both Stanley brothers intended to be on the winning side. If Henry's battle line showed serious signs of collapsing, I think it's reasonable to assume that he was not going to be king.

So, with preparations made and prayers offered on both sides, battle was about to commence.

Chapter 41

Bosworth, Part One

THE BATTLE OF Bosworth, fought on 22 August 1485, is rightly regarded as one of the most important battles fought upon English soil. You can read various accounts of the battle, but I would heartily recommend the very informative and detailed description in Chris Skidmore's book *Bosworth*.

Almost every account of any battle seeks to describe in an orderly way a sequence of events which was rarely anything like orderly. Medieval battles, like most battles, were often complicated and unpredictable affairs – and Bosworth was very complicated. Why? Well, partly because of the unequal numbers of the two sides, but also because the role of several key participants remained shrouded in doubt until the battle itself unfolded, and even then it was a real cliff-hanger.

To add to all that confusion, our main sources of information about the battle – chroniclers – generally only understood warfare in broad brush strokes. Rather like modern tabloid newspapers, chroniclers were looking for a story and thus they tended to concentrate on episodes of bravery and treachery. So, as always, we must regard all accounts, if not with suspicion, then certainly with great care.

Foremost in our minds must be this principle: we should not confuse actions with motives. As you will have gathered, the whole topic of the Wars of the Roses is frequently subject to such confusion. My point is, that even if we can piece together which participant did what and when, we cannot always be sure *why* they acted as they did. In this battle there were several key moments when the motives were far from clear.

Given that even the two main protagonists – Richard and Henry – were not entirely sure who was on their side, we can hardly be confident about it more than 530 years later. Well, you may say, surely it's obvious now, because we know who did, in the end, fight on each side – or did not fight at all. That is true, but we don't always know why. Therefore, everything seems much more clear-cut than it actually was at the time. Battles often turned on small incidents, local decisions made in haste and luck. Once the fighting started, neither Richard nor Henry could actually control the other players in the game. As we shall see, they could only control what they individually decided to do.

So, with those provisos in mind, let's explore the battle.

As we know, Wars of the Roses battlefields are sometimes a bit hard to pin down, and Bosworth has been no exception. The traditional site was Ambion Hill near Market Bosworth, not far from Leicester, but, after much argument, and literally years of work by the Battlefields Trust, I think we can now be pretty certain that the centre of the battle was fought probably a mile or two to the south-west of Ambion Hill. Archaeological finds – especially a lot of cannon shot – have helped to pinpoint the location.

Richard's army had mustered at Leicester and it was from there that Richard rode out on the morning of 21 August. He must have looked pretty impressive, in full armour and wearing the crown on his head. Ceremony was important in the fifteenth century and the powerful image of Richard as king was designed to stiffen the resolve of his army.

You will recall that Richard's army was much larger than Henry's – even leaving aside the uncommitted Stanleys – and may well have amounted to some 15,000 men. He arrayed his forces on the higher ground on the slopes of Ambion Hill, but bear in mind that an army of that size would have covered several large open fields. Just consider how much space a hundred people take up, then multiply that by 150 and add horses, cannon, supply train and so on. Imagine trying to communicate with the various companies gathered there. A considerable amount of organisation was required just to ensure that the troops arrived anywhere near where they were supposed to be. Many of Richard's soldiers were commoners, who were less well-trained and therefore more difficult to control in the heat of battle. Oh, and once the cannon started firing, you could see precious little of the battlefield at all...

Richard's vanguard was led by the experienced John Howard, Duke of Norfolk, and Sir Robert Brackenbury. Norfolk was a veteran of several campaigns and had actually fought for Edward IV at Barnet in 1471 – ironically against the Earl of Oxford, who would be his direct opponent at Bosworth. I doubt either man had forgotten that.

Richard was in the centre of his army, behind the vanguard, and surrounded by his hand-picked household knights.

The rear guard, to his left, was commanded by Henry Percy, Earl of Northumberland, and although it is said that he had about 10,000 men, they were still lagging behind the rest of the royal army.

Below Richard's army on the lower ground, near the River Sence, known as Redemoor at the time, was a green and marshy plain. It was through this unpromising lowland area that Henry's army had to advance.

The Stanley brothers – Thomas and William – positioned their forces in between the two main armies to Henry's right – and therefore, Richard's left.

Henry's speech to his troops on the day of the battle – according to the sixteenth-century chronicler, Edward Hall, included the following telling words: 'Backward we cannot fly so that here we stand like sheep in a fold... between our enemies and doubtful friends.'

What did he mean? Well, earlier that morning – 22 August – Henry had invited Thomas Stanley to join his army and lead the vanguard. Stanley politely declined, replying that he would join the battle once Henry's army was committed. Hence the Stanleys were the 'doubtful friends' he referred to. How much could he rely on the Stanleys' promises?

Henry's position, as I've already hinted, was not very promising: the king held the high ground, had the wind in his favour and vastly superior numbers. Indeed, Henry's army was so small that instead of forming up into the traditional three medieval units (or battles, as they were called) – the vanguard, main battle and rear guard – he could only form his army into one battle line, split into a left-wing and a right-wing. Without the Stanleys, Henry was massively outnumbered.

Let's take a moment to consider Thomas Stanley's position in more depth. His son, Lord Strange, was still Richard's prisoner on the morning of the battle and Thomas had no way of knowing what had happened to him. When Richard saw that Stanley's forces had not joined the royal army, he regarded it as clear evidence of treason and was minded to execute Stanley's son, Lord Strange, on the spot. Yet Stanley had still not actually committed himself; positioned as he was, midway between Henry's right flank and Richard's left, he could still play a decisive part in turning the battle either way.

Now the Stanleys in general, and Thomas Stanley in particular, have taken a lot of stick about Bosworth – and a few other things too. Ricardians blame them for Richard's defeat and Henry's supporters blame them for being lukewarm in their support. As always, I try to bring a modicum of common sense to all this nonsense.

Let's be clear: the Stanleys intended to support Henry. Why else would they take such outrageous risks in keeping in touch with him, thereby putting in jeopardy their lives and legacies by angering the king. Of course, you could argue that the Stanleys were just showing Richard how vital their support was, but that would be a very dangerous game indeed. And why bother, since the king already knew that.

Richard must have thought Stanley's defection was likely long before the battle, or he would never have taken the extraordinary step of holding Stanley's son and heir, Lord Strange, hostage. After that, does anyone seriously believe that Stanley and Richard could ever trust each other?

All things being equal, Thomas Stanley would support his step-son, Henry Tudor, and he told him so several times. But all things were not equal; they were very far from equal, because the king's army was very large and, though the Stanleys' forces were considerable, they had no intention of sacrificing themselves in a doomed cause. If Henry's army – a rag-tag collection of Welshmen, Englishmen, Scotsmen and French – there must be a joke in there somewhere –was able to stand against Richard, then the Stanleys would support him, but if Henry was quickly routed, then the Stanleys would fall back on Plan B.

Plan B was Thomas Stanley telling the king that he was simply blocking Henry's road to London and that he was always ready to join Richard in battle if needed. Well, it was true that the Stanleys were sitting next to Watling Street, which was indeed the road to London. While Richard might not have been amused by the explanation offered, there was little he could have done about it since Stanley was still sitting at the head of a very considerable army.

Of course, Thomas Stanley's policy may be seen as cynical, but he survived – as he had on several other previous and equally dodgy occasions. As I said of Northumberland, sometimes we have to get off our moral high ground and enter the real world of the fifteenth century, where royal favour brought land, power and wealth. A great family who ended up on the wrong side in a key battle would no longer be a great family; there was far more to lose than just their lives. Furthermore, Richard simply did not inspire loyalty among many of his other subjects. It was not just the Stanleys who spent a while sitting on the fence at Bosworth. Some lords did not even answer the king's summons.

The battle itself began with the customary exchange of arrows, which proved inconclusive, and was followed by Richard's artillery. Many don't realise that warfare in this period included plenty of cannon. The archaeological evidence proves that Richard had many cannon of varying size and range. They were even able to fire balls of lead packed with lead shot or pebbles – which of course were wholly designed to maim or kill.

Henry was therefore seriously outgunned, but under such heavy fire his men seemed to acquit themselves surprisingly well. We should not underestimate how terrifying such an artillery bombardment was for the participants. But in this respect, the small size of Henry's army helped because it enabled them to mass on their left flank where the lie of the land shielded them from the worst effects of the cannon fire. A larger army could not have done that. We're told that it was the French mercenaries, who had faced such cannon fire before, who gave them that handy tip. And, of course, in the smoke of battle the king's gunners would not have been able to see their targets very clearly at all.

So the arrows came and went; and then the cannon shot came and went. Since neither were in any way decisive, it was time for cold steel.

As Henry's army advanced, they passed a very marshy area on their right flank which would make it difficult for Richard's forces to outflank them there. Remember that Henry's forces had concentrated on their left flank to avoid the cannon fire, so when they attacked it was Richard's right flank which bore the brunt of their assault. Since Thomas Stanley had passed up the opportunity, battlefield command of Henry's armies fell to John de Vere, Earl of Oxford, who was a very experienced and capable commander.

Oxford was also very much a man with a mission – in fact, several missions.

Firstly, you will recall that Oxford was a Lancastrian through and through. If he was a stick of rock he would have had Lancaster written through him in red letters. He genuinely believed in Henry's cause.

Secondly, at Barnet in 1471 he had come close to destroying the house of York – including the present King Richard, then Duke of Gloucester. But in that fog of a battle he had lost control of his troops and, while they were off celebrating, the battle was lost. Oxford was determined to make sure that he did not repeat that mistake at Bosworth.

But there was also a third mission for Oxford – a very personal one. Oxford had lost his lands to the Yorkists, notably to Richard himself, but also to his rival for control of East Anglia, John Howard, Duke of Norfolk, against whom he was about to be pitted in battle.

So, for many reasons, Oxford was determined to use all his considerable military skill and experience to win this battle. The first action came when Oxford, leading a large number of Henry's men, massed as we have said on his left flank, attacked the Duke of Norfolk's position. The assault was full-on and Oxford's men pressed Norfolk back. But Oxford, anxious to prevent a repeat of Barnet, gave the order that no man should advance more than four feet in front of their battle standards – which might well have been one of the few things any man was still able to see.

Because of that order, the fighting appears to have ground to a halt with Oxford's men holding back and Norfolk's wondering what the heck was going on.

Further up the slope, King Richard would not have been able to see much, but one thing he did notice was that Thomas Stanley's banners were exactly where they had been since early that morning. Why, he wondered, had Stanley not helped out Norfolk by putting Henry's army under pressure on their right flank – which was very close to where he was? There was only one answer to that and Richard, already half-expecting it, now knew that he might have to win without Thomas Stanley's help.

Though the battle on Henry's left had stalled, the contest was only just starting. Oxford might have paused, but he wasn't finished. Again, his men, still massed on Henry's left flank, attacked Norfolk, but at the same time Oxford ordered another assault by a small force who would try to break through Richard's main battle line. Since he did not have enough men for a broad, frontal attack, Oxford could only spare a single column to drive like a wedge at Richard's line. The aim was to punch a hole in the royal line and cut off King Richard from Northumberland's rear-guard. There is some suggestion that it was the Welshmen of Rhys Ap Thomas who made this charge, but we cannot be certain.

Some of the sources suggest that this concerted attack on Richard's lines coincided with his decision to execute Lord Strange. Apparently, there was a bit of a discussion in Richard's camp about whether they should execute him or not, but either way we're not too sure what happened next. Somehow, Lord Strange contrived to escape and it is difficult to understand how that could possibly have happened unless he had help from within Richard's own ranks. Richard was thus unable to carry out his threat, which must have been extremely annoying. But by then, he had other things to worry about.

Norfolk's vanguard was outmanoeuvred and turned around by Oxford; and, because of the success of the other attack on Richard's line, Norfolk became isolated. Many of his men were killed and Norfolk himself perished too, whether in the fighting or by summary battlefield execution, we don't know. What we do know is that Oxford wanted him dead.

The royal vanguard had thus been destroyed and men were fleeing the field, but the battle was by no means over. In his attack Oxford had used a large part of Henry's army, which meant that Henry had only a very small force as his rearguard. In contrast, Richard still had thousands of men at his disposal, including those of the Earl of Northumberland. And of course, the two Stanley brothers had not yet committed any of their men to the fight one way or the other. So, the battle was still finely poised.

Chapter 42

Bosworth, Part Two

ONE OF THE pillars of King Richard's regime, John Howard, Duke of Norfolk, had been killed and the royal vanguard routed by John de Vere, Earl of Oxford. Some of Richard's men on the field may have seen that happen and perhaps also took flight. Richard must have been waiting for his leading magnates to weigh in and support him.

We've already established that the Stanleys, if they supported anyone directly, would support Henry, so the collapse of Richard's vanguard would hardly have persuaded the Stanleys to support the king. However, they did not yet support Henry. What does this tell us? It tells us that Richard had not yet lost the battle. The Stanleys would have been watching closely to see what Henry Percy, Earl of Northumberland and commander of the king's rear-guard, was going to do. They would not have seen much, however, because Northumberland was not doing anything.

It is worth turning this situation on its head. Let's go wild for a moment and forget about Richard and Henry and instead focus on Northumberland and Thomas Stanley, two of the political heavyweights of their age. Each had thousands of men under his command and the armies were not very far apart. At this pivotal moment in the battle, with the royal vanguard in pieces, either man could have ridden to support Richard, but neither did. As much as they were focused on the battle, they were also watching each other. If either committed to the fight, the other might join with them or – equally possible – attack them from behind and destroy them. It is hard to grasp this, but neither man was thinking about the battle: both were thinking about what would come next.

Whoever was the victor at Bosworth, both men wanted greater influence in the kingdom and that is why they played this waiting game. We have examined Stanley's motives already, but what about Northumberland?

Northumberland, like Thomas Stanley, had to consider what outcome was in his best interests. And there is an interesting – though utterly unsubstantiated – theory that Northumberland, wary of Richard's tarnished reputation as king, saw an opportunity to ensure that neither Richard nor Henry became king. Certainly, if Henry became king without his help, Northumberland's position would be weaker than it already was, for he would not want the Stanleys to gain power at his expense. But remember that King Richard depended upon the support of the Nevilles – the traditional northern rivals of the Percys – and, if Northumberland saw Richard's kingship as flawed, perhaps he had found another solution.

In the north, Richard had his nephew, the Duke of Clarence's son, Edward, Earl of Warwick, locked up – most likely at Sheriff Hutton castle. The suggestion is that Northumberland had in mind the idea of putting Edward, Earl of Warwick on the throne and marrying him to his own daughter. He, not Stanley, would then be the kingmaker at Bosworth, providing he ensured that everyone else destroyed themselves. Of course, there is no actual evidence of such a plot by Northumberland, but why else did he do nothing?

There may be a simple and more practical reason why neither Northumberland nor Stanley intervened. To get to Henry both of them would have to cross the marshy ground on Henry's right flank. Perhaps they simply could not do so, or regarded it as too much of a risk.

Whatever the reasons for Northumberland's inactivity, it was of course vital to Richard. He would already have suspected that the Stanleys would desert him, but when he and his most loyal supporters saw that there was no help coming from Northumberland either, they must have been devastated. Much evidence suggests that, at this point, several key men advised Richard to flee while he could – live to fight another day, as they say. Richard had personal experience of this because he had fled before, with his brother Edward, when faced with overwhelming odds against him. In the end it comes down to a mindset: Edward accepted that he might flee to regroup, but Richard had an entirely different view. He was determined to see the battle through. If he won, he was brave; if he lost, he was foolish.

However, Richard's decision to stay might have been a little more sensible than it appears in hindsight. We have already said that most of Henry's army was committed upon his left flank and that he had few men with him in his position at the rear of his army. It seems that at this critical moment in the battle, Richard saw Henry's standard in the distance. Oxford's fight was away to the king's right, but straight ahead of him his opponent, Henry, stood exposed with relatively little support. Richard saw a genuine – if risky – opportunity to strike down his enemy and end the battle. Thus he led a mounted assault with his household knights, and, riding around the ongoing struggle with Oxford, he charged directly at Henry's small force. Wearing his crown on his helmet, he was determined to live or die as king.

As Richard made for Henry's standards, the Stanleys – despite Thomas's earlier promise to Henry – had still not intervened. For Richard, the aim was simple: kill Henry Tudor. Well, he certainly tried to; but Henry was well defended by his leading knights. Sir William Brandon, his standard-bearer, was killed and one of the greatest – and indeed largest – knights of his day, John Cheyney, was knocked down. It seems that there was a very real threat to Henry's life at that point, but it is nearly impossible now to distinguish fact from fiction in that final sequence of events.

It was in the interest of Tudor chroniclers to big up Henry's role, and to accentuate his resistance and bravery. To do that, it was also necessary to exaggerate the threat. How close did Richard get to killing his opponent? We've no idea, but it is reasonable to suppose that those he did kill – like Brandon – would have been very close to Henry indeed. A reasonable conclusion must be that Richard's brave gambit came very close to success. In the end, it did fail; but not through any particular heroism on Henry's part, or any weakness on Richard's. It failed because, finally, the Stanleys intervened.

It was Sir William Stanley who launched an attack with his 3,000 men and destroyed both King Richard and his men. Sir William arrived in the nick of time, but that could not possibly have been deliberate. It's equally likely that Henry could have been killed before he arrived, because William Stanley had no way of knowing what the exact situation was when he began his charge.

But why did the Stanleys leave it so late, and only act when Henry was in dire peril? Is it likely that William Stanley would have acted without his elder brother's permission? Well, yes perhaps, because remember that Sir William had already been revealed to Richard as a traitor by his nephew, Lord Strange. Sir William was doomed if Richard won, so perhaps he was more personally committed to a Tudor victory than his elder brother Thomas. It's also possible that Thomas Stanley received word of his son's escape and decided he could act freely. Even if he thought his son had been executed, he might still have decided to intervene.

After the event, of course, it became a perfectly-timed intervention, but the Stanleys basically got lucky. Throughout the battle they had waited and waited, and only when Henry's death seemed imminent did they move. Even then Thomas Stanley himself remained aloof on higher ground, still perhaps nervous about Northumberland's nearby superior force.

It appears likely that Richard and any survivors were driven into the marsh by William Stanley's sudden attack and there they were cut down. After the battle a lot of men claimed they had delivered the blow that killed the king – a favourite choice was the Welshman Rhys Ap Thomas – but even at the time hardly anyone would actually have known who killed Richard.

Meanwhile, Northumberland quietly withdrew from the field. Did he know Richard was actually dead? Almost certainly not, but he would have realised that from the moment William Stanley intervened Richard was doomed. Had Richard stayed on the slopes of Ambion Hill, Northumberland could still have supported him. But as it was, there was not much he could have done to save him. So he sensibly withdrew.

Meanwhile, across the battlefield many others surrendered and the king's crown was discovered and ended up in the hands of the Stanley brothers – who else? The chronicles argue about which brother placed the crown on Henry's head, but most likely it was Thomas Stanley, who by his absence from battle had given Henry victory.

The battle had not lasted very long – perhaps a couple of hours. The death toll was certainly not as great as Towton, or even battles such as Barnet or Tewkesbury. Far more were killed on the king's side – most when his vanguard was routed. Perhaps a hundred of Henry's men were killed to a thousand of Richard's. This was one of those strange battles where those who looked on vastly outnumbered those who actually fought.

The death of Richard, of course, was all that mattered. Though in the final mêlée, both men could easily have been killed, which would have left Northumberland with the genuine possibility of putting Edward, Earl of Warwick, on the throne.

Richard's body, once discovered, was stripped and put on public display at Leicester; this was only partly done to humiliate his memory. It was also to scotch any rumours that he had escaped the field.

Two of Richard's most committed supporters, Richard Ratcliffe and Robert Brackenbury, were killed with their lord in the final fighting. Some other notables managed to escape, including Francis, Lord Lovell, and John de la Pole, Earl of Lincoln, Richard's nephew and his named successor. Since many others had surrendered, there was a long list of prisoners, most notably Henry Percy, Earl of Northumberland, John Howard's son the Earl of Surrey and a leading councillor of the king, Sir William Catesby.

Surrey was eventually pardoned and Northumberland too, but not until Henry had secured possession of Edward, Earl of Warwick and kept Northumberland in the Tower for a few months. Sir William Catesby, however, was not so fortunate. His influence with Richard and his very prominent role in both the seizure of power in 1483 and Richard's subsequent reign, meant that he had to be executed. The deed was done on 25 August. Most other prominent men were not hounded by Henry, who was desperate to unite the nobility and gentry behind him.

So, what was the significance of Bosworth? Well, if on 23 August 1485 – the day after Bosworth – you asked a nobleman, or noble lady for that matter, whether the battle was important, they might have replied: 'I'll let you know in ten years' time'.

Folk of the late fifteenth century had become a little wary of so-called decisive battles: Wakefield in 1460; St Albans and Towton in 1461; Barnet and Tewkesbury in 1471. All had seemed decisive in one way or another, yet none had ended the period of crisis. So why should Bosworth be any different?

Well, readers will know that just because Richard III was dead does not mean that was the end of the matter. Because there were always others who were keen to press their claim to the throne.

Part Five
After Bosworth

Chapter 43

What Next?

THE STORY OF the Wars of the Roses might reasonably be awarded a subtitle – to borrow from the author, Roald Dahl – 'Tales of the Unexpected'. Because just when you think everything is settled, you discover that it's not.

In August 1485, on the field of Bosworth, Henry Tudor was proclaimed king. He had staked his claim on the battlefield and it was manifest to all that God had given him the victory while striking down his opponent in the most decisive manner. Yet what a strange battle it was – how many battles can you think of where most of those present did not actually take part?

So what did the events of Bosworth actually mean? That was probably a question posed by many at the time.

Did it mean that Henry was acceptable to those who stood and watched events unfold? Or did it signify that neither Henry, nor Richard, commanded particular support? Or did it mean that no one cared any more who was king? And if not Henry, then who? What alternatives were left? Well, Henry might be the undisputed Lancastrian claimant, but there were several members of the House of York who could still throw their hats into the ring – or rather, have it thrown in for them.

Mindful of this, as soon as his victory was assured, Henry sent loyal men north to Sheriff Hutton Castle in Yorkshire, where several people of note had been housed by Richard III. The chief Yorkist representative was Edward, Earl of Warwick, the fifteen-year-old son of Richard's attainted elder brother George, Duke of Clarence. By birth no living Yorkist had a better claim, so once Henry had lodged Edward in the Tower it would be difficult for any diehard Yorkists to rally around another candidate. Difficult, but not impossible. Richard had named his nephew, John de la Pole, Earl of Lincoln, as his successor, but for the time being Lincoln seemed content to submit to Henry and accept him as king. But would Lincoln remain loyal?

Let's not forget that although Henry's entourage included several prominent Lancastrians, such as his uncle, Jasper Tudor, Earl of Pembroke, and John de Vere, Earl of Oxford, the majority of his leading advisers were ex-servants of Edward IV – men who had only supported Henry in the first place as a means of opposing Richard. They were essentially Yorkists, but now Henry must bind them together with his Lancastrian supporters if he wanted to keep his throne. The prospect of the

What Next?

Tudor coalition fracturing very soon after victory was a genuine possibility. Tudor possession of the throne – which seems so inevitable with hindsight – did not look at all inevitable in 1485.

With the demise of several of the great Yorkist magnates of England – Hastings, Buckingham and Norfolk – only two men of such influence were left in 1485: Lord Thomas Stanley and Henry Percy, Earl of Northumberland. At the moment of Henry's victory, Stanley was very much in the ascendant and Percy was a prisoner. Stanley's eldest son George, Lord Strange – effectively King Henry's step-brother – was even briefly given Northumberland's command as Warden of the Northern Marches.

However, fortunes were easily reversed in this period and, by December 1485, Percy was a free man and reinstalled as Warden of the Northern Marches. Why would Henry do that? Well, because the northern borderlands were a constant source of trouble between England and Scotland. Though the Scottish king, James III, was in theory an ally of the new king Henry, his leading border subjects desired peace about as much as they liked their English counterparts – in other words, not very much. With his political future in the balance, Henry could not risk the north – which he already suspected of being hostile to his regime – being destabilised by Scottish border attacks.

Lord Strange, however, was not the man for such a weighty task, because the Stanley name hardly sent Scottish raiders into a fit of panic – more likely a fit of laughter. What Henry needed to strengthen his northern defences was a Percy – a name which inspired courage on one side of the border and trepidation on the other. Fortunately, King Henry happened to have a Percy at his disposal, so he unleashed him in the north – but how loyal would the unreliable Henry Percy be?

In the early days of the new Tudor regime, many of those who had joined Henry in exile now got their rewards, whether by appointment to prominent positions, or by receipt of lands. Chief among these supporters was John de Vere, Earl of Oxford. Oxford claimed the major credit for the victory at Bosworth, though it was probably not lost on Henry that, despite Oxford's efforts, the would-be king might have been killed without the last-ditch intervention of Sir William Stanley.

Nevertheless, Oxford was showered with rewards: he was appointed Great Chamberlain, Lord Admiral of England and Constable of the Tower. Meanwhile, Henry's loyal uncle Jasper was elevated to Duke of Bedford, a title with close association to the House of Lancaster since it had been that of Henry V's brother. Jasper, now in his fifties, had sacrificed all to establish his nephew on the throne. So he next decided to look to his own life and legacy. With that in mind, he married the twenty-seven-year-old widow of the Duke of Buckingham, Katherine Woodville. You have to feel a bit sorry for Katherine, sister of Queen Elizabeth Woodville. She was first married at the age of seven to a 10-year-old boy, and now to a man twice her age.

Jasper was not the only recipient of a new title. Edward Courtenay, a staunch Lancastrian, received the earldom of Devon, while Thomas Stanley was made Earl of Derby and Constable of England. One man who did not receive a peerage, nor much else in the way of reward, was Lord Stanley's brother, Sir William. Had it not been for him then Henry would most likely have perished on the field of Bosworth. Yet William Stanley was overlooked and merely retained the offices he had held under Richard – and even those he had to ask for. For such an ambitious man, that might well rankle in the years to come.

On Sunday 30 October, Henry was crowned king with much ceremony. Prominent in this lavish state occasion were the usual suspects: Jasper Tudor, Thomas Stanley and John de Vere.

In November, Henry met his first parliament and asserted his right to be king both by inheritance and God's verdict in battle. Parliament, no doubt weary of such matters, simply ignored all the rival claim nonsense and just declared that Henry was king. He insisted that his reign was backdated to the day before Bosworth – 21 August – so that those who fought against him might be seen in law as traitors. This was not a very popular decision, since most of those who supported Richard at Bosworth did so in good faith, believing him to be their anointed monarch. If such matters could be changed after the fact, then where would it all end? In addition, all Crown lands granted since 1455 were to be taken back – though, for obvious reasons, there was a very long list of exceptions.

There was, however, one piece of the royal jigsaw missing: where was the new queen? Had Henry not sworn an oath to marry the heiress of Edward IV, Elizabeth of York? Yet there was no queen, and some of Henry's Yorkist supporters were most disgruntled about it, especially since all the pageantry they saw seemed to show the old Beaufort symbol of a portcullis, the red rose of Lancaster and the Welsh dragon of Tudor. Quite reasonably they wondered: where was the white rose of York?

There are several issues here, the main one being Henry's reluctance to imply that his crown depended in any way on Elizabeth's Yorkist claim. So while a marriage might heal some old wounds, it was not to be the basis of Henry's kingship. There was also a legal impediment yet to be removed. Richard III's act of Titulus Regulus had – among other things – declared all Edward IV's children to be illegitimate. This needed to be repealed and Henry left parliament in no doubt that repeal was only the half of it. The act 'was to be void, annulled, repealed... burnt and utterly destroyed.' We can deduce that he didn't like it very much...

By the time, the House of Commons eventually petitioned Henry to marry Elizabeth in December 1485, negotiations were already underway to remove another obstacle to the marriage: the Pope needed to grant a dispensation.

The papal dispensation was not finally granted until March 1486, but Henry married Elizabeth in mid-January. After all the delay, the sudden haste might perhaps be explained by the birth of his first son only eight months later. Elizabeth would not be crowned queen, however, until November 1487.

What Next?

Even after the king's marriage to a Yorkist heiress, there were still a few Yorkists who presented a genuine and immediate threat to Henry's regime: men such as Lord Francis Lovell, who had been a long-time friend and loyal supporter of Richard III. As Richard's Lord Chamberlain and close confidant, he was inextricably linked with the Ricardian regime. After Bosworth, Lovell and Humphrey Stafford fled to seek sanctuary in Colchester, where they remained for some months. But in April 1486, the two men escaped with the intention of raising a revolt against the new king. Francis Lovell headed north to stir up trouble in Yorkshire, where support for Richard had been strong, while Stafford joined with his brother Thomas to raise a rebellion in Worcestershire.

By April 1486, Henry himself was already on a trip north, keen to stamp his authority on what he expected to be a difficult region to control. In the end, Henry's mere arrival in York on 23 April was enough to scatter the very limited force that Lovell had managed to scrape together. Since Northumberland greeted the king upon his arrival in York, it was clear that a rebellion would not have any Percy backing. Without it, there was no chance of success.

When Jasper Tudor rode out with a handful of pardons, even some prominent gentry families who had been close to Richard, like the Conyers, the Metcalfes and the Huddlestones, had had enough. Seeing no point in further resistance, they accepted their pardons and went home. After all, who would these dyed-in-the-wool Neville men be fighting for now? The old Earl of Warwick was long dead and his two Neville daughters as well. Were they prepared to fight and die to see one of Richard's nephews on the throne? Clarence's son, Edward, might have inherited the Warwick title, but he was a mere shadow of a youth, and John de la Pole, Earl of Lincoln – what was he to those northern Neville gentry? Where the likes of Conyers and Metcalfe feared to tread, many others too were inclined to hold back and accept the new king. Only a few remaining diehards, like Lovell, fled abroad.

But what of the Stafford brothers? Well, their attempt at rebellion collapsed just as easily. They then tried to take sanctuary again, this time at Culham near Abingdon, but Henry wasn't having that a second time. In a scene reminiscent of Edward IV's actions at Tewkesbury, the right of sanctuary was ignored and the conspirators were dragged out. Though the rest were pardoned, Humphrey Stafford was executed because an example had to be made.

Overall, Henry must have been very satisfied with the ease of his triumph over a couple of significant rebels and, with his most prominent rival claimant, Edward, Earl of Warwick, in his pocket, Henry could at last rest easy. Er, well, not quite...

Chapter 44

Trouble in Ireland

THE FAILURE OF the Staffords and Francis Lovell to galvanise Yorkist support against the new Tudor king did not mean that any attempt to unseat Henry was doomed to failure. Henry himself knew that all too well. As ever, hindsight affords us the luxury of knowing that all attempts failed, but folk of the time – especially the key political players – could be forgiven for thinking that perhaps another king was only just around the corner. We must therefore put ourselves in their shoes to grasp why they did what they did.

Some Yorkist supporters believed – and I can understand why – that the revolts failed because the rebels had not been able to rally around an actual Yorkist prince. Clearly, the new king had possession of the most obvious Yorkist heir, Edward, Earl of Warwick, son of George, Duke of Clarence. It would be difficult therefore for the young earl to be put at the head of a rebel army. But there were other possible claimants, notably a plethora of de la Pole brothers, the sons of Richard III's sister Elizabeth, Duchess of Suffolk. The eldest of these, John, Earl of Lincoln, had been named heir by Richard III, but had made his peace with Henry VII after Bosworth, as did his brother, Edmund de la Pole. But how long would these two Yorkist relatives remain loyal – would they be tempted by the prospect of royal power?

What we can say is that there were not hordes of people urging them to lead a rebellion, nor did they seem to attract a great deal of personal support. We can assume this because when John, Earl of Lincoln did eventually rebel, it was not to press his own claim, which is a bit of a disappointment for us all really, because otherwise, we might have had a second King John.

But I digress. What Lincoln did do was attempt to put on the throne a 10-year-old Oxford boy: a commoner who – it was claimed – was the real Edward, Earl of Warwick. His actual name was Lambert Simnel, but in May 1487 he was crowned King Edward VI in Dublin in Ireland. Now, of course John, Earl of Lincoln, must have been very well aware that the real Edward, Earl of Warwick, was under close supervision in the Tower of London. So what on earth was going on, because this sounds crazy even by War of the Roses standards.

Trouble in Ireland

In order to explain, we need to take a diversion and look into what was going on in Ireland in this period. To do that, we have to go back forty years – now don't panic because we're not going back there for long.

Back in 1447 our old friend Richard, Duke of York – the architect of the Yorkist bid for the English throne – was appointed as the king's lieutenant in Ireland. At the time, Henry VI and his advisers intended for York to be banished from the main arena of power – to be side-lined and made irrelevant in English politics. This plan backfired spectacularly because what York achieved in Ireland was the exact opposite: he established a significant and lasting power base there. In fact, he already had a connection with Ireland as the Earl of Ulster.

The most powerful men in Ireland were the Anglo-Irish lords – men who had their lands and titles from the English king – and the English king was very rarely in Ireland, which was why he was represented by a lieutenant. So when York was lieutenant, he was increasingly acting in his own interests rather than those of Henry VI, and he was thus able to make Ireland a Yorkist stronghold – a place of refuge and a source of support.

During the late 1440s and 1450s, York gained the personal support of many of the key Irish lords, in particular Gerald Fitzgerald, Earl of Kildare. The support of these lords when York's fortunes were at a low ebb in 1459 was undoubtedly helpful to him, but it meant that the Irish lords were certain to want something in return – something he was in no position to refuse. What they wanted was the virtual independence of Ireland from English rule. Thus, when York's son Edward IV became king in 1461, he was in an awkward position. The Anglo-Irish lords expected to be given more or less a free hand in Ireland. Edward's attempt to re-establish royal control by the appointment of the brutal John Tiptoft, Earl of Worcester, as his new lieutenant, did little more than alienate some of the Irish lords.

By the 1470s, Edward IV had stopped worrying too much about Ireland and left it very much under the control of the local man, the Earl of Kildare. Richard III, during his brief tenure as king, was also not in a position to reassert royal control of Ireland. In 1485 the new King Henry VII, despite his hard core of Yorkist supporters, emphasised his Lancastrian descent. This gave Kildare and his fellow lords in Ireland a decision to make: should they cut all ties with York and support the new king, or should they emphasise their Yorkist connections – which had bought them some independence – and attempt to remove the Lancastrian king?

In 1486 the lords decided to throw in their lot with the disaffected elements of the House of York and, by doing so, hoped to keep their control over Ireland. Edward, Earl of Warwick, had a special appeal to the Irish because his father, Clarence, had been born in Dublin. Thus the lords saw Clarence's heir as 'one of their own.'

However, the boy they crowned wasn't Warwick: he was an imposter. He had been trained up by a priest, Richard Simons, but it seems unlikely that Simons woke up one day and off his own bat decided to train up an imposter to the English throne.

John de la Pole, Earl of Lincoln, must have been involved early on. The first Henry seems to have heard of it was in January 1487 and even a month later he clearly had no inkling that Lincoln was involved, because the earl was at a council meeting at which the plot was discussed. Henry responded to the rumours by parading the real Earl of Warwick through the streets of London – though who among the common people would have slightest idea what Warwick actually looked like?

Not long after, Lincoln fled to Flanders to join Francis Lovell and seek support from that eternal Yorkist optimist, Richard III's sister Margaret of Burgundy. Consequently, throughout April 1487, Henry expected an attack to be launched from Burgundy upon East Anglia, or perhaps Essex. In that region the Earl of Oxford's loyalty was beyond doubt, but what about Lincoln's father, the Duke of Suffolk? Though Suffolk was not a man likely to rebel against anyone, it would surely have put him in a difficult position. And then there was Thomas Grey, Marquess of Dorset, who had shown himself to be untrustworthy in the past. Henry arrested Dorset just in case and I can't say I blame him.

Nevertheless, the anticipated attack in the east never materialised because Lincoln and Lovell went to Ireland instead, assisted by the Duchess of Burgundy, who provided a couple of thousand German mercenaries. Their arrival must have given Kildare and his fellow Irish lords much encouragement, which is why they went on to crown Simnel as Edward VI and to provide soldiers for an invasion force.

Henry waited at Kenilworth, knowing that the invasion, since it was coming from Ireland, must now come on the west coast. Sure enough, by 4 June 1487, Lincoln and his allies landed at Furness in Lancashire. They were attempting to do to Henry VII what he had done to Richard III: in other words, arrive with only a small army and gather more support en route from disaffected supporters of Richard III, before forcing a showdown with the king in battle.

Once he heard of the landing, King Henry moved to Nottingham to wait for the Stanleys to join him and to see which way Lincoln would go. Lincoln crossed the Pennines into Yorkshire where he hoped to swell his army considerably, then he headed south towards Newark.

On 14 June Lord Strange – you'll remember that he was Thomas Stanley's eldest son – joined Henry at Nottingham with a large army. Also present were at least three earls, including Oxford who would command Henry's vanguard. Later acts of attainder suggest that no earls – apart from Lincoln himself – were in the rebel ranks.

Henry, confident of his support, advanced towards the rebels and the two armies met near Stoke on 16 June. Little is known about the battle itself – no surprise there – but it does appear that beyond those men the rebels brought with them, they received minimal support in England – and small wonder, less than two years after Bosworth.

It seems likely that only a small part of Henry's army was involved in the actual battle and a few historians have commented that perhaps some were waiting to see how the battle went – as at Bosworth – but that seems unlikely. Nearer the mark is the fact that he simply did not need to use the rest of his army because the rebels, though determined, were simply too heavily outnumbered. The rebel ringleaders were killed including John de la Pole, Earl of Lincoln, and possibly Francis Lovell. Whether Lovell was killed or not, nothing more was ever heard of him. The boy, Lambert Simnel, was put to work in the royal kitchen, presumably to emphasise his common origins. But since he ended up as the king's falconer, I suppose you could say that he did alright out of the whole fiasco – unlike his mentor, the priest, Richard Simons, who was imprisoned for life.

So, what did this little episode mean in the context of Henry's reign? Since it did not come close to unseating the king, you could argue that it was an abject failure, which was dealt with effectively by the king. However, I'm sure it would have had a serious impact upon Henry himself who, in the period leading up to Bosworth, had lived through the experience from the opposite point of view. He knew very well that such madcap schemes could succeed if the conditions were right.

It must have rocked Henry to know that a lord sitting within his own council had secretly been plotting against him. A stray arrow was all that was needed to end a dynasty. The fact that there was no repeat of Bosworth in 1487 was not because Henry VII was a popular king – he wasn't really – but more because of the policies he put into effect to prevent such an event occurring again. The Wars of the Roses did not end by accident, but because of a combination of factors – one of which was how Henry ruled his barons.

Let's remember that Henry VII was probably the least experienced king England had ever seen. Even Henry VI knew a lot in theory about kingship and government; he was just useless at doing it. Henry Tudor had not even run a baronial estate, let alone a kingdom. But unlike his earlier namesake, Henry was smart – and he became a smart king.

So what did the smart king do next? Well, in his next parliament in November 1487, the rebels were attainted – no big deal there, since rebels nearly always were. Next, an act was passed to give certain members of the king's council special powers to investigate and deal with anyone acting against the king or stirring up unrest. He then went ahead to plan the coronation of his Yorkist queen, who had been the mother of his heir for over a year. It was time to formalise the union with York.

Since the most recent threat had been launched from Ireland, where his lords were clearly hostile to their king, it also made sense to try to bring Ireland back under royal control – sensible perhaps, but in reality far from easy.

Henry asked the Pope to excommunicate the Irish bishops who had been involved in crowning Simnel and by January 1488 his request had been granted. He then had to bring to heel the rebel Irish lords – which was pretty much all of them. In June 1488, Henry sent a trusted member of the royal household to Ireland.

Lest there be any confusion here, a member of the household did not mean a valet or lavatory attendant. The men of the royal household were trusted knights and squires upon whose personal loyalty the king could utterly depend. Remember how many of Edward IV's household men had risked everything to actively oppose

Richard III's takeover in 1483. Many, in the end, had joined Henry in exile. In Richard III's last stand at Bosworth, it was his own household knights who fought to the end by his side.

So Henry sent one of his trusted household men, Sir Richard Edgecombe, to Ireland with 500 men. His task was to offer pardons to those who would submit and take an oath of loyalty to Henry, and to arrest those who would not. By the end of July, Edgecombe was able to return to England with Ireland loyal once again – at least in theory. Gerald Fitzgerald, the all-powerful Earl of Kildare, decided to make his peace with the king, and the rest of the lords followed his lead. What did that mean exactly? It meant that Kildare remained the king's deputy in Ireland and acknowledged allegiance to the new king. Despite his treason, normal service was resumed.

Inevitably, Henry's security in the future would also depend on his relations with neighbouring powers. He was acutely aware how much his own bid for the throne owed to Brittany and France. Yet he found himself in an awkward position with a debt to both states. France, as ever, was keen to annex the two significant duchies on its borders, Brittany and Burgundy. While Henry was no friend to Burgundy – as Margaret's support for the Simnel rebellion shows – he was not keen to see Brittany absorbed into France. Not only had Brittany kept him from harm for years, but clearly the acquisition of Brittany would make France much more powerful. Though France was an ally at that time, what if it stopped being an ally? If he fell out with France, which had supported him against Richard III, what was to stop France supporting a rival against him? And possession of the Breton ports would make France an even greater threat to England.

Thus diplomacy was a bit tricky and, in the end, most of what Henry attempted was pretty half-hearted. In 1489 he promised to support Brittany against France, but his resources to do so were so meagre that before he managed much support, the Breton cause was already lost and the heiress of Brittany, conceding defeat, married the king of France, Charles VIII.

So that was that. Henry made a significant treaty with Spain in 1489 which was directed at France and included the suggestion of a marriage alliance between the two countries in the future. More importantly though, from Henry's immediate point of view, it agreed that neither country would aid the rebels of the other.

It is perhaps worth noting that one unintended consequence of Henry trying to raise tax revenue so that he could afford to support Brittany was the death of the Earl of Northumberland in April 1489. The earl – not exactly a popular man at the best of times – was attacked and killed in Yorkshire, partly because of resentment of the additional taxes. Given his precarious position, Henry was obliged to punish the perpetrators and did so, though one managed to flee and – like all the other disaffected English exiles – ended up at the court of Margaret, Duchess of Burgundy.

By the end of 1490, it had been a dodgy couple of years for Henry but he had survived and could at least hope for better news in the future. It won't surprise you to hear, however, that he didn't get any…

Chapter 45

Perkin Warbeck

IN 1487 HENRY had seen off the threat of a Yorkist pretender to the throne – except that, as we have seen, Lambert Simnel had no royal blood in his veins because he was an imposter. Henry must have thought: phew, got away with that one – an imposter? That's pretty unusual, just as well they don't come along very often. But of course, rather like infrequent buses, there's always that one in a million chance that two will come along in quick succession. And sure enough, in the autumn of 1491, another imposter popped up in Ireland, which clearly must still have seemed to be a strong Yorkist base.

I am, of course, referring to a chap called Perkin Warbeck, who appeared in County Cork sometime in October or November 1491, posing as the younger of Edward IV's sons, Richard, Duke of York – one of the so-called 'princes in the Tower'. Like his elder brother, Edward V, young Richard was assumed to be dead, though no one could actually confirm that – at least as far as we know.

So where did this Perkin Warbeck come from? There is some evidence that he was employed by Sir Edward Brampton – a Yorkist lately pardoned by Henry VII. Brampton is one of the most colourful and bizarre characters of the whole period and his story is well worth exploring for its own sake. Brampton picked up the teenage Perkin Warbeck in the Netherlands and one suggestion is that he was used as a sort of male model since his master was involved in the cloth trade. Anyway, Brampton knew the Yorkist kings pretty well and most likely shared a thousand anecdotes about them. Was it him who first put the idea in young Perkin's head? Did he say one day: 'My goodness, you're the spitting image of Richard, Duke of York?' We'll never know, but we do know that, by the age of seventeen, Warbeck had arrived in Cork on a Breton silk merchant's ship. That was appropriate since he was originally the son of a boatman from Tournai in France.

After his arrival in Cork, we are told that the leading citizens of the town were struck by the youth's royal bearing and suggested he might be the Earl of Warwick, but no one was falling for that old chestnut, so the smart money went instead on the idea that he was Richard, Duke of York. It is worth pointing out that absolutely no one in Cork – or anywhere else really – would have had the faintest idea what Prince Richard looked like as a child, let alone how he would look as a young man.

You might suspect that someone of note had to be the instigator of the deception, but however unlikely it seems now, a new pretender was born and gradually seemed to grow into the role. Because he was older than Simnel, Warbeck clearly presented a more plausible alternative king, though his story was, in the end, that of a rather naïve man being used for the purposes of several European rulers.

In Ireland, Warbeck received some early support from one of the Anglo-Irish lords, the Earl of Desmond, and perhaps the Earl of Kildare was interested too, though he later denied it. Overall, the Irish lords gave Warbeck only lukewarm support – perhaps it was a case of once bitten, twice shy. By early 1492 Warbeck had started looking for support elsewhere, notably from James IV of Scotland. Soon he received an invitation from the French king, Charles VIII, who received him in 1492 as a prince.

Did Charles VIII actually believe that Perkin was the long-lost duke of York? I suspect that the French king didn't really care either way; what he wanted to do was put pressure on Henry VII. In October 1492, Henry had finally made good on his commitment to assist Anne of Brittany against France, but it was too late, since Brittany had already capitulated. Nonetheless, his invasion of France in October 1492 was massive – thousands of men in hundreds of ships sailed to Boulogne under the command of the Earl of Oxford.

Bear in mind that war with France was pretty much expected of every new king and, though Henry was not exactly a warrior king, making a genuine show of force against France boosted his image. But it was also very expensive, and when Henry withdrew his forces a month later, having exacted payment from Charles VIII to do so, there was a sense of anti-climax very similar to that felt when Edward IV's invasion ended in a similar fashion in 1475. Henry proceeded to make a treaty with France in November 1492 – the treaty of Etaples – in which Charles and Henry agreed, among other things, not to support each other's enemies.

Obliged to leave France, Warbeck then turned up in neighbouring Flanders – part of the Duchy of Burgundy – where the duchess, Edward IV's sister Margaret, accepted him as her nephew. At least it was possible that she had actually seen Prince Richard on her last visit to England in 1480 when he must have been about seven years old. It's surely doubtful that she would have seen a great deal of the boy, however, and I know from decades of teaching adolescents that by eighteen a boy's appearance can change so radically as to be almost unrecognisable from the seven-year-old he once was.

Whether Margaret was genuinely taken in or not, we'll never know; but she did school Warbeck about young Richard's childhood and obviously provided him with other family background. Margaret was not the ruler of Burgundy, but she had always been close to her step-daughter, Mary, who was. Mary had married Maximilian of Austria and, after Mary's untimely death, their son became Philip IV of Burgundy. Because Philip was still young, his father, Maximilian – fast becoming a major player in European diplomacy – directed Burgundian affairs. Like the

French king, Maximilian was interested to see how useful Warbeck might be. Maximilian, who hoped to create an alliance of powers to limit French expansion, was incensed that Henry had made peace so easily with France. Perhaps, if Henry was not willing to join the coalition against France, a new ruler might be.

Up to this point, although Henry was obviously aware of the existence of a young man claiming to be his brother-in-law, he had no idea who he actually was. Word of the apparent survival of Richard, Duke of York, spread like wildfire. Men who had committed to Henry's cause in the belief that the sons of Edward IV were dead, now found themselves rather conflicted. If this man truly was the heir of Edward IV, then he was clearly their rightful king.

For Henry, Warbeck was much more difficult to counter than Simnel because he could not display the dead Richard, Duke of York, and nor could he provide confirmation of Richard's death. Did he even begin to wonder if Warbeck was for real? In the end, in July 1493, the king's spies determined who Perkin Warbeck actually was. Henry was so incensed by the fact that Margaret of Burgundy had recognised Warbeck as her nephew that he broke off all English trade with Flanders – which was a bold step, since it was a very important area of English trade.

In November 1493, Perkin met Maximilian, who received him as the rightful king of England and by the summer of 1494 he was in Flanders sporting a white rose and the coat of arms of Richard IV. Meanwhile, he was trying to spread his influence even more widely and wrote to other monarchs, such as Queen Isabella of Castile, to seek their support. Despite Henry's best diplomatic efforts, he was finding it hard to undermine the belief that Edward IV's heir existed.

Recently some so-called 'new' evidence has come to light, which claims to support the idea that Perkin really was the son of Edward IV. In my view all the evidence does is tell us what we already knew – Maximilian and Margaret of Burgundy supported Perkin as Richard IV. Though it suggests that both might have believed him, it ignores the fact that Maximilian did not care whether he was really Richard or not. All he was concerned with was exerting pressure upon Henry VII and Perkin was useful in that regard.

As long as Warbeck was under the protection of a foreign power, it was very difficult for Henry to get to grips with him; but what he could do was try to make it difficult for the pretender to gain any support within his own kingdom. His initial response to Warbeck's appearance in Ireland had been to despatch a small force to drive the pretender out and by June 1492 the Earl of Kildare had been removed from the office of royal deputy in Ireland. Nonetheless, Ireland remained a real concern and by late 1494, when Warbeck appeared more of a threat, Henry committed to effecting genuine change in Ireland. He sent Sir Edward Poynings with about 700 men. It was not, however, a quick fix, and Poynings did not leave Ireland until a year later, in December 1495, by which time Ireland was no longer a viable base for a Yorkist invasion.

Henry's spies were also hard at work trying to winkle out Warbeck's sympathisers in England. Many were suspected and watched closely in an atmosphere reminiscent of Richard III's last year in power. Some plotters were identified and later attainted in the parliament of 1495. By far the most significant plotter was Sir William Stanley – I'm sure you've not forgotten him. He was Henry's own chamberlain and the man who more than any other had intervened at Bosworth to save Henry's life and cause.

Perhaps it was not that surprising that a man who had been so committed to the Yorkist cause in the past, and who felt that he had never been sufficiently rewarded by Henry, might consider alternatives. His contact with Perkin Warbeck began in March 1493 when he sent a representative to meet him in Flanders. As it turned out, his representative, Sir Robert Clifford, was either a royal agent from the outset, or soon decided to become one. It was his evidence which condemned Stanley, and the demise of Stanley early in 1495 effectively killed off the plot.

The advantage Henry had over his predecessor was that he already had two healthy male heirs in princes Arthur and Henry. In November he made great show of this by parading his 3-year-old second son through London before bestowing the dukedom of York upon him on 1 November. In a flurry of ceremony he was telling the world that here was the true Duke of York, his son Henry. Did it make much difference to what ordinary folk believed? Who knows, but it is fair to say that support for Warbeck within England never appeared more than lukewarm at best. Thus, even when Warbeck landed in Kent to raise his standard in July 1495, with a little support from Margaret and Maximilian, the escapade was an abject failure.

When even the folk of Kent, where many a rebellion had found some support, were unwilling to risk all for Perkin Warbeck, he must have known he was in trouble. The inexperienced Warbeck panicked, deserting those few who had turned up for him, and fled to Ireland again. But Edward Poynings was still there, and thus Warbeck found no support.

A desperate man now, Warbeck travelled to Scotland where he met with James IV in November 1495. For King James – like all the other monarchs – Warbeck was a useful bargaining chip in his relations with Henry VII. Did James ever believe that he had the real Richard IV in Scotland? Possibly for a while he convinced himself – after all, let's not forget that Margaret of Burgundy had already accepted Warbeck, and surely she was better placed than most to know?

The situation within Scotland was far from stable and young James IV had been crowned after a virtual civil war with his father, James III, who had been well-disposed towards Henry VII. Since many leading Scots favoured a more hostile relationship with England, James IV had to tread carefully if he was to retain his own Scottish crown. Giving aid to a Yorkist rebel therefore seemed like to good plan to unite the Scots behind him. So James IV accepted Warbeck as the real Richard, Duke of York, and even arranged a favourable marriage for him to a royal relative. For Henry VII, having Perkin Warbeck in Flanders was one thing, but having him just across the border in Scotland was quite another. There he presented a much more serious threat, since he was so close to any possible lingering Yorkist support in the north.

All the while, as we have seen, there was an international element to this whole story. Several European powers were attempting to balance the growing power of France by establishing an alliance against it. Maximilian and the Spanish monarchs, Ferdinand and Isabella, were keen to get England on board. A marriage alliance had already been proposed between Henry's eldest son and heir Arthur, and Katharine of Aragon, daughter of Ferdinand and Isabella.

How, you might ask, does all that tie in to Perkin Warbeck's activities in Scotland? Well, the Spanish monarchs were worried that Henry's Tudor regime was under threat and, if it was, the last thing they wanted to do was marry their valuable daughter off to a king who was shortly going to lose his throne. The genuine threat posed by Warbeck in Scotland, which, as it happened, was a long-time ally of France, seriously undermined Henry's negotiating position. Thus all the major powers were watching to see how Henry would handle the impending crisis.

By September 1496, the diplomats were working overtime because several actions were in play. Firstly, as I've said, there were the negotiations for a Spanish marriage. However, there was another marriage proposal being considered at the same time: between James IV of Scotland and Henry VII's daughter Margaret. Even while those negotiations were going on, however, James was preparing to launch an invasion across the border to support Perkin Warbeck in his bid for the English throne, and Henry was preparing to counter it.

Confused? Basically, James IV had two irons in the fire: if the Warbeck invasion came to nothing, he could revert to a policy of peace and rapprochement with England by proceeding with the marriage.

In September 1496, the Scots, bolstered by a small contingent from Margaret of Burgundy, crossed the border under the banner of Richard IV of England. To call this an invasion would be a serious breach of the English language for, in essence, it was little more than a border raid. A couple of towers were captured, land was laid waste and, having penetrated less than five miles into England, the Scots withdrew. It was a disaster for Warbeck but a welcome relief for Henry. On 1 October 1496, on the back of the Scottish defeat, the Spanish marriage between Arthur and Katharine was agreed.

However, Henry could not assume that the threat was over. Perkin Warbeck was still at large and nominally supported by both Scotland and Burgundy. There was no guarantee that he would not try again. As a result, Henry demanded high taxation from his parliament in January 1497 to finance a military effort in the north. In the months that followed, in the first half of 1497, no further attacks came from Warbeck, but serious trouble of a different sort was heading Henry's way from an entirely opposite direction...

Chapter 46

The Spectre of the White Rose

HAVING THWARTED THE threat of Perkin Warbeck on his Scottish border – at least for the time being – Henry VII's attention was dragged back to the rest of his kingdom by a catastrophic event in the south. The heavy taxation raised in January had hit many folk hard and, in particular, those in faraway Cornwall were extremely angry that they were required to pay for a war from which they expected to get no benefit at all.

It is difficult to comprehend now how the various far-flung regions of the kingdom saw themselves in the late fifteenth century. Just as Wales and Ireland had distinct identities which did not always chime with the wishes of the English king, so we have already seen that other areas distant from London – such as the north – could present problems for central government. In the far south-west, Cornwall was exactly such a place. Fiercely independent, the Cornish always resented royal interference in their affairs and, in 1497, Henry's taxation in Cornwall became a serious bone of contention.

A large number of Cornishmen – possibly as many as 15,000 – showed their displeasure by marching to London. Let's face it, it was a long way from Cornwall to London, so they must have been pretty fired up. The leaders included an outspoken lawyer who argued that the Cornish should not have to pay for Henry's war on his northern border. It would be more appropriate, he suggested, for northerners to pay for their own protection. Henry became aware of the insurrection in May 1497 but was probably unsure how serious it was.

The Cornishmen did not see themselves as rebels and most certainly had no link to the Yorkist cause in general, nor Perkin Warbeck in particular. Nor were they soldiers, but mainly common men armed with only bows and working tools. For the most part they made their way peacefully across southern England and as a result gathered more support along the way. They persuaded Lord Audley – another man who felt undervalued by the king – to lead them. When they arrived in Kent, they intended to draw the king's attention to their grievance in the hope that he might dismiss the 'evil advisers', as they put it, who had persuaded him to implement the tax. As ever, advisers who argued for higher taxes tended to be branded 'evil'.

Henry arrived in London to find it in panic mode. Various bridges along the Thames were swiftly blocked – for example at Henley and Staines – to prevent the rebels from crossing to the north of the river, though there is no real evidence that they ever intended to do so. Queen Elizabeth and Prince Henry were sent to the safety of the Tower of London and the Lord Mayor organised the defence of London Bridge. Henry ordered Lord Daubeney, who was on his way north with an army for the Scottish border, to divert southwards to defend London and meet the rebels south of the capital at Blackheath. Meanwhile the Earl of Oxford was dispatched south to cut off the rebels' retreat.

It appears that the rebels might have offered to hand over their leaders in return for a pardon, but Henry rejected that. On 17 June Lord Daubeney attacked them and, after some initial hard fighting, routed the Cornish army. Perhaps 2,000 or so men were slaughtered. The ringleaders were captured in the field and executed once Henry had reassured himself that the revolt was completely unconnected to the Yorkist cause. The rest were allowed to leave with a pardon but those pardons came at a heavy financial price, which would ruin many Cornish families for generations to come – which, of course, was the intention. As an added bonus, the fines Henry imposed on the truculent Cornish would more than cover the expenses he incurred in suppressing the revolt.

With the Cornish revolt dealt with, Henry now needed to wrap up the whole Warbeck fiasco as quickly as possible, because the fact that 15,000 armed Cornishmen could march across England unopposed made his regime appear very vulnerable. In early July, he sent two senior bishops, of Durham and London, to negotiate with James IV for the surrender of Perkin Warbeck. As it happened, Warbeck had already left the court of James IV and an elaborate – for which, read hare-brained – scheme had been set in motion. James would launch a new attack on the northern border while Warbeck would make a landing at the opposite end of the country in disaffected Cornwall, which was clearly ripe for rebellion.

What could possibly go wrong with this cunning plan? Well, pretty much everything, as it turned out.

James IV launched his invasion in August 1497 and laid siege to Norham Castle in Northumberland. It did not go well. Thomas Howard, Earl of Surrey – Henry's commander in the north – advanced swiftly from Yorkshire with 20,000 men and forced the surprised James IV to retreat. After that, James was obliged to negotiate a truce with England.

Warbeck meanwhile, clearly in no hurry, decided to return to Cork at the end of July – where, as they say, his dream had begun. He expected to receive support from the Irish to improve his chances of success in Cornwall. Without any further information about Warbeck, that should be enough to convince you that he was an unrealistic fool. Bear in mind that by then Henry's agent, Sir Edward Poynings, had already calmed affairs in Ireland and Warbeck was lucky to escape with his life, never mind any significant Irish support. Undeterred, he landed on the Cornish coast at Whitesand Bay on 7 September 1497 with perhaps a hundred supporters. This was only a few months after the surviving Cornish rebels had arrived home clutching their expensive pardons. How keen would they be to risk all in rebellion again?

Henry knew very well that Warbeck was on his way – especially since four of his own ships had followed the pretender all the way to Cornwall. Across the country, Henry had all bases covered with loyal commanders at every possible trouble-spot. Although, never forget that Richard III felt just the same about his preparations in 1485...

Anyway, ever the optimist, Warbeck marched to Bodmin where he was declared Richard IV and persuaded as many as 3,000 men to support him. Within ten days of landing, Warbeck arrived at Exeter, the most important town in the south-west, which was held for Henry by the Earl of Devon. Some of Warbeck's men forced their way through the east gate, but were repelled during close hand-to-hand fighting.

After that the rebels gave up and turned towards Taunton instead, but when Warbeck learned that Lord Daubeney's royal army was only twenty miles away at Glastonbury, he did what he had done several times before in his career: he panicked and during the night escaped, hoping to find a ship in one of the southern ports. When that appeared impossible he was forced to take sanctuary at Beaulieu Abbey near Southampton. But even then, since many folk knew he was there, he decided to surrender to Henry and hope for mercy rather than wait for capture.

Warbeck met Henry at Taunton on 5 October and was sent, with his Scottish wife, to London while Henry basked in the glow of success. It must have been a huge relief to Henry to finally nail Warbeck, who had been a thorn in his side for many years.

By the end of November, Warbeck had confessed to being an imposter, though of course since he was Flemish he could not really be charged with treason. Henry made sure the deception was well known and dealt leniently with him because it helped to minimise his importance. Rather than an actual Yorkist claimant to the throne, Warbeck was presented as just another out-of-luck loser. Thus Warbeck gave his word not to flee and Henry allowed him simply to reside at court. His wife, Lady Catherine Gordon, was placed within the orbit of Queen Elizabeth.

But, oh dear, Warbeck being Warbeck, he soon tired of being a nobody at Henry's court and in June 1498 he did a runner. Needless to say, he was easily caught and this time Henry's clemency had run out. Warbeck was sent to the Tower.

Despite some fanciful suggestions that Warbeck really was Richard, Duke of York, all along, I can see no reason to doubt Warbeck's confession; nor the letter he wrote around the same time to his real mother, telling her all about his exploits and enquiring whether she might have any spare cash. For me, this sums him up: he was a con man – and a pretty good con man too. Like most successful con men, he persuaded others by his charm and wit, but he lacked the substance to amount to any more than that.

It has always seemed to me that if Henry believed that there was any possibility that Perkin Warbeck actually was Richard of York, then surely the best person to judge was his queen, Elizabeth of York, who would have seen a great deal more of young Richard than Margaret of Burgundy. It's also possible that Henry was already certain of Richard's death but could not prove it.

I have said before that, for me, there was absolutely no possibility of Elizabeth Woodville supporting the claim of Henry Tudor in 1483 if there was even the slightest chance that one of her boy princes was still alive.

Novelists and others have suggested that young Richard was spared a grisly death in the Tower and somehow spirited away to safety – as if such things were simple or commonplace. I just don't believe it, because it was jolly tricky to get out of the Tower – and that neat segue brings me to the full stop at the end of Perkin Warbeck's sentence.

Warbeck was in the Tower along with the real Edward, Earl of Warwick, until 1499 when apparently the two young men decided to try to escape – or at least, so we are told. There was a conspiracy by several Londoners to free them, but there is a whiff of a frame-up in that story. Though neither man actually presented a genuine threat to Henry in 1499, both were inconvenient prisoners for him – especially as the arrangements for the much-awaited Spanish marriage continued slowly. Would it not be a happy coincidence if the two prisoners made a noose for their own necks? We'll never know for sure, but Warbeck was certainly foolish enough to try to escape.

And what of his fellow inmate, Edward, Earl of Warwick? Much has been made of some flimsy evidence that he was a simpleton, but I suspect that, having spent most of his life under house arrest, he was probably just not very worldly wise. A charmer like Warbeck had convinced plenty of people who were far from simple to support him, so we should not dismiss Warwick's intellect so easily. I do wonder whether Warwick, after so many years of not living a normal life, simply said: 'to hell with it, I may as well try to escape; it's better than staying here for the rest of my days.'

The swift trial and execution of Warwick and Warbeck in November 1499 may have been the postscript to one tragic story, but sadly it was only the beginning of Tudor paranoia about possible rivals. Had previous kings adopted the same lethal approach as Henry and his successors, it's doubtful whether there would have been any royalty or nobility left at all. While Henry was by no means the first to use judicial murder against his opponents, he was the first to lay down the means by which his son, Henry VIII, could remove any potential – rather than actual – rivals merely on the suspicion that they might be a threat. Once you go down that road, it's truly impossible to stop, as Henry VIII discovered.

There is also an argument that executing Edward, Earl of Warwick, was the stupidest thing Henry VII could have done, because as long as the senior Yorkist claimant was alive, all other lesser claims could not be advanced. Once Warwick was dead, the poisoned chalice of York passed to the five surviving de la Pole brothers, the eldest of whom, Edmund, Earl of Suffolk, had thus far remained loyal to Henry. Suffolk clearly had a few thoughts about the throne as early as the summer of 1499 when he fled abroad for a time. Though he returned briefly, in 1501 he left once more, this time taking his younger brother Richard with him.

They went to the court of Maximilian, who had been angered by the execution of his protégé Warbeck. Henry imprisoned their brother William de la Pole in the Tower, where he remained for the remaining thirty-eight years of his life – though he had not made any attempt to rebel.

In his last decade, Henry's spirit – not to mention his legacy – took a serious bashing from events. In June 1500, his third son, Prince Edmund, died. Though the longed-for Spanish marriage finally took place in November 1501, by April 1502 the bridegroom, Prince Arthur – England's great hope – was dead. He was probably struck down by the sweating sickness. The king and queen were devastated by the news – it was one of the few moments when Henry's humanity showed through his armour of formality.

Aside from the sheer personal tragedy of Arthur's death, it also meant that the entire Tudor regime now hung by a single thread: the life of the king's second son, Prince Henry – a not terribly robust boy of ten. Some later writers saw in the sudden demise of Arthur and thus the Spanish match, a terrible symmetry – was Henry Tudor reaping what he'd sown when he killed the innocent Warwick? If God was indeed punishing Henry, He wasn't finished yet.

News that the queen was pregnant cheered everyone up, but shortly after her confinement began in February 1503 she died along with the daughter she bore. Henry, clearly utterly devastated by this new blow, retired alone, inconsolable, to Richmond and left the funeral arrangements to his mother, Margaret Beaufort. In the weeks after Elizabeth's death, Henry himself fell ill – perhaps he was even close to death. At Richmond, his mother organised everything with the help of his most loyal servants including Arthur Plantagenet, the late queen's half-brother, who proved himself to be both supportive and loyal. For many weeks the king was weak, but he survived. I think though that it would be fair to say that he never really recovered from the deaths of Elizabeth and Arthur in such quick succession – and truthfully, who would?

Now Henry had to find the strength to apply himself to rebuilding the Tudor future around Prince Henry – a son destined for the church until fate intervened, raised with his two sisters, and whom Henry knew very little about. Henry considered remarrying, but as the years passed it seemed that everything must depend upon Prince Henry.

What a deathly place the court of Henry VII must have been after Elizabeth's death. In August 1503 his elder daughter, Margaret, was finally married to the Scottish king, James IV so she too left the court. Henry, desperate to secure his dynasty against the Yorkist threat, stepped up his efforts to capture Edmund de la Pole, Earl of Suffolk. While he did so, his spies winkled out anyone who might conceivably have a connection to any scheme to put Suffolk on the throne. Eventually, in 1506, chance intervened to deliver the earl into Henry's hands, but even with Suffolk in the Tower, his younger brother Richard de la Pole was still at large. The spectre of the white rose of York hung over Henry until the day he died in 1509, as it was to haunt his son throughout his reign.

Part Six
Conclusion

AFTER THE MANY pages I have spent describing, and attempting to explain, the series of crises which took place during the second half of the fifteenth century, I hope I have managed to provide some insight into the causes and the nature of the Wars of the Roses.

Perhaps because they are commonly referred to by that single, all-embracing title, the Wars of the Roses appear, at a superficial level, to be one event. As we have seen, they were most certainly not. Though I quite like the title, even I have to admit that it is wholly misleading. Since the wars have nothing much to do with roses, there has been an attempt in recent years to change the name of the conflict to 'The Cousins War'. For me this is a folly and no less misleading, since countless medieval – and even some relatively modern – wars were fought between 'cousins'. However inappropriate the name is, it has stuck for a long time and remains the easiest way to identify the subject.

In any case, as we have seen, the events of the period should not be lumped together as if they were part of some ongoing struggle for the throne. Clearly, while a claim to the throne might have provided a vehicle for opposition, it was not a requirement. Why then has the period been regarded as a struggle for the crown between the two noble houses of York and Lancaster? Well, I suppose have to blame the Tudors for that, at least in part – or more particularly, Edward Hall. It was in Hall's sixteenth-century chronicle that the events were presented for the first time as a coherent story. It was not though, a deliberate attempt to brainwash the population – then or now. It was merely a reflection of what many folk believed after decades of relative political peace under Henry VIII.

The fifteenth century was not the first time that a medieval English king was deposed. It had happened with Edward II in the 1320s and again at the end of that tumultuous fourteenth century with Richard II. In both instances, the personality of the king was relevant, but more important was that both those kings had lost the confidence of a significant number of their leading noble subjects. Only when that happened was it possible to overthrow a king.

In the 1440s Richard, Duke of York, believed that he had an excellent claim to the throne but he did not attempt to overthrow King Henry VI. Why? Because not a single lord would have supported him. Also, York was relatively content as long as he was given a role which he believed reflected his position as the senior peer of the realm. Until the rise of Edmund Beaufort, Duke of Somerset, York was the obvious candidate to succeed to the throne if Henry VI should die childless.

The emergence of a rival to York, both as England's leading nobleman and as potential successor to the king, changed how he regarded his position. But that did not happen overnight; York's opposition began around 1450, but he did not openly seek the throne until 1460 – and even then he only succeeded after Henry VI died.

The difference between 1450 and 1460 was that, during that decade, York found a few powerful barons to support him politically against the Beaufort faction. The emergence of two rival factions vying for control of Henry VI was what led to the main crisis of 1455–64. Some of the blame for that has to lie with Henry himself because, like Edward II and Richard II before him, he failed to manage his most powerful subjects effectively. Let's not pretend though that it was a simple task!

The second major crisis came about because the overweening Earl of Warwick, Richard Neville, was disgruntled about his waning influence over the first Yorkist king, Edward IV. Let's not blame Edward's choice of wife, or Clarence's vacillating loyalties, because without Warwick, there would have been no crisis in 1469–71. Yes, there were several royal claimants around, notably Henry VI himself, but I can't see any of them causing a problem for Edward IV without Warwick. He is known to history as the 'Kingmaker', which is ironic because he didn't actually make any kings. What he was spectacularly good at was *unmaking* kings. So, for me, Warwick was a largely destructive force, motivated by the need to protect his vast inheritance.

The third great crisis of the period arose – in some ways like the second – not out of some ongoing rift between York and Lancaster, but from division among the Yorkists themselves. Richard, Duke of Gloucester, despite his previous impeccable loyalty, felt insecure about his future under the new king, young Edward V. So seriously did his seizure of power divide the Yorkist faction that many preferred to support the unknown Henry Tudor rather than the Richard of Gloucester they thought they had known.

Whatever one thinks about Richard III, there is no doubt whatsoever that his rule polarised political opinion in England. The far too often discussed issue of whether or not he killed his brother's sons is, politically, a complete red herring – perhaps the greatest historical red herring of all time. Because, from summer 1483 onwards, it did not matter whether he was actually responsible for their deaths or not. The key factor was that enough of the politically aware classes believed either that he had killed them, or that he might have done. Their actions were founded upon belief not fact. Richard might have been innocent of the crime and has thus been slandered and misrepresented throughout history. But at the time, in the years 1483–5, it really did not matter.

Some have blamed Margaret Beaufort or Elizabeth Woodville – or both – for stirring up opposition to Richard in the months that followed his seizure of the throne. But we have only to see the speed and determination of the reaction from supporters of the late Edward IV at a local level to understand that, if the two women were active, then they were pushing at an open door. Important local knights and squires – especially in the south – risked all they had to oppose the new king. You don't do that on a whim. It was unprecedented and it reveals the level of suspicion and outrage that existed against Richard.

Even after the king put down the misfiring rebellion of October 1483, many significant men had decided to support Henry Tudor: a man about whom they knew nothing at all. Some went to join him in exile in Brittany, others kept their powder dry and joined him in August 1485, but still more, though they did not fight for him, did not fight for King Richard either.

Henry Tudor, more by luck than judgement, managed to defeat Richard III at Bosworth. Richard, Henry's leading opponent, was killed at Bosworth and had no surviving direct male heir. Though he had named his nephew, John de la Pole, as his heir, the latter did not immediately challenge Henry Tudor. After 1487 Henry had most trouble from rebels who were not actually Yorkists at all but imposters. Henry then managed to live just long enough for one of his sons to succeed as an adult.

By Henry VIII's reign, it seemed obvious to others, not just Hall, that by marrying the heiress of Edward IV, Henry VII had ended the political strife and unified the warring houses of York and Lancaster. But with hindsight, we can separate those two ideas, because the marriage of Henry Tudor with Elizabeth of York was not the reason that warfare ended. It merely marked the occasion with a symbolic ceremony. Henry Tudor's pledge to marry the heiress of York was important, but it did not create the schism which doomed the House of York. While the prospect of the marriage encouraged some Yorkists to throw their support behind Henry, the real division took place in the summer of 1483.

Nevertheless, the accession of Henry VIII was not as certain in 1509 as it appeared by the time he had ruled for several decades. Chance could still easily have reignited the political divisions of the time. Henry VII was acutely aware of the fragile legacy he was passing on which explains – though does not excuse – his paranoia towards the end. The paranoia exhibited by his son, however, had more to do with being a self-obsessed and cruel spoilt brat of a king rather than any genuine threat to his kingship.

But how much did the wars really affect the people of England, and what did ordinary folk think about the interminable circus of political musical chairs?

The warfare of the Wars of the Roses was often bloody because it was fought largely between massed ranks of armoured infantry knocking or carving lumps out of each other with fearsome weapons as they fought hand to hand. Add in massed archers and an increasing amount of ordnance and you end up with quite high casualties. But not every battle was as destructive as Towton in 1461 or Barnet in 1471. Others, though still brutal affairs, would have had far fewer casualties, especially among the common soldiers, for whom survival was a good yardstick of victory.

At times, there were large armies traversing the country and they certainly would have had an adverse impact on the places they passed through, for example Queen Margaret's northern army, which marched south to St Albans and London in 1460. But the type of warfare that caused most local deprivation was a siege, and there were very few of those during the Wars of the Roses. For the most part, the military campaigns were short and sharp; though there were certainly several towns which suffered considerably, such as Ludlow and St Albans.

To consider how much impact the Wars had on the people of England, it is worth going back, just for a moment, to where we began – which seems a very, very long time ago now.

Conclusion

We started, not by focussing on any political event, but by considering the seismic effects of the Black Death in the second half of the fourteenth century. That scourge not only killed a significant proportion of the population, but also prompted catastrophic social upheaval, including a serious revolt by peasants against an oppressive Poll Tax.

Events such as these do not necessarily unseat kings, but they do have a profound effect on people's lives and their perspective. It would be fair to say that almost everyone in England – as in most of Europe – was directly affected by the Black Death. Many would have lost siblings, parents or children. Thus, in a society which readily accepted death as part of man's lot, and as an inevitable part of the spiritual process, the Black Death was just way too much. Long-held beliefs did not seem to explain a phenomenon so aggressive towards rich and poor alike. For some – though by no means all – it significantly undermined their view of the world and their place within it.

Death, famine and poverty were constants of the medieval period, but in the fourteenth century they reached an all-time high – or low, perhaps. The savagery of the French wars which dominated the middle of the fourteenth century also seemed to reflect a society that had already been through hell.

Naturally, the Wars of the Roses had significant political effects – both short and long term – but essentially, after the chaos of the previous century, the fifteenth century was a time of recovery. I think, in our modern age, we tend to get carried away with 'sexy' political events and lose sight of how people lived their lives. In a game of football, if you change the referee at half-time, it doesn't change what game you're playing. Ordinary folk might have been vaguely aware of the sweep of events, but the vast majority of the population never even saw a king, or even any great lords. They couldn't have picked them out in a line-up.

For the gentry class, however, whose role was to keep order and oversee local law enforcement and administration, the political changes at the top were a great deal more significant. Being on the 'wrong' side could ruin such families utterly; and the intermittent wars thus caused them considerable trouble. In medieval times, family was everything. No lord or gentleman wanted to be the one who doomed his family to extinction or penury.

Nevertheless, despite the risks to the gentry, the vast majority did not suffer disaster during the period. That was perhaps because they were such a vital element of government. When new lords rose to prominence in the realm, they had to be rewarded with land befitting their new status. A good example of this is Edward's brother and heir presumptive in the 1460s, George, Duke of Clarence, who was showered with new lands, especially in the southern counties. But while Edward might have initiated some changes of gentry personnel – to reward his own loyal supporters – there was by no means wholesale change. Hence, at gentry level – as at noble level – some families benefited and others lost out.

The only occasion when new local appointments created genuine hostility was during Richard III's reign when he attempted to control the southern counties by appointing a number of northern men to positions of local influence. But even then, as we have seen, he had limited people that he could use in such positions of local power. Aside from anything else, the gentry were numerically very thin on the ground and their continued survival was essential to ensure stable local government.

Why do I tell you all this? Well, to put the Wars of the Roses into some perspective. Did the Wars affect people's lives? Yes, they did, but they did not kill half the population. This great period of repeated political crises may have featured violent changes of ruler and even a breakdown of the rule of law but, compared to the biblical upheaval of the previous century, it was pretty small beer. During the periods of so-called 'crisis', merchants continued to sell their goods, farmers tilled the soil and grew their crops and – basically – life went on. Of course, it was disruptive occasionally to all those normal activities of medieval life, but it did not fundamentally change how people lived.

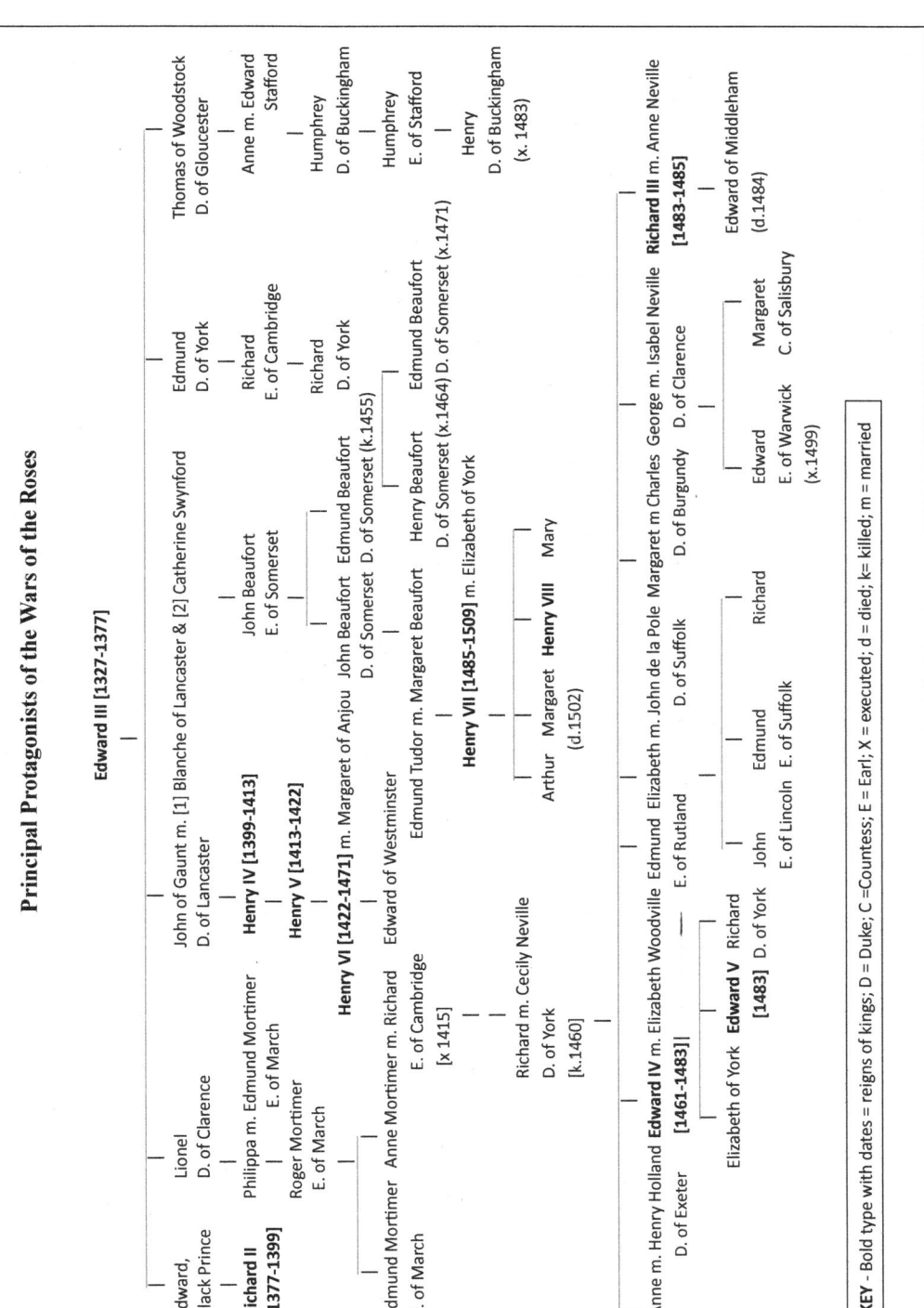

Bibliography

Chrimes, S.B., *Henry VII*, (Eyre Methuen Ltd, London, 1972)
Cook, David R., *Lancastrians and Yorkists: The Wars of the Roses*, (Longman, 1984)
Davies, C.S.L, *Peace, Print and Protestantism 1450-1558*, (Hart-Davis Macgibbon, 1976)
Dockray, Keith, *Richard III A Source Book*, (Sutton Publishing Ltd, Stroud, 1997)
Gillingham, John, *The Wars of the Roses*, (Weidenfeld and Nicolson, London, 1981)
Hancock, Peter, *Richard III and the Murder in the Tower*, (The History Press, Stroud, 2011)
Hicks, Michael, *Richard III*, (The History Press, Stroud, 2003)
Higginbotham, Susan, *The Woodvilles*, (The History Press, Stroud, 2013)
Jacob, E.F., *The Fifteenth Century: 1399-1485*, (Oxford, 1969)
Johnson, Lauren, *Shadow King The Life and Death of Henry VI*, (Head of Zeus Ltd, London, 2019)
Kendall, P.M., *Warwick the Kingmaker*, (Sphere Books, London, 1973)
Licence, Amy, *Anne Neville*, (Amberley Publishing, Stroud, 2014)
McFarlane, K.B., *The Nobility of Later Medieval England*, (Oxford, 1973)
Orme, Nicholas, 'The Education of Edward V' *Bulletin of the Institute of Historical Research 57* (1984)
Penn, Thomas, *Winter King The Dawn of Tudor England*, (Penguin Books Ltd, London, 2012)
Pollard, A.J., *Richard III and the Princes in the Tower* (Alan Sutton Publishing Ltd, Stroud, 1991)
Ross, Charles, *Edward IV*, (Eyre Methuen Ltd, London, 1974)
Seward, Desmond, *Richard III England's Black Legend*, (Country Life Books, London, 1983)
Skidmore, Chris, *Bosworth*, (Weidenfeld and Nicolson, London, 2014)
Storey, R.L., *The Reign of Henry VII*, (Blandford Press, London, 1968)
Weir, Alison, *Lancaster and York*, (Vintage Books, London, 2009)
Wolffe, B.P., *Henry VI*, (Eyre Methuen Ltd, London, 1981)

Index

Act of Accord 52, 56

Barnet, battle of 98-101, 177
Bosworth, battle of 171, 173-182
Beaufort, Edmund, 2nd Duke of Somerset 13, 14-18, 20-24, 27-32, 37, 204
Beaufort, Edmund, 4th Duke of Somerset 93, 98, 103-5
Beaufort, Henry, 3rd Duke of Somerset 33-4, 42, 46-9, 52, 55, 60, 65-71, 74
Beaufort, Lady Margaret 151, 153-4, 161-2, 205
Black Death 3, 173
Blackman, John 9

Cade, Jack 11-12, 14, 46
Calais 32, 34, 38-9, 43-47, 81-2, 89, 108, 124, 141-2, 163
Charles VII of France 11, 63
Clarence, George, Duke of 5, 75, 77-90, 92-3, 95-7, 112-114, 116-120, 123, 126, 205
Cornish Rebellion 198-201

De la Pole, John, Earl of Lincoln 160, 182, 184, 188, 190-1
De la Pole, William, Duke of Suffolk 10-12
De Vere, John, Earl of Oxford 92-3, 95-6, 99-101, 163-4, 176-180, 184-5, 194

Edgecote, battle of 82
Edward Hall 7, 174, 204
Edward III of England 7, 13, 114, 155
Edward IV of England 5, 43-4, 47-8, 52-62, 66-70, 74-135, 150, 152, 205
Edward V of England 114, 123, 131-140, 145-9, 154
Empingham, battle of 87-88

Gloucester, Richard, Duke of
  see Richard III of England
Grey, Thomas, Marquess of Dorset 113, 123-4, 131, 136-7, 141-2, 161, 164

Hastings, William, Lord 63, 75, 93-96, 99, 113, 123-4, 131, 136-8, 140-3, 147-8, 151
Henry IV of England (Bolingbroke) 2, 7, 13, 15, 19, 95
Henry V of England 3, 6-9, 11, 13, 102
Henry VI of England 3, 4, 6-9, 11-19, 21, 26-32, 34-7, 42-4, 48, 50-3, 56-60, 62-71, 74, 90. 93, 96, 98-102, 107-9, 112, 204
Henry VII of England 5, 109, 151-2, 154-190
Holland, Henry, Duke of Exeter 22, 23. 25, 33, 47, 55, 60, 63, 93, 96

211

House of Commons 6, 14, 24, 28, 186
House of Lancaster 2, 7, 12, 64, 90, 106, 112, 185
Howard, John, Duke of Norfolk 125, 131, 143, 148, 160, 172, 174, 177-9, 182
Hundred Years War 2, 3, 10, 16-17, 21

Kent 11, 38, 39, 46, 103, 196

Lambert Simnel 188, 190-193

Margaret of Anjou 11-12, 16-17, 21, 23, 31-4, 36-8, 42-3, 50, 52-8, 60-65, 68-71, 79, 90-94, 98-9, 101-105, 107-9
Mortimer's Cross, battle of 4, 54, 58

Neville, Anne, Queen of England 91, 93, 117-8, 126-7, 165-6
Neville, Isabel, Duchess of Clarence 81, 89, 117, 119
Neville, John, Marquess of Montagu 55-6, 68, 70-71, 75, 81, 84, 89, 92-3, 95-6, 99-102, 127
Neville, Richard, Earl of Salisbury 19-20, 23-5, 27-8, 32, 35, 38, 43-4, 47, 52-4
Neville, Richard, Earl of Warwick 19-23, 29-35, 38, 43-4, 47-58, 63, 65, 67-8, 71, 75-103, 108, 116-117, 205
Neville, William, Lord Fauconberg 28, 47, 75, 106

Patronage 7, 8, 21, 24, 55
Peasants' Revolt 2
Percy, Henry, 2nd Earl of Northumberland 20, 25, 27-8, 30
Percy, Henry, 3rd Earl of Northumberland 33-4, 38, 49, 52, 55, 60
Percy, Henry, 4th Earl of Northumberland 84, 92-3, 96, 106, 114, 118, 124, 128, 131, 138, 141, 143, 152, 160, 171-2, 177-182, 185, 187, 192
Perkin Warbeck 193-199
Poll tax 2
Propaganda 10, 16, 24, 37, 47, 49, 57, 80-81, 167

Richard II of England 2, 7, 15, 19, 39, 51, 81, 116, 204-5
Richard III of England 5, 77, 84, 93-4, 97, 104, 113, 115, 117-18, 124, 126-131, 134, 136-162, 166-182, 205

Shrewsbury, battle of 2
Shrewsbury, Richard of, 1st Duke of York 141-4, 193, 196, 200
Stafford, Henry, Duke of Buckingham 78, 114, 122, 125, 136-138, 140, 148, 151-7
St Albans, battle of (1455) 13, 15, 29-34
Stanley, Lord Thomas 43, 84, 89, 92-5, 114, 125, 128, 138, 143, 145, 148, 151-6, 160, 167-172, 174-176, 179-181, 185-6
Stanley, Sir William 168, 170, 174-5, 181

Tewkesbury, battle of 104-5
Towton, battle of 59-60, 62, 65
Tudor, Henry, Earl of Richmond
  see Henry VII
Tudor, Jasper, Earl of Pembroke 33, 52, 54-5, 63, 66, 74, 92-3, 95, 103, 108, 161, 169, 184-5, 187

Index

Warwick, Edward, Earl of   180, 182, 184, 187-9, 201
Westminster, Edward of   23, 24, 33, 36-7, 49-52, 55, 61, 71, 74-5, 90-3, 95-96, 101-2, 105
William Shakespeare   4, 9, 36
Woodville, Anthony, Earl Rivers   66, 76, 79, 83, 94, 99, 107-8, 113, 123-4, 130-33, 136-143, 145
Woodville, Elizabeth, Queen of England   76, 78, 93-4, 113, 121, 124, 130, 133, 136-9, 141, 144-5, 151, 153-4, 164, 166, 205
Woodville, Richard, Earl Rivers   76, 79, 82

York, Elizabeth of, Queen of England   161, 165-6, 186, 191, 200, 202
York, Richard, 3rd Duke of York   12-18, 22-39, 42-6, 49-54, 74, 137, 149, 204